Technology as a Substitute

Nukes, Missiles and other Stories

Technology as a Substitute

Nukes, Missiles and other Stories

Air Vice Marshal
Samir K. Sen

Manas Publications
(We Convert Fighters into Writers)
New Delhi-110002 (INDIA)

MANAS PUBLICATIONS
(We convert Fighters into Writers)

(Publishers, Distributors, Importers & Exporters)
4402/5-A, Ansari Road (Opp. HDFC Bank)
Darya Ganj, New Delhi-110 002 (India)
Off. 23260783, 23265523, Res. 23842660
Fax: 011-23272766
E-mail: manaspublications@gmail.com
manaspublications@yahoo.com
Website: www.manaspublications.in

ISBN 978-81-7049-516-1
₹ 995/-

Designed at
Innovative Processors

Printed in India at
R.K. Print Services, Delhi and
Published by Mrs Suman Lata for
Manas Publications, 4402/5-A, Ansari Road, (Opp. HDFC Bank),
Darya Ganj, New Delhi-110 002 (INDIA)

To the memory of my long-departed parents

and

to my wife

Contents

Foreword

I authored several papers but have so far written only one book, all of those writings focused on technology-driven issues of international politics. This, therefore, is my second book. Broadly on the same theme but written in the first person singular, this book gives a brief account of my own experience in the development of our own guided missiles, in particular, with occasional forays into other stories.

For one who had belonged to the engineering branch of our Air Force I have had the rare privilege of having worked as a scientist of our country's military technology enterprise for the most part of my Air Force service. And, thereby, I had had the unique opportunity of having worked for almost two decades in those two areas of our military technology, which, curiously, have seen an unalloyed success, namely the guided missiles and the missile-warheads. In this book, therefore, there is a necessarily-selective and a brief account of the technology development activities by our scientists in both guided missiles and missile warheads in their early years.

Further, after my superannuation from our Air Force at an early age of 57 years and the consequent closure of my work in military technology enterprise way back in

December, 1988, followed by a short stint in engineering consultancy, I had taken to scholarly work. And, in doing so, I had switched from science and technology to the social sciences and joined scholarly work in an area of international politics, which is profoundly influenced by development of technology. Consequently, in addition to researching and writing occasional papers and a book, I had, also, given invited lectures at graduate schools on some of those issues of international politics which are impacted by technology. One chapter of this book, therefore, deals briefly with that experience.

There is one important feature of our country's military technology enterprise, which is singularly absent from the DTIBs (Defence Technology & Industrial Bases) of the industrially developed countries, and it is none other than the absence, in our country, of an integrated management for the development-cum-manufacture of weapon systems of the conventional kind, a phenomenon which has largely contributed to the delays and the failures of most of our weapon development projects. As stated, however, there has been one notable exception, namely our guided missile and our missile-warheads, where our development projects have met with success despite the drawback of that dysfunctional organizational structure of our higher defence management. I have, therefore, discussed in this book the reason why there is, on the one hand, an apparent disconnect between the near-failure of our MBT and LCA projects, for instance, and the success of our guided missiles and missile-warhead development programmes, on the other.

And, in doing so I have argued that the success of our guided missile development programme, in particular, has been possible, primarily, because of one reason: Whereas the absence of a built-in system of integrated-management in our country's DTIB, in particular, has disrupted the progress of most of our weapon development projects till now, the uniqueness of the leadership of our guided missiles programme had managed to bring about a virtual integration of both the development management and the manufacture management for the duration of that programme, thanks to the personal attributes of the leader of that programme, the late Dr Abdul Kalam, and the astonishing work that he had put in during his DRDO years.

Chapter 1

An Overview

My 34 years in the Indian Air Force (IAF) were especially interesting because of one unexpected development: Although I had been on the active list of our Air Force through all of those years and fully engaged, during the first fifteen years, in our Air Force's engineering and technical maintenance operations, I had worked as a scientist of our Defence Research & Development Organisation (DRDO) during the last two decades of my Air Force service. A period that had turned out to be the best years of the build-up and growth of military technology in India and had yielded spectacular success in two of our DRDO's most productive development programmes, namely the guided missile and the missile-warhead. And, I had, probably, done reasonably well in both of those roles:

During my early years – as an engineer in a fighter-Squadron, two different Wings (ie bases), the quality assurance unit of our Air Force at a cluster of three Ordnance Factories, two explosives maintenance units of our Air Force and on staff duties at the Air Headquarters, while I had, also, done, sandwiched between those postings, post-graduate studies in engineering, twice, by having been deputed by our government to an institute of armament technology in India once and at an engineering university in the UK the second time.

And, during the later years of Air Force service – as a scientist in two high-technology weapons research laboratories of our country, namely the DRDL (Defence Research & Development Laboratory) and the TBRL (Terminal Ballistics Research Laboratory), with a stint between those two at the headquarters of the DRDO in our Ministry of Defence (MOD).

Looking back, I am aware that working as a scientist in two of the most important areas of military technology, while continuing to remain on the active service list of our Air Force, had been a unique career opportunity. And, although I had been generally aware of it I had not thought too much of that, either, immersed as I had been in the daily routine of keeping up with the challenges of an engaging, if exacting, work-schedule.

So, it was only at the end of my Air Force service, when I had reached my superannuation as an Air Vice Marshal of our Air Force at an early age of fifty seven years, that the realization had dawned on me that I had been one of the few among my contemporaries in our Air Force and, indeed, among many others in our government's service then, who had had a lot of satisfaction, most of the time, while doing his job.

I was then the Director of India's Terminal Ballistics Research Laboratory (TBRL) for nearly four years, and although under the terms of our country's military service, then in force, I had to retire an year earlier than any civil-services officer of our country then and, more to the point, three to five years too early for a senior civilian scientist, holding a major R & D Laboratory's Director's position either in my own organization, the DRDO, or in one of the other R & D organizations of our country, eg the Indian Space Research Organisation (ISRO), the Atomic Energy Organisation (AEO), the Council of Scientific & Industrial Research (CSIR) etc., I had no issue on that account. On the other hand, I had been aware that I had the privilege of serving my country for an extra one year, since, unlike now, the retirement age of an Air Vice Marshal of our Air Force then was only fifty six years.

I have noted over the years that the fact that my career in our Air Force's engineering branch had taken an unusual turn, albeit, within the perimeters of our defence establishment, had surprised some of my own countrymen who had not known of another one like I. But, the fact is that there had been, in those early years, a handful of other university-educated engineers, too, in our military's engineering cadres, who had served our government in the same manner. They, too, had acquired the appropriate post-graduate engineering degrees and had then been deputed to serve in one of our DRDO laboratories as scientists. Typically, each one of those few had, prior to his joining our Army or Navy or Air Force, acquired an undergraduate degree in engineering from one of the reputed universities of our country and then served for some seven to ten years in the military's engineering services before being selected by our government for post-graduate studies in engineering. Typically, also, the completion of that post-graduate education had been followed, in the case of a few of those engineers, by a placement in a DRDO laboratory and the rendering of satisfactory service as scientists and the consequent rise through the ranks of the civilian defence scientists cadre before one or two of them could make it to the position of the Director of a Laboratory. For example, the Gas Turbine Research Establishment (GTRE) in Bangalore, the Defence R & D Laboratory (DRDL) in Hyderabad, the Naval Science & Technology Laboratory (NSTL) in Vishakhapatnam and the Aeronautical Development Establishment (ADE) in Bangalore were some of the weapon-systems laboratories of our country, which had, in their early years, found it necessary to induct a few young and post-graduate qualified engineers of our armed forces as mid-level scientists (ie equivalent to a Scientist C) to help build those laboratories from scratch and to help commence work on the development of the relevant hardware (ie the weapon systems). Consequently, each of those laboratories had, in due course, also, seen one or two of those highly qualified scientists, originally inducted from our military, rise through the combined ranks of scientists, including those of the DRDS (Defence R & D Service) cadre, and getting selected as the Director of the Laboratory.

I ought to mention here that, as known, in our country such lateral moves by a selected few of our military's engineering cadres have been few and far between. However, that has not been the case in the industrially developed countries of the world. In the UK, the USA and France, for instance, quite a few of the university-educated engineers of their armed forces, who had possessed post-graduate engineering qualifications and had demonstrated, thereafter, good capabilities in scientific research and technology management, had worked, during the later years of their military service, as scientists in the weapon R & D establishments and prototype manufacturing centres of their respective country. In fact, one of the most advanced R & D programmes of the world to date, namely the so-called Star Wars project of the USA of President Reagan's era, had a well-qualified senior of the Corps of Engineers of the US Army, namely Lt Gen Abrahamson, as its first Director. And, as known, the Star Wars project, which had lasted a little over a decade then, had made phenomenal progress during the late nineteen eighties under the leadership of General Abrahamson, and the success of that enterprise had contributed substantially to the winning of the so-called Cold War by the USA and the consequent disintegration of the erstwhile Soviet Union. It goes without saying that the spectacular success of that Star War research project of that era had come about largely because Gen Abrahamson had both successfully managed the selection of appropriate technologies for the sophisticated space weapons of the USA that were then developed by the USA and ensured the utilization of the talents of some of the most competent among the American scientists of that era, many of whom, as known, had been outstanding professors and researchers at some of the best known US universities then.

The truth of the matter is that in our country it is mostly the members of one particular branch of our civil services, ie the Administrative Service, who are routinely placed, in large numbers and at senior levels, in appointments outside their cadre. But, in the industrially developed countries both the civil services and their equivalents in the military share that obligation and that opportunity. In fact, it is precisely because of that equitable practice of the developed countries that non-discriminatory selection of individuals with appropriate background – from both the civil services and the military – takes place routinely in the developed countries, and only the meritorious among them are, more often than not, placed in appropriate positions of responsibility outside their parent cadres. But, for me, an university-educated engineer of our Air Force, who had, apparently, possessed the requisite degrees and the appropriate skills but had no strings to pull, it was, probably, no more than a combination of random chances, rather than a deliberate design, that had made it possible for my career to take the turn it had taken. Whatever the reasons, however, that realignment in my professional career had proved good. Consequently, I have had both the good fortune of having performed satisfactorily during the early years of my Air Force service, dealing with the challenges of a military service in operational (or 'forward', as it was then known as) areas, and the opportunity, in the later years of my Air Force service, to work as a scientist in the much-awaited build-up of our country's guided missile R & D, in particular, and in the upgrading of our DTIB, in general, and, through it all, to participate in the making of two of our advanced weapon systems, namely the guided missile and the missile-warhead.

As known, during those highly-charged years of the Cold War a non-aligned country like ours could neither purchase a long-range surface-to-surface guided missile with a deterrent warhead from any one of the three nuclear-empowered, developed countries of the West then, namely the USA, France and the UK, nor obtain their know-how from their adversary, the less-developed but equally militarized former Soviet Union. Our successes, therefore, in the making of those two advanced systems for our own national security enterprise were, therefore, rightly regarded by the world at large as two important milestones in our country's march towards achieving self-reliance in weapons and equipment. And, although in my case both of those two unique opportunities which came my way, namely to participate in the first-ever build-up of our country's infrastructure for guided missile R & D and to work, thereafter, for the development of two high-technology weapon systems, namely the guided missile and its warheads, had come about somewhat accidentally I am deeply grateful to both our Air Force and our DRDO for having given me that privilege.

It ought to be mentioned in this connection that our country's success in the making of our own deterrent warhead, unlike our success in our guided missiles development programme, had remained totally unknown till 1998, when our Prime Minister had startled the world by suddenly disclosing that India had already developed and just then successfully tested two of its own miniaturized nuclear warhead prototypes and, thereby, become a nuclear-weapon nation in its own right. However, the fact remains that it is the combined success of both of those high-technology R & D programmes of our country, namely the guided missile and the strategic warhead, that has made it possible for our country to acquire a deterrent weapon capability on her own and, thereby, to prevent two hostile nations in our immediate neighbourhood, namely China and Pakistan, from making any inroads into our nation's security and sovereignty.

As mentioned, the news of our guided missile development enterprise, namely the Integrated Guided Missile Development Programme (IGMDP), including the story of our longer-range SSM (ie the Agni missiles), had figured prominently in our news media from time to time. However, there are a few items of interest, pertaining to our weapon development programmes, in general, which still remain largely unknown. For instance, despite the widely-held belief that the IGMDP, which had been launched by our country in the early nineteen eighties, was the DRDO's first ever major weapon system development programme, the fact is otherwise. That distinction, probably, goes to another major weapon development project of our country, namely the main battle tank (MBT), Arjun, which programme, initiated under a sanction given, possibly, at about the same time or a little earlier than the IGMDP's, had, actually, been launched a little before the IGMDP. But, it had receded into the background largely because of a series of bottlenecks and unforeseen delays that the project Arjun had suffered in its early years. Similarly, although it seems curious now that – between the IGMDP and its contemporary, the MBT (Main Battle Tank) Arjun – it is only the IGMDP which had received wide publicity in our media, the fact is that there are many reasons why that had happened. For instance, though it had become known by all interested observers in the early nineteen sixties that the development of guided missiles had made considerable headway in industrially developed countries like the UK, France and the USA, it was not known by most of our countrymen that our defence scientists, too, had initiated preliminary work on guided missiles almost at the same time, ie in the late nineteen fifties, thanks entirely to the foresight and genius of our first Scientific Adviser (SA), the great visionary Professor DS Kothari, who had been selected as our country's first SA to the Defence Minister and, also, the chief of our newly-formed Defence Science Organisation (DSO) by our first Prime Minister, Jawaharlal Nehru. Curiously, Prime Minister Nehru had done that selection soon after he had consulted the British Scientific Advisor and decided to make a small beginning in the development of military technology in our country.

In short, although it is not widely known, even, today that Professor Kothari had not only founded our country's first defence R & D Organisation, then called the DSO, but had, also, constituted a study group for an early commencement of the development of our own guided missiles the fact is that he had done so and had located it in Delhi inside the precincts of one of our laboratories and had named that study group a Special Weapons Development Team (SWDT). And, the reason why he had called that study group the SWDT was that during those early years of the development of guidance and control technologies it was popularly believed, even, in some of the industrially-developed countries, engaged in the development guidance and control technologies, that, unlike other weapons, including the unguided rocket, the guided missile constituted a 'special' weapon in that it both seeks and destroys the enemy-target.

In other words, it is possible that the association of the term 'Special Weapon' with the name 'Guided Missile' had been the reason, basically, why the IGMDP had evoked greater interest than the MBT project and had, thereby, received more publicity in our media than the MBT Arjun project. However, it is, also, possible that the IGMDP received more attention simply because it was our country's first major-weapon development programme which had met with more success, right from its beginning, than any other weapon development project of our country till then.

In any event, as known, that success in the making of our own guided missiles – which had come about after nearly four decades of our Independence and three decades or so after the formation of the SWDT – had yielded for our country, at a critical juncture of our nation's history, a much-needed launch-vehicle for our own strategic warhead and, thereby, made it possible for our military to acquire its own strategic weapon for the defence of our sovereignty. And, that, in turn, has provided our national security enterprise its much-needed strength, more strength, in one sense, than all of our other weapon development programmes, put together. Further, while it is widely known that the IGMDP had been sanctioned as a consolidated programme for five projects, namely four projects for tactical-application guided missiles and one project for a 'technology-demonstrator' surface-to-surface missile (SSM), popularly known as a ballistic misslie, there is one interesting aspect of that story, which, probably, remains largely unknown.

Of the five projects of the IGMDP two, as stated, pertained to guided missiles of the SSM class, namely the Prithvi and the Agni. However, although both of those two SSMs operate in the 'ballistic' mode they differ from each other in one important respect, namely the distance that each type of missile could travel, that is, in respect of their range: While the range of the Prithvi is much shorter, 50 to 150 kilometers, say, making it ideally suitable for carrying both conventional but sophisticated (ie a high-explosives filled) warheads and, in case the range is extended a little further, to 250 kilometers, say, for tactical nuclear application, too, the longer-range surface-to-surface guided missiles, eg the Agni, are necessarily much costlier and suitable only for delivering strategic-application warheads. However, unlike the four tactical missiles, comprising the Prithvi SSM, the Nag Anti-Tank Missile (ATM), the Akash medium-range Surface-to-Air Missile (SAM) and the Trishul short-range SAM, which, together, had constituted the originally-envisaged 'core' of the IGMDP, the question of including a fifth project for the development of a Agni-like ballistic missile (ie a longer-range SSM), which is cost-effective only in strategic mode, had not been settled for quite some time.

In other words, in the beginning the intention had been to develop only four tactical-application guided missiles which were then urgently required and, therefore, to launch only a four-missile development programme to enable our country to achieve self-reliance, as early as possible, in those four types of guided missiles. However, when those deliberations on the proposed IGMDP had been in progress a handful of our guided missile scientists of those early years, especially a few 'seniors' among them, had, also, thought of the necessity for adding a fifth project to the IGMDP, namely a project for undertaking an experimental study pertaining to the development of a comparatively longer-range SSM (ie a SSM of much longer range than the Prithvi) in order that our country acquired the capability to develop at a short notice, if required, such a longer-range missile for possible use as a launch vehicle of a deterrent weapon. Further, the same guided missile scientists of that era had, also, envisaged that it would be logical to designate that project as a technology-demonstrator missile development project, since, in the absence of a firm requirement for such a launch vehicle, it would not be possible to seek a sanction for the full-scale development of a long-range SSM, popularly known as a ballistic missile.

In short, the fifth project had been envisaged as a limited R & D activity towards the development of an experimental missile that would enable our missile scientists to conduct limited studies pertaining to the design of a ballistic missile. And, that thinking had come about largely because of the reason that it was known by the world by then that our neighbor, communist China, having already developed its own deterrent weapons, had been surreptitiously assisting our other neighbour, Pakistan, with the know-how and materials required for assembling a nuclear warhead and, also, encouraging its ally, namely communist North Korea, to supply to Pakistan, clandestinely, some of its own ballistic missiles of the kind that carried nuclear warheads.

The reason why that particular development project, ie the fifth project, had been described by our missile scientists of that era as a technology demonstrator project was none other than the fact that it was an apt description of the objective of the proposed project: Since the full-scale development of a ballistic missile was not feasible then, the only way our scientists could have helped matters had been to get a sanction for limited funds and undertake some experimental work for a longer-range SSM. In any case, both the Scientific Advisors of that era, Professor MGK Menon and Dr Raja Ramanna, each an eminent physicist in his own right, had been convinced that the IGMDP must include a fifth project for the development of such an experimental SSM.

However, although the stated purpose, for which the Agni missile project had been included as a fifth project of the IGMDP, had been to undertake an experimental study pertaining to a longer-range ballistic missile, as known, our missile scientists, by undertaking the work on that fifth project, have, actually, achieved much more than that the limited objective. As known, it is the success of that modestly-funded fifth project of the IGMDP for developing a technology-demonstrator longer-range SSM, so diligently undertaken by the our scientists, which had ensured that our country would get a head-start in the development of our own ballistic missiles of longer ranges, should our government, later, have perceived a necessity for acquiring our own strategic weapon.

The IGMDP will have been formally concluded well before the publication of this book. This would be a good time to mention, therefore, that way back in the nineteen sixties and the early seventies it was only a few guided missile scientists of the DRDL of that era, who, as pioneers of India's guided missile R & D, had envisaged that their efforts and the efforts of the scientists of the associated DRDO and non-DRDO laboratories, alone, would, finally, lead to the successful development of our country's own guided missile systems for both tactical and strategic applications. It is, also, a good occasion to acknowledge that it was largely due to a combination of their hard work and optimism and, equally importantly, the foresight of the three SAs of that era, namely late Professor BD Nag Chaudhuri, Professor MGK Menon and late Dr Raja Ramanna, the third, the fourth and the fifth SAs who had led the DRDO during an exciting period of its build-up and growth, that our country could successfully undertake an IGMDP-like comprehensive development programme a few years hence. And, those scientists of that era and the three SAs had achived the success through ensuring both the meticulous planning of the infrastructure build-up by the concerned DRDO laboratories, namely the nodal laboratory, DRDL, and the supporting technology laboratories, mentioned later, and the energetic execution, thereafter, of those plans by all of those DRDO laboratories.

And, as for the success of the IGMDP, it was undoubtedly the selection and induction by the SA of the relevant time, namely Dr Raja Ramanna, of a person of the stature of Dr Abdul Kalam, who had had the rare distinction of combining in himself all of the required technological prowess and human attributes of an out-standing leader, as the Director DRDL, that had contributed the most to it.

Incidentally, the timing of Dr Kalam's induction into the DRDO, as the Director of the DRDL and the ex-officio leader of the IGMDP, had been fortuitous, too. It had enabled Dr Kalam, as the incoming leader, to put the required finishing touches to both the planning for the IGMDP, including the defining of its management structure, and the technology and infrastructure build-up work that had been successfully undertaken by the DRDL for nearly a decade by then, albeit, in cooperation with the associated laboratories within the DRDO and a number of other R & D and manufacturing centres outside the DRDO. And, all of that work had been done just in time for the IGMDP to be formally launched.

Undertaking a development programme of the size and the complexity of the IGMDP in a developing country like ours has not been an easy task, to say the least. Since there is a large variety of technologies that needed to be indigenously developed and made use of, a process which had necessitated the co-option by the nodal laboratory, ie the DRDL, of a number of other laboratories and work-centres, both in and outside the DRDO, as equal partners of and major contributors to the IGMDP and its success, the chief of our IGMDP had to set up an appropriate management structure and to navigate through that complex structure to get things done on time by both the public-owned institutions and by the private sector companies. Whereas the work centres which were within the DRDO (ie the DRDL and its sister-laboratories) were government-owned institutions, each with its own charter of technology or system development responsibility and each functioning independently of the DRDL, the work centres which were outside the DRDO were a mixed lot. Some were owned by our central government (eg the laboratories of the ISRO, the CSIR, our institutes of technology, other university-colleges of engineering, the Ordnance Factories and Defence Public Sector Units (DPSUs), eg the BHPV, the HAL, the BEL etc which made prototypes, while the others belonged to the private sector (eg the Larsen & Toubro). Therefore, Dr Kalam, who had been given two sets of responsibilities, namely those of the Director of the DRDL and the duties of the Chief of the IGMDP, had to be well-supported by the SA throughout the duration of the IGMDP, both as a Secretary to the government and as the DG DRDO, a support which had been given in full measure by the SA, Dr VS Arunachalam, even though Dr Arunachalam had himself been new in his job then, having succeeded Dr Ramanna as the SA only a few months after the induction of Dr Kalam. Finally, since Dr Arunachalam had, in due course, as known, earned the rare distinction of having been the youngest Secretary to our Government and, also, the longest-serving Secretary-cum-SA, both the IGMDP and its leader, Dr Kalam, had, benefited greatly from the fall-out of that occurrence, namely the stability and the continuity of Dr Arunachalam as the SA, effectively, over the entire duration of the IGMDP.

As known, the prototypes of three state-of-the-art tactical missiles (ie guided missiles embodying state-of-the-art-technologies) of the IGMDP have been successfully tested and accepted by our military, and the indigenous missiles have now gone into production. While one of those three, the Prithvi surface-to-surface missile (SSM), had, as known, received the acceptance of our military well on time and been deployed, too, the acceptance and the production of the other two missiles, namely the Akash and the Trishul, had occurred an year or two later, probably, because those two missiles have had one or two variants and embodied certain changes in staff qualitative requirements that have resulted in improvements in performance. As known, the nominated production agency for the bulk production of all three missiles is the Bharat Dynamics Limited (BDL), a DPSU which had been constituted in the early seventies. It is likely that in the case of both of those two missiles the actual deployment of the indigenous missiles by our Army/Navy/Air Force has, also, taken place.

In the case of the anti-tank missile Nag, which had, as mentioned, involved for the development of a set of 'futuristic' technologies, related, primarily, to missile guidance, that our development team is yet to score an unqualified success. One has a reasonable expectation, however, that the final version of the Nag prototype, a prototype which would meet our own scientists' original expectations, would, also, be made ready in the future, although developing an ATM which guides itself all the way from the missile launcher to the enemy tank, unassisted by an operator, ie the missile 'pilot', and strikes the armoured target at its most vulnerable spot in order that the vehicle is either destroyed or immobilized was not an easy task. As known, no ATM, comparable in sophistication to the Nag's projected performance, has yet been developed by any country.

Finally, unbelievable as it may seem now, the fifth project of the IGMDP had been given a lower priority for execution, in the beginning, in compliance with the initially prioritized objectives of the IGMDP, namely the development of the four types of tactical-application guided missiles, as mentioned. However, it is the success of the comparatively-lower priority, fifth project of that very missile programme, the one which had aimed at developing an experimental longer-range SSM as a technology-demonstrator missile, which has turned out to be the harbinger of a series of longer range ballistic missiles, as known. And, the development of those longer range ballistic missiles has, arguably, turned out to be the most significant contribution of the IGMDP, although the inclusion of that fifth project in the conclusive stage of the planning and deliberations on the IGMDP proposal had appeared then to have been almost a product of an afterthought. Further, strange, as it may seem now, the trigger for including that fifth project in the IGMDP as a technology-demonstrator project – and not a full-scale missile development project – had, primarily, been the intuition of a few senior missile scientists of that era and the foresight of the then Scientific Advisor. And, it is possible that the same missile scientists who had pressed for the inclusion of the Agni technology demonstrator project in the IGMDP had, during the finalization of the IGMDP proposal, framed the broad parameters of that technology demonstrator missile, albeit, in some consultation with other specialists. However, although those technical and operational parameters of the first prototype Agni missile, as drafted by our misile scientists of that era , had, presumably, undergone changes along the way the resulting technical document had incorporated all of the features, more or less, that would typically feature in a staff QR for a shorter-range ballistic missile, as drafted by any military planner.

It ought to be mentioned here that although the sanction for the IGMDP had been obtained during the early eighties the deliberations on the IGMDP proposal had been undertaken over a number of years prior to that, keeping in view the fact that the DRDO would be required to develop, simultaneously, a few types of tactical guided missiles to meet our military's immediate requirements. However, even before that, ie probably a decade earlier, our missile scientists had thought that, in addition to the need for tactical-application guided missiles, a need will, also, be felt in the not-too-distant future, for, also, a class of longer-range guided missiles for strategic application, ie an Agni-like long-range SSM. However, although that thought had occurred in our scientists some years back it was only much later, when the final deliberations on the IGMDP were under way, that the seniors among our missile scientists had thought, in concrete terms, of the details of the development work that it would be necessary for our scientists to undertake to develop such a missile under a separate and an appropriate development project. And, it was only when work on the finalization of the IGMDP proposal, including its cost estimation, had commenced that a firm view on the inclusion of that fifth project in the proposed IGMDP for the development of that experimental missile, albeit, on a lower priority, was taken.

In short, although by including the Agni technology demonstrator-project in the IGMDP at a comparatively later stage of the planning process we had succeeded in achieving the objective of obtaining the sanction for a limited amount of funds for that project and although it was the Agni project that had, at that point of time, been given a lower priority, albeit, for valid reasons, it was the early success of that very technology-demonstrator, Agni missile, development project, a project whose success, as known, has now resulted in the undertaking of a number of succeeding projects for developing, even, longer-range Agni missiles, that has, in the eyes of our countrymen, become, arguably, the most meaningful event of our country's march towards achieving self-reliance in weapons and equipment. More meaningful, probably, in some ways than, even, the success of all of the other (ie the tactical-application guided missiles) projects of the IGMDP.

Finally, unbelievable as it may seem today, there were other reasons, too, why the Agni project was initially thought of as a lower-priority project and, also, why there was some hesitation, in the beginning, about making the Agni prototype development project a part of the IGMDP. First, the missile scientists of that era were afraid that in view of our country's resource constraints our government may not be in a position to favour the incurring of additional expenditure on an Agni-like technology demonstrator project, notwithstanding the fact that it was known that the cost estimates for the IGMDP proposal, as a whole, were well below the expenditure that were known to have been incurred by developed countries like the USA and France some years earlier while developing similar missiles. Second, since at that point of time the strategic thinkers and planners of our country had not yet pronounced that a need for developing a ballistic missile as a launch vehicle for a strategic weapon exists, our missile scientists were afraid that the fact of the absence of such a requirement in our military's threat perception then would make our guided missile scientists' case for including the additional cost for the development of such a prototype ballistic missile in the IGMDP proposal weak.

To be fair to all concerned, however, there were valid reasons why our military had not suggested that a Agni-like development project be undertaken at that particular stage of the DRDO's technology development capability. Due to the decades-long denial of resources to the DRDO post-Independence, our defence scientists, in those early years, had had no opportunity, sadly, to acquire technology development capabilities by undertaking the required infrastructure build-up, let alone pursuing meaningfully the development of specific missile-related technologies, capabilities that needed to be acquired as a pre-requisite for achieving success in the development of any type of sophisticated weapon or equipment. And, consequently, our Army/Navy/Air Force had – even, as late as the early-seventies, ie nearly three decades after the advent of the DSO/DRDO – carried a poor impression of the DRDO's capabilities. In fact, our military had, in those early years, felt largely unsure, as I recall, of our ability to develop, even, a low-technology weapon system, let alone a guided missile for tactical application or a long-range ballistic missile, on schedule.

However, although our users, the Armed Forces, were still sceptic then the fact was that things had changed rapidly after the arrival of Professor Nag Chaudhuri as the first-ever empowered SA in the early nineteen seventies. And, it was no longer business-as-usual for a perceived side-lined R & D Organisation, not any more: In fact, the DRDO had suddenly transformed itself into an efficient and meaningful development organization, duly supported by our government and ready to produce results in right earnest, by the time Professor Nag Chaudhuri had handed over charge as the SA.

As known, by the early nineteen nineties the news of our country's success in developing an Agni-like ballistic missile prototype had become a household word. And, in some important ways, it was that success that had ensured that the Agni technology demonstrator missile project would be the forerunner of a series of longer-range Agni missiles, which, at this point of time, are, probably, the mainstay of our delivery systems for deterrent weapons. That, we, the erstwhile members of the missile scientist community of that era, had the unique opportunity, in those early years of our country's military technology build-up, to engage in the development of our country's first ever R & D infrastructure for guided missiles and, equally importantly, that I, along with a very few others of my ilk then – ie a handful amongst the young university-educated engineers of our Armed Forces then, who had been trained, also, for a scientist-career by our government and were members of that group of early missile scientists – had the additional privilege, also, of participating in our guided missile development, while remaining on the active-service list of our armed forces, has been an unique privilege, to say the least.

In this connection it ought to be mentioned that the grounds for the success of the IGMDP had been truly laid a decade or so prior to the commencement of the IGMDP, ie during the early to late nineteen seventies, although some of the basic work had, necessarily, been done prior to that. That was so, largely because the missile scientists of those early years, especially the young lot, including the first two batches of young scientists, recruited by our laboratory fresh from our university campuses, had participated, for the first time in the history of the DRDO, in the execution of a full-scale multi-technology development project for an indigenous version of a complex missile system like a medium range SAM, complete with its launch vehicle, ground-based tracking system etc. And, that typically complex development project, named Project Devil, had been undertaken partly because a perception had arisen then that a need for making a sizeable number of such an indigenous missile in the next three to four years for our Air Force, in particular, and, therefore, the need for developing a prototype of such missile would likely become an inescapable necessity in the near future. But, the need for undertaking that project had mainly arisen because the undertaking of such a wide-ranging project activity by our missile laboratory, the DRDL, on a tight schedule would provide a much-needed opportunity for our scientists to gather on-the-job experience for undertaking thereafter a large-size integrated development programme for a few tactical-application guided missiles in order that the tactical guided missile requirements of our Army/Navy/Air Force may hereafter be met on a war footing by undertaking at the earliest the large-scale manufacture of a few, selected types of missiles of our own design. Further, because of the manner in which the development of that indigenous medium range SAM system had been carried out, using successfully our scientists' technology-development cum project-management skills, Project Devil had turned out to be fore-runner of the IGMDP.

As stated, Project Devil had, also, been planned as a time-bound exercise, incorporating in its scope, for the very first time in our history, both the establishment of the infrastructure for technology development, albeit on a bare-minimum basis, and the full-scale development of all of the technologies, relevant to a complex medium-range SAM, including the transfer of those technologies to respective production agencies. Two objectives were achieved thereby, namely (a) the indigenous design, development and prototype production capabilities, pertaining to a medium range SAM, albeit of an obsolescent kind then, had been established, and (b) an opportunity had been provided to our scientists for acquiring expertise in developing technologies and managing the development of a complex, high-technology guided missile system on a tight schedule, leading to an efficient transfer of technology and the establishment of bulk production by a target date. The envisaged task, therefore, had implied that our laboratory would be able to undertake, simultaneously (a) the building of the required R & D infrastructure including scientist manpower of the required kind, on a tight schedule and (b) the full-scale development of a typically complex guided missile system, in co-operation with both the associated laboratories of the DRDO and the relevant national-level technology centres and production agencies, in and outside the government-owned establishments. By participating in that first-ever multi-technology, multi-sourced, weapon system development programme of our country, which had laid the foundations of the now-renowned IGMDP, our scientists had had the cpportunity of working under the leadership of some of the most eminent scientists and visionaries of our country of that era. The following chapter deals briefly with that experience.

Chapter 2

Project Devil: The Training Run

While most people are aware of the name IGMDP and of some of its successes and achievements, thanks to the extensive news-reporting by our media on the tests and the trials with the prototype missiles of the IGMDP, the story of an earlier, comprehensive, competence-building activity for the development of guided missile systems for our country remains largely unknown. And, that enterprise, code-named Project Devil, had, as its focus, the indigenization of a typically complex medium range SAM but had, essentially, been an infrastructure-cum-competence-building project whose success had, in a large measure, laid the foundation for the IGMDP and its successor guided missile development programmes of our country. That project, I may explain right away, had been conceived as soon as the distinguished nuclear physicist of that era, the Late Professor B D Nag Chaudhuri, had taken over the reigns of the DRDO in the early nineteen seventies as the Scientific Adviser to our Defence Minister-cum-Secretary to the government in the

MOD and, therefore, as the first-ever 'empowered' ex-officio DG of the DRDO. That had happened consequent to his relinquishing his first job with the Govt of India, namely a Member of our Planning Commission, that he had held earlier. Although before obtaining the sanction for Project Devil due diligence had been exercised by the new SA by way of assessing both the capability of his own organization, the DRDO, and its guided missile laboratory, the DRDL, in particular, and by consulting the other stake-holders, eg the Army, the Air Force, the Navy, the ISRO etc, it was largely his own intuition that had made the selection of that project, namely Project Devil, an excellent choice.

By putting in place a complex project like the Project Devil as an urgent development project to be undertaken by the DRDL and, thereby, forcing the pace of technology build-up and infrastructure development for guided missiles in our country Professor Nag Chaudhuri had, in effect, also, triggered then the much-awaited process of the development of military technology by our country on a war-footing. That was a task which had, right at the beginning, most assiduously been pursued, as already stated, by our first Scientific Advisor, Professor Kothari, but had then suffered an immense set-back for over a decade after his departure from our MOD and return to the Dept of Physics of the Delhi University as its chair. As a result, by the time the third SA, Professor Nag Chaudhuri, had, also, moved on, only about two years later, the Project Devil had, by re-starting the interrupted process of building military technology in our country, realized an additional goal over and above its primary goal: It had hugely succeeded in engineering the revival of our guided missile laboratory, the DRDL on a fast track and, through it, both a national-level drive towards the development of technologies pertaining to guided missiles and the growth of military technology in all its facets. In a quick order he had, also, forced the revival of all of the other high-technology laboratories of the DRDO by ensuring through persuasion that our government mend its earlier policy and accept the allocation of resources for weapons development as an integral part of its nation-building agenda. Thus, in his relatively short tenure of only about two to three years Professor BD Nag Chaudhuri, the third SA, had managed to lay the foundation for the indigenous development of a variety of high technologies, pertaining to advanced-armaments of all kinds for our Army/Navy/Air Force. He had, of course, singled out such subjects as aeronautics, aircraft and rocket propulsion, avionics, naval science and technology as our priority area and thereby directed investments, for the very first time, in those areas, all of it with one objective in view, namely the attainment of self-reliance in advanced weapons and equipment.

As regards guided missiles, as mentioned, he had, presumably, consulted beforehand all of the stake-holders in both the development of our own guided missiles, namely the Chiefs of our Army, Navy and Air Force, on the one hand, and the associated technologies, on the other, namely the Chief of the Indian Space Research Organization (ISRO) and the Directors and the senior scientists of his own laboratories, concerned with the development of technologies pertaining to guided missiles. But, interestingly – and this needs to be mentioned – before taking a final view on the competence of his own nodal laboratory for guided missiles, the DRDL, and its associated laboratories to pull themselves up by their bootstraps through undertaking such a gigantic task, he had, also, consulted each one of us in the DRDL, a handful of mid-level and one senior scientists, who, between them, had then constituted the heads of the six or seven technology divisions of that miniscule laboratory, namely a laboratory which had very little to show then by way of either infrastructure or technology development activities.

As mentioned, at that point of time I had already spent an year in the DRDL as the head of its missile-propulsion group, having returned from the UK with a MSc degree-by-research in rocket technology. As I recall, like most others in our Air Force then, I had, prior to that, neither known what exactly were then being done by the scientists of that laboratory nor been familiar with its past achievements, if any. And, the tragedy was all the more because I had expected to be posted at a good fighter aircraft station or an engineering base of our AirForce while, unbeknown to me, our Air Force had agreed, in advance of my return from the Cranfield university, to my being made available to the DRDO and posted with at that laboratory. It had, therefore, given me the shock of my life, as I recall, when I had landed, in December, 1969, on that ill-equipped laboratory on the outskirts of the old city of Hyderabad. There were only a handful of scientists, probably no more than 15, comprising mostly junior and middle-level scientists, who were thinly spread over some seven or eight technology-disciplines. So, by the time Professor BD Nag Chaudhuri had taken over the reigns of the DRDO and unfolded his plan to energize the activities of our laboratory for developing our own guided missile I had been all too aware of the enormity of the task involved in making a success of that venture, namely (a) transforming our ill-equipped laboratory, on a fast track, into a somewhat-adequately equipped development centre for guided missiles with, at the least, a bare-minimum of qualified scientists on its payroll and (b) getting that laboratory, also, to simultaneously engage in the development of a complex guided missile system, code-named the Devil missile. However, as I recall, all of us in the laboratory then had been thrilled beyond measure as we had learnt of that imminent change of circumstances for our laboratory and the commencement its work for the development of a guided missile.

For a totally-ill-equipped laboratory, as we then had been, thanks to the continued denial of resources to the DRDO and the DRDL, in particular, by our government over the previous two decades then, it was, indeed, a daunting task. A task which had involved, as stated, the immediate build-up of that laboratory's infrastructure from scratch and, simultaneously, the undertaking of the Project Devil, ie the development of a full-fledged missile system, albeit, with the support of a network of other laboratories in and outside the DRDO, which dealt with a host of technologies relevant to guided missiles, eg gound-based electronics like the radar, aviation electronics, explosives of various kinds including high explosives for warheads and solid-rocket propellants, several types of special materials, mechanical and electro-mechanical devices etc. The task was even more daunting, in a way, because, unlike the ISRO and the AEO (Atomic Energy Organisation), which were, from the beginning, well-funded and fully empowered by our government to commence their mandated tasks without loss of time, the DRDO had lacked both the financial resources and the scientist-manpower that were required for developing indigenously the high-tech components and subsystems of a complex system like the guided missile. A task which, as known, calls for a network of R & D institutions and other work-centres that are endowed with one or the other technology-capability as well as a host of prototype production facilities.

And, as regards co-operation and collaboration, ie the deriving of benefit from the other national-level R & D organizations, especially the ISRO, the picture was bleak: There was such a watertight separation between the ISRO and the DRDO prior to the arrival of the new SA, Professor B D Nag Chaudhuri, that there was no way by which our laboratory, the DRDL, could take advantage, in concrete terms, of either the infrastructure resources or the technology expertise of the SSTC, the ISRO's space launch vehicle research centre, in any one of the fields which are common to the guided missile and the space-launch vehicle. I will have more to say later on that curious situation that had prevailed then, but, coming back to our problem in hand then, we had no option in those early years but to depend entirely on our own resources for undertaking both of the following two activities simultaneously:

1. Establish some of the essential but comparatively-low-cost facilities inside the Laboratory for the fabrication and the testing of some of the components and sub-systems of a guided missile and identify similar, ie fabrication or testing, facilities for the other types of components both inside and outside the DRDO including institutions in the public and the private sectors of our industry, and
2. Develop, on a fast track, the prototypes of all of the components and subsystems of the missile and the complete system, while, also, initiating measures for establishing within our country the required bulk production facilities for guided missiles through the transferring of technologies with a view to ensuring that the production of Devil missile at a short notice, if it became necessary to do so, would be feasible.

It would be obvious that our intention was to achieve through that process two important objectives, namely

(a) training ourselves, the scientists and the technology managers of the DRDL, and, where applicable, of the allied laboratories, too, in the handling of a large-size missile development project, starting from its beginning to its end, ie from the stage (1) the users formulate their qualitative or operational requirements (QR or OR) through the stages of (2) analytical studies and designing and developing components/subsystems including their functional testing before and after their environmental treatment, (3) the integration of those prototype components and subsystems into a complete prototype of the indigenous missile system, (4) subjecting that prototype missile including its ground-support equipment, successively, to technical and operational (ie flight) trials, (5) the preparation and the handing over of the required number of prototypes of the indigenous missile system to the users and then participating, as observers, in the users' trials and, finally, (6) completing the process of transfer of technology of manufacture to the selected bulk-production agency and assisting that agency in the establishment of free-flow production of the indigenous missile, and

(b) following the successful completion of Project Devil, enabling each one of the associated DRDO-laboratories which had supported the DRDL by developing components and/or subsystems which called for the application of their respective technology-expertise to participate, in the near future, in the development of our own tactical-application guided missiles to meet the requirements of our own Army/Navy/Air Force under an integrated missile development programme.

Although the logic behind the sanctioning of Project Devil, as briefly enumerated in the previous paragraphs, was in conformity with an universally adopted practice, the business of getting our government to sanction, for the first time, a development project of such a magnitude in those early years, ie during 1971-72, probably, had been an altogether new, if an humbling, experience for us. After all, the DRDO, in the absence of resources, had waited for nearly two decades in the wilderness, and then, suddenly, a project which would enable the DRDO and the DRDL, in particular, to commence the build-up of some of its long-awaited test and fabrication facilities and, at the same time, to undertake an actual development of a complex-system guided missile, almost in its entirety, needed to be sanctioned by our government. It is precisely for those reasons that the Devil project, both for the DRDO and our country then, had been an unprecedented experience, thanks to the vision and the leadership of a new and empowered SA. I may, also, mention here that first step that he, the new SA, had taken then was to select and put in position a new Director for our laboratory, namely Air Commodore (later Air Vice Marshal) VS Narayanan of the Engineering branch of our Air Force, who had the required credentials for the job and, as expected, had hit the ground running. But, while giving the approval for the Devil project, our government then, had, also, stipulated that a continuous review would be undertaken by expert committees at every stage of progress on a pre-determined path.

The idea was that although a few approvals for expenditure would initially be given for a limited build-up of the DRDL our government would not be in a position, unless there were enough indicators along the way to show that the DRDL would be able to take up the Project Devil and bring it to its logical conclusion, to make further investments towards the augmentation of facilities in the DRDL and associated DRDO laboratories and , also, in the establishment of bulk production facilities for the indigenous missile system in our Ordnance factories and our public sector production units.

The logic had been that a combination of (a) the availability of resources, consequent to the sanctioning of funds for the Project Devil by our government, and (b) our being able to successfully make use of those resources within the stipulated time-frame will enable our country to immediately, thereafter, commence the task of 'making' of a few, tactical-application, guided missiles of our own with a view to achieving a reasonable degree of self-reliance, in the foreseeable future, in both unguided rockets and guided missiles. In short, the objective was to do away with our continuing dependence for guided missiles on developed countries. However, indisputably, also, a dose of caution, on the part of our government, had been a matter of prime importance while it had given the go-ahead for an expenditure of that magnitude, making it abundantly clear that the decision-makers, at the highest level, had some reservations at that point of time (1971-72) about the DRDO's ability to make a success of such an unprecedented programme which called for the simultaneous utilization of funds for hardware development and the selection and induction, on priority, of a large amount of manpower resources of the right kind. What it had really implied was that our government needed to see if (a) the DRDO scientists were, in fact, capable of designing and developing all of the subsystems and components of a complex guided missile system on their own while, also, designing and building some of the items of the much-needed infrastructure for the first time, and (b) the senior scientists and technology managers of the DRDL, in particular, and the managements of all of the other associated laboratories were capable of handling successfully such a time-bound, multi-technology development-cum-manufacture programme.

Although, at that juncture, it was essentially a matter of decision-making in relation to spending a total of about three crores of rupees, no less, by way of expenditures related to the project Devil, a sum which, in terms of today's rupee-value, would amount to two hundred crores of rupees, probably, in reality our government, by giving that sanction – albeit, after nearly three decades of inaction – had suddenly broken away from its earlier mind-set and had signaled the start of the much-awaited development of military technology in India in a planned and meaningful manner. Further, at that point of time our government had, also, committed itself, in principle, to our undertaking, in the very near future, a comprehensive guided missile development programme for the development of a selected few types of guided missile for tactical applications. As known, our Armed Forces have been in need, for many years by then, of quite a few types of guided missiles and were importing a few of those missiles. And, that had to be changed, and the dependence on foreign suppliers must cease. That was why, at that juncture, decisions pertaining to the incurring of expenditure for the development of technologies of guided missiles could be taken by our government without loss of time, keeping in view the criticality of the need for building self-reliance in guided missiles. It ought to be noted that at that point of time we were focused on tactical application missiles only, and the question whether we ought to be able to develop in future a guided missile for a strategic application, also, had not arisen and, therefore, not figured in our planning.

Fortunately for us, Project Devil had met with enough success by early 1974, both in terms of the targeted infrastructure build-up and in respect of the development of technology and of selected components and subsystems, signaling that the work had progressed well. Some of the activities which were undertaken during that phase by the DRDL and some of its supporting laboratories were (a) the design and construction of a static test facility, fit for testing large-thrust solid propellant rocket engines, eg the booster engine of the 'Devil' missile, (b) similar work pertaining to the static test facility for sustainer type of liquid propellant rocket engine, (c) test facilities for a number of electro-mechanical, electronics and mechanical engineering devices of the 'Devil' missile, (d) testing and identification of materials and formulation of their specifications including those of solid and liquid propellants, electronic components and subsystems etc (e) design studies related to both the electronics and the rocket engines and of their hardware fabrication techniques, and, finally, (f) the outsourcing of several development activities including those pertaining to the electronic components and sub-systems etc etc. Incidentally, the outsourcing of most of the critical materials, components and subsystem development had meant, in effect, utilising the capabilities of quite a few other high-technology laboratories of the DRDO itself. Incidentally, the ERDL had, also, been asked then to set up a facility for exploring cast double base (CDB) propellant as an alternate technology for extruded double dase (EDB) propellant. It ought to be mentioned in this connection that both the DRDL and a network of its supporting laboratories in and outside the DRDO had, for the first time in the history of military technology development in India, played an equally important role in this all-embracing venture. Some of those supporting laboratories were the ERDL, the Armament R & D Establishment (ARDE), the TBRL, the Defence Electronics Research Laboratory (DERL), the Electronics Research & Development Establishment (LRDE) and the R & D (Engineers) Establishment of the DRDO and a few academic institutions and R & D establishments outside the DRDO, a few of the manufacturing companies in the private and the public sector of our country which had assisted the DRDL in developing some of the prototype hardware fabrication techniques.

Because the Devil project had met with enough success, during the first phase of its work, by early 1974, our government had signaled an agreement, early on, to invest funds, without further loss of time, in the next stage of our infrastructure build-up activity and to our taking up work for the next phase of Project Devil. As far as the infrastructure build-up was concerned, therefore, it was only at that point of time that (a) the design and construction of some additional accommodation for housing additional facilities, complete with access roads and augmented water and power supply facilities, were taken up on the highest priority, and (b) the work on the setting up of additional fabrication and test facilities, which were comparatively costly but were unavoidably required for the development of the next lot of subsystems and components, were planned in greater detail, and (c) the design and the construction work which were related to those facilities had been started.

To our pleasant surprise, we had, once again, made a success of those ventures, too, and had done that in record time. Therefore, most of those facilities were built and commissioned by us during 1974-75. To illustrate that point I may provide two examples from two different areas of missile technology:

1. In the case of missile propulsion, we had, at that stage, invested in two major facilities, namely (a) procuring a set of special equipment, which were essential for the fabrication of the hardware of liquid propellant rocket (LPR) engines and (b) a state-of-the-art instrumentation facility for real-time data acquisition, which was required for a state-of-the-art test facility for static testing of solid and liquid propellant rocket engines.
2. In the field of electronics and electro-mechanical test facilities we had made substantial progress in the development of one important guidance device, namely the inertial navigation system (INS), by designing and then setting up the required test facility for the indigenous INS prototypes, making use of both indigenously fabricated components and, most

importantly, by managing to procure from the open market in developed countries some of the critically important components, an altogether a fine piece of development work that was carried out successfully by our guidance and control engineering specialists.

It would be evident from the examples, quoted herein, that those bought-out equipment were meant to equip and set up the kind of test facilities which, in fact, ought to have been built and put into use by our DRDO, at least, a decade back but were actually being established only during 1972-76, that is just in time for making it possible for the DRDO to train its scientists and be in readiness for undertaking the IGMDP. It may, also, be evident that the reason why we could commission and put into use, in such a short time, most of those sophisticated test and fabrication facilities – or, for that matter, the reason why the DRDO could have set up those facilities and commissioned them much earlier, say in the mid-sixties, if the required funds were made available – is none other than this: Unlike all of the other developing countries, India, even in those early years, had possessed the intellectual capability for assimilating knowledge and undertaking the design of complex technology systems, even though our country had lacked the wherewithal for translating that design capability into the making of the hardware for the prototype of sophisticated components and equipment, eg the components of a state-of-the-art rocket engine or an INS.

Thus, Project Devil was the project which had provided the DRDO – and our country's military technology and industrial base – with both the essential tools (eg an array of test and fabrication facilities) and the learning process (ie the experience in planning for and the execution of a complex guided missile development project) for managing a multi-technology, multi-vendor development and technology-transfer process including the establishment of large-scale production. And, since a number of Indian R & D institutions including some of our civil-sector R & D laboratories and the manufacturing enterprises in the industry at large had necessarily to be involved in this process, Project Devil had proved to be an excellent enterprise. It had, in the process of its execution, helped our country and, therefore, a large number of our R & D institutions within and outside the DRDO and, also, manufacturing facilities in various fields, which would, in a matter of a few years thereafter, collectively make it possible to develop successfully quite a few types of indigenous guided missiles under the IGMDP. Some of those institutions where work had been successfully outsourced during the Devil Project were:

(a) the network of DRDO laboratories dealing with associated technologies, ie the Explosives R & D Laboratory (ERDL), the Defence Electronics Research Laboratory (DLRL), the Defence Metallurgical Research Laboratory (DMRL), the Electronics & Radar Development Establishment (LRDE), the Terminal Ballistics Research Laboratory (TBRL), the Armament R & D Establishment (ARDE), the R & D (Engineers) Establishment (R&DEE) etc, and

(b) the non-DRDO research institutions, eg our CSIR laboratories, some of our PSUs, well-equipped academic institutions, and the centres of excellence in our manufacturing industry at large.

As mentioned, the pre-requisite for the success of the IGMDP had been the success of the Project Devil. The basis for the planning and the execution of Project Devil had been the acceptance of an assumption that the success of the Project Devil would be immediately followed up by our undertaking a programme for the development and production of a few types of tactical application missiles with a view to meeting the immediate requirements of our Army/Navy/Air Force and, thereby, achieving self-reliance in an important area of weapons and equipment. In short, the IGMDP had been the logical follow-up of the Project Devil. And, it had been planned and undertaken by the DRDO squarely on the basis of the experiences and expertise gained by the DRDL during the execution of Project Devil. The fact that the IGMDP had been designed as a much larger task and had constituted much more of an ambitious programme than Project Devil only reinforces the fact that Project Devil had repaid, many-fold, the investments our country had made into Project Devil and the related infrastructure build-up.

I ought to mention another fact. Because of the reason that the IGMDP, with its four tactical-application guided missile projects and one project for the development of a technology-demonstrator longer-range SSM, had involved outsourcing of prototype manufacture in some cases to some of the research institutions and manufacturing centres of our country on a much larger scale than what the Project Devil had done, the DRDO had to take on an additional responsibility, in the case of the IGMDP, in one important respect, namely the guarding of classified information while dealing with government-owned non-Defence work centres and academic institutions, eg the national laboratories, the IITs etc and, even, non-government institutions, eg specialized research institutions and our industries in our private sector. And, we had learnt how difficult it was to persuade non-defence organizations and private-sector institutions, which had little or no experience earlier in the handling of defence-related classified information, to agree to put in place special administrative measures for ensuring full-proof security of information in compliance with all of our national-security maintenance regulations.

By the early 1976 I had completed a little over six years of work at the DRDL, six eventful years which had proved to be the most satisfying in terms of technology development-cum-management experience. And, at my initiative and after considerable efforts on my part at convincing my seniors, especially, the then Director of the DRDL, I could make all concerned to agree to my moving away from the laboratory to the headquarters of the DRDO, where I had a job cut out for me as regards coordinating and undertaking activities in support of our laboratories, eg the DRDL and its associated laboratories, in relation to future projects for the development of both guided missiles and unguided rockets, progressing ongoing dialogue with the headquarters of the three user services, namely the Army/Navy/Air, etc. Incidentally, of the unguided rocket projects the most important project had been the development of a vehicle-mounted multi-barrel rocket launcher (MBRL) system. As known, the successful completion that development programme by the DRDO laboratories has yielded, a few years back and soon after my retirement, an important weapon system for our Artillery, namely the Pinaka Multi Barrel Rocket Launcher (MBRL) system.

However, I may mention here that I had departed from the DRDL at a point of time when I had reached a sense of some satisfaction at having completed my task as a senior scientist of that laboratory successfully: On one hand, I had participated fully in the build-up of the infrastructure and test facilities of the DRDL from its earlier state of near-non-existence into a reasonably well-equipped laboratory with a sizeable strength of young and qualified scientists and, on the other, the development of the particular subsystem of the Devil missile, namely the indigenous prototype of the solid propellant booster rocket engine, which had been the responsibility of my technology-division, had been successfully completed in that it had undergone all tests including its flight trial successfully and the process of technology transfer for the establishment bulk production of the indigenously developed propellant as well as the rocket-engine hardware to the respective production agency had been completed. In other words, my work, both as the head of my own technology-division and as one of the deputies, responsible for the planning and execution of the build-up of the laboratory, in general, and of the solid-rocket-propulsion facilities including the establishment of a detachment of a propellant development facility, manned by its own specialists, had been successfully completed. Incidentally, two of the highlights of the solid-rocket development facility had been the setting-up of a large-thrust static test facility with its sophisticated instrumentation within the laboratory and the development of fabrication techniques for the hardware of the large-impulse solid rocket engines' hardware outside, namely at an outsourced production facility, located in one of our pressure-vessel manufacturing PSUs. In addition, propulsion scientists of the division had, also, commenced work on the development of solid rocket ramjet engine for a future tactical-application guided missile. I may, also, mention in this connection that I had, also, initiated a number of collaborative research programmes on missile-propulsion related technologies at selected centres of excellence in our country including two reputed academic institutions.

Way back in December 1969, when I had joined the DRDL, that guided missile laboratory was, practically, a notional laboratory, not equipped for serious R & D work. However, only a year or so later, in 1971-72, probably, ie soon after the arrival of Professor BD Nag Chaudhuri and the commencement of the much-awaited build-up of that laboratory, I had, as a member of the first-ever campus-recruitment team of the DRDL, comprising three senior scientists of our laboratory representing various technology disciplines, visited the campuses of most of our country's better known engineering-universities including the IISc and selected young undergraduate and graduate engineers to fill the newly-created posts of entry-level and young mid-level scientists in all of the technology-divisions of our laboratory. And, with two more of such on-campus recruitments of young scientists in the following three years, the DRDL had, by the time I had moved away in January, 1976, acquired a substantial strength of qualified young scientists, spread over all the relevant technology divisions. The making of that erstwhile ill-equipped laboratory grow into the largest laboratory of the DRDO and, probably, one of the few of its size in our country then – in a matter of five or six years – had, in a sense, prepared me well for my new assignment. I had, therefore, taken over my new assignment in the Directorate of Rockets & Missiles with enthusiasm.

At this point I may, again, point out, however, that but for the twists and turns that my career had taken in the first half of my Air Force service I would, probably, not have been selected twice by our government for advanced studies, not have had the opportunity to have done well in both those courses and, therefore, not have received the entry into work on military technology. As for the opportunity to play an active role in the building of our country's guided missile enterprise during its early years, it may have eluded me, too, unless a person of Professor BD Nag Chaudhuri's stature and capability had taken over the DRDO as our country's first-ever empowered SA cum DG DRDO an year or so after I had been posted by our Air Force at the DRDL. That was, in fact, the more likely reason why I had received both the opportunity to work shoulder to shoulder with some of our best scientists of that era and the privilege of seeing from close quarters the good work that had been done by some of our country's outstanding Scientist-managers then. Apart from the fact that those early years of military technology activities by a newly-revived DRDO were exciting times for an Indian scientist, the fact that during the later part of that period I had a better perch for seeing from close quarters some of those technology development activities had, unsurprisingly, given me an excellent opportunity, also, to see for myself how the four SAs of my time had, each in his own style, nurtured the growth of military technology in India during those early years. For instance, it was evident that two of our Scientific Advisers who had led the DRDO at two critical junctures, namely Professor B D Nag Chaudhuri and Dr Raja Ramanna, had contributed more effectively to the development of military technology in our country than some of the other seniors during their respective watches. By inspiring our bright and hard-working scientists of those decades, most of them young scientists who were both talented and dedicated, these two seniors amongst our senior scientists of that era had promoted excellence in quite a few of our DRDO's laboratories and establishments during their time.

Consequently, both of those SAs were successful in launching some of the critically-important, if ambitious, development programmes and in ensuring that the concerned laboratories and their competent scientists were well supported in their work. Although it is a matter for the posterity to make a final judgement on such matters, it was clear to us that those two outstanding leaders of science and technology of our country then had contributed in a major way to our country's success in both the guided missiles and the strategic weapon development programmes and that, but for their efforts, the unflattering record of some our country's early policy-makers' failures and delays and, in the case of a few of our other development projects, our own failures and lapses wouldn't have given way, finally, to a somewhat bright picture of our DRDO's success. Not surprisingly, both of those SAs had, each in his turn, taken inspiration from – and had excelled under the leadership of – the same Prime Minister, namely late Indira Gandhi, who had inducted both of those SAs, in their turn, as empowered SA-cum-DG DRDO. And, largely because it was she who had, in the first place, hand-picked each of them for the SA's job, and, also, because it was largely due to her that the DRDO had received the much-needed resources for building infrastructure and developing self-reliant military technology in our country that the conditions required for achieving self-reliance in weapons and equipment had, finally, materialized during the early nineteen seventies. As for the contributions that those two outstanding leaders of India's defence science and technology, Nag Chaudhuri and Ramanna, have made, it ought to be acknowledged that both have strengthened our DTIB and reinforced India's national security and sovereignty like none before had done.

There were others, too, who had done their bit, some within the government establishment and others outside, both in our universities and at other centres of excellence. Barring a few, however, who were within the establishment as senior functionaries of other scientific departments of the government, such as Professor Satish Dhawan, the rest are largely unknown faces but yet deserve full credit for having given a big push to our country's military technology development at its early stage. In the case of the late Professor Dhawan, the Chairman of the Indian Space Research Organisation (ISRO) then, the opportunity to play a big role in our missile technology development, in particular, had, also, come about at the very beginning of the DRDO's coming into its own. In other words, Dr Dhawan had not only been an witness to both the end of an earlier era of a moribund DRDO and its sudden revival but had, also, observed from close quarters the magnificent efforts put in by our scientists. Like one of his predecessors in the IISc, an illustrious Director and a jewel of a scientist in earlier era, Professor Homi Bhaba, Professor Dhawan had been active in promoting scientific education and research and had functioned as an outstanding teacher and researcher in his earlier years. And, like Homi Bhaba of an earlier era, Satish Dhawan, too, had been lifted by the nation's Prime Minister of the time – Nehru and Indira Gandhi, respectively – from a world of teaching and academic research to a place of leadership in our nation's industrial research. Thus, each of them had been entrusted with leading an important national endeavour, namely our Atomic Energy in the case of one and our Space Science enterprise in the case of the other, each move aimed at promoting the socio-economic transformation of India through the application of science and technology. While Professor Bhaba had laid the foundations of both the organizations soon after Indian independence and, later, built the Atomic Energy organization of our country into a first-ever successful nuclear power enterprise, developed by an economically challenged country, while earning for its world-renowned research centre, later renamed Bhaba Atomic Research Centre (BARC), an international recognition, a few decades later Professor Dhawan, albeit a person with lesser fame, had, as mentioned, successfully nurtured the nation's space sciences enterprise as an worthy successor, in that venture, to another physicist of repute, Dr Vikram Sarabhai, who, as a contemporary of Dr Bhaba, had been in engaged in building the Indian Space Research Organisation (ISRO) from a scratch and had achieved phenomenal success but, like Bhaba before him, had died unexpectedly. As known, Dr Dhawan, following in the foot-steps of Dr Sarabhai, had contributed his share of leadership at all levels of the ISRO and made our space programme a spectacular success and an envy of, even, the industrially developed world.

What is not so widely known, however, is that Professor Dhawan had, also, made his presence felt well beyond the call of his duties in the Space Research organization by influencing in an important way the course of our country's guided missile development programme in its early years. That was the reason why I have mentioned Professor Dhawan in connection with this brief discourse on Project Devil. As for those who had helped us from outside the pale of our government establishment, most were either young scientists and teachers in universities and institutions of technology or, as in one or two cases, managers in manufacturing companies dealing with sophisticated engineering or materials-related production processes. In almost all of those cases they had already excelled in their chosen fields and then come forward to lend a hand in the national effort to acquire self-reliance in military technology. Those are the people whose names would never appear in any Honours list but whose work in critical areas had been of inestimable value to our development projects and is yet unsurpassed. In the case of the institutes of technology and university colleges of engineering, some of those brilliant scientists, while continuing to work as inspiring teachers, had, often, at our behest, come forward and helped develop cutting-edge technologies that had benefited the national endeavour at achieving self-reliance in sophisticated weapon systems. Thus, their contributions to the IGMDP have helped the DRDO in no small measure.

It is a fact, however, that in a vast country like ours, with its abundance of scientific talent, there ought to have been many more of them to assist in the nation's efforts to develop weapons and equipment, as evident from the experience of the developed countries where military technology often rides on the shoulders of their universities and corporations. Our failure to follow their example was rooted in the fact that there were too many cobwebs in our colonial past, which had acted as impediments and, reinforced by other shortcomings in our country's higher defence management structure, had prevented us from making full use of our nation-wide resources during all of our post-Independence years. Hopefully, some of those outdated modes have since been abandoned and given place to rules and regulations which no longer prevent our defence technology and industrial base from making the best use of more and more of our intellectual assets and technology capabilities, outside the government-owned institutions but within the country.

Of the few who had, from outside the establishment, contributed in a big way to the build-up of our military technology base during those early years, I readily recall one who, then, had been a young assistant professor of computer science in one of our well known university colleges of engineering. He and his group of young and bright researchers had helped solve one of our critical design problems by successfully developing an algorithm for a target acquisition and prioritization system of an advanced-technology SAM prototype. That prototype missile which exemplified one of the most sophisticated systems of guidance and control had, at that point of time, been in its early stage of design and reflected our military's perception as regards a future, state-of-the-art SAM with multiple-target handling capability. Although in an initial stage of development then, as mentioned, the design studies on the guidance system for that prototype of an advanced missile had been based on the premise that a number of cutting-edge technologies, which then were yet to be developed by our country (eg a phased-array radar) but were in advanced state of development in the USA and one or two other developed countries, ought to be made use of.

The reason was that there were quite a few imponderables. And, the likelihood of attaining success in developing the required software and high technology hardware within the stipulated time frame had seemed not so bright either, for the simple reason that the infrastructure for developing those advanced technology hardware components was not yet available either within the DRDO or outside, eg in other R & D laboratories in our country's non-defence sector or in centres for innovation in our industry at large. Therefore, although most of our missile scientists were fully confident of our eventual success, a few had felt that there were some imponderables which would make it difficult for the concerned scientists to abide by the projected time-frame. And, unfortunately, that had turned out to be true, going by the reports of tests and trials, published in our newspapers from time to time. Apart from the fact that down the line the users had changed some of the parameters reflected in their original qualitative requirement (ie the QR), the DRDO's efforts at crossing the technology hurdles had, also, not met with easy or early success in those specific areas. In short, the results obtained during the technical and users' flight trials over nearly two decades have often led to further development work and delays. And, although the most recent news reports in our national dailies paint a more hopeful picture, it is not clear if the Akash prototype missile which has, finally, gone into production has earned our military's seal of approval in respect of all of the user-specified parameters. However, as mentioned earlier, over the time our Akash system may still feature as one of the few, state-of-the-art, surface-to-air missiles of its class in the world and, eventually, fare as well as the Patriot missile system of the USA/Israel joint venture.

A word about the state of our military technology preparedness will, probably, be in order here. Although India, admittedly, is yet to achieve, even, a semblance of self-reliance in conventional weapon systems India has, nevertheless, taken indisputably big strides in developing some of the high-technology weapon systems for both tactical and strategic application, namely the guided missiles of the IGMDP, the MBT Arjun, the LCA Tejas etc and the ballistic missile Agni and the nuclear warhead. And, as acknowledged now the world over, it is in those two areas, precisely, that we have, on our own, successfully demonstrated our technology capability. Areas where the ability of a nation to achieve self-reliance on its own steam alone matters – and not its ability to finance a purchase. In short, as a nation we have thus managed to attain what, admittedly, is the most difficult and, arguably, the most important goal, namely a reasonable degree of self-reliance in strategic weapons. A capability which, beyond doubt, is more critical for a non-aligned country like ours, encircled, as we are, by two nuclear-armed nations led by hostile rulers, since our very existence as a sovereign, secular and democratic nation will continue to depend on our ability to sustain that capability. Although a full account of my two-decades-long association with the people and the processes that had been involved in the building of this capability – and the stories of the successes and failures of our scientists of those early years – ought to make an absorbing reading, a brief recounting of some parts of that story is all that has been attempted in the following chapters of this book.

Chapter 3

Technology as a Substitute for War-Fighting

Digressing for a while from the story of my two-decades-long experience as a military technologist to take a look at my present work as a social science person post-retirement, I ought to mention that although my connection with military technology had ceased altogether with my retirement from our Air Force and the consequent bidding of goodbye to the DRDO, I had successfully switched, thereafter, from my earlier, active-life profession in science and technology to that of a free-lance, unpaid academic in the social sciences. And, I had done so by taking up reading of and writing on some of the technology-driven issues of international politics.

To illustrate the point, one of the studies in the field of Intnl Politics that I had taken up early on in my new avatar as an analyst, had culminated in my writing a paper which would bear the title 'Technology As A Substitute For Political Action: A Counterview Of US Policy & Strategy & Their Impact'. It had been published many years back, in the end of 1994 or early 1995, probably, in a US journal, called 'Comparative Strategy'. And, that article had, I believe, served the purpose for which I had got it published, in the first place, in an US journal which had considerable reputation then: It had managed to attract the attention of some of the American scholars of international politics, who specialized in US foreign policy studies and were either members of the US academia, ie the US universities and think tanks, or working for the policy-studies wings of the US government's State Department or the Department of Defence (DOD) or the Department of Commerce. My intention had been to highlight one particular aspect of the US foreign policy of those years, which had considerably harmed our country right from our inception (ie India's Independence) through the Cold War years and until very-recently and, curiously enough, had worked against the USA's own economic and political interests, too. And, it had done so by unfairly targeting a secular and democratic country like ours for all of those five decades and more. I refer here to the US-sponsored and US-allies-supported technology control regimes of those post-WW-2 years, each one bearing a different name coined by the Pentagon or the State Dept or the Dept of Commerce, but all specifically designed, or so it seemed, to achieve only one purpose, namely to throttle any attempt at developing dual-use high technologies made by any nation outside the US-led alliance of developed nations.

As it had turned out, that article became the first of the four articles on technology-related issues of international politics, that I had contributed to that journal during the period 1995-2000. However, it was almost two years before that, in 1993, probably, that I had made my debut, post-retirement, as an ISS analyst and occasional lecturer at universities and graduate schools, after I had switched to the social sciences. And, I wish to deal here with the kind of scholarly work that I have been engaged in since then, ie post-retirement and as a free-lance analyst. Work that I had taken up full-time, only after my retirement from government service, followed by another three years of professional engineering work as a senior in a reputed engineering consultancy organization in our private sector.

Interestingly, I may mention here that although it was only in early 1993 that I had taken up full-time scholarly work, albeit unpaid, it was, in fact, way back in 1962-63, ie in the eighth year of my service in the engineering branch of our Air Force, that I had written my first paper on a technology-related issue of international security and had it published in the Journal of the USI (United Service Institution) of India. And, that article, to my joy, had been well-received then, as I recall, considering that I was only a young and 'untutored' analyst of defene studies then, ie a Flight Lieutenant with only a good undergraduate degree in engineering, who had belonged to our Air Force's engineering branch. And, to my surprise, that article had been regarded then as one of the very few analytical pieces, written by an Indian scholar on that very subject. Admittedly, that article, which had been written by me in the late 1962, to be precise, had dealt with what had then constituted an important topic of international security studies by the nuclear-armed developed countries, namely the advent of nuclear and thermo-nuclear warheads and their impact on future war-fighting. In this connection it may be recalled that the subject of that article had great topical interest during the early nineteen sixties, because thermo-nuclear weapons had just then been developed by the USA and, probably, the Soviets, too, and that paper had dealt with the applicability of the time-honoured principles of war to the conduct of future war-fighting, using nuclear and thermo-nuclear weapons. Here I may add that the basic staff for writing that article had, in fact, been researched by me a couple of years earlier, ie in March 1960, probably. And that was because I had conducted that piece of research, in the form of a search of published literature on nuclear and thermo-nuclear bombs, written by social scientists, in preparation for a mandatory dissertation-writing in fulfillment of an important requirement of a junior staff course, namely our Air Force's Junior Commanders Course (JCC) of that period, which I had been detailed to undertake, by our Air Force, during Jan-March 1960. As in the case of most officers undergoing the JCC, I had then been a Flight Lieutenant, and I was posted as an engineering officer of a fighter squadron at a large Air Force base in West Bengal.

However, as already mentioned, it was nearly two years later, in 1962, that I had written that article, the product of my very first scholarly effort in strategic studies, which was unrelated to my primary avocation as an engineering offiicer of our Air Force. By then, however, I had already been transferred from the fighter base, not far from Calcutta, to the city of Calcutta itself, to take over my work as our Air Force's Technical Liaison Officer (TLO) at the headquarters of the Director General Ordnance Factories (DGOF), later renamed the Ordnance Factories Board (OFB), and, concurrently, the work of the officer-in-charge of what then used to be known as the Eastern India detachment of our Air Force's Inspectorate of Explosives, whose primary function, in those early years, had been the supervision of the in-house quality-assurance measures and the acceptance inspection of the engineering components of air armament stores, the special alloys etc, which were under production then at the three large Ordnance Factories, in and around Calcutta, and their vendors. And, I had written that scholarly article, using the materials that I had researched and collected during January-March, 1960, as an officer-student of the Junior Commander's Course (JCC) of our Air Force in connection with the writing of an end-of-course dissertation. That article, entitled 'Principles of War & Nuclear Weapons', had been published and sent by me from my previous station, Calcutta, to the USI, in New Delhi, in late 1962, probably. But, I had completely lost track of it after a while, partly because soon after that I had been posted out of Calcutta and promoted Squadron Leader at a forward maintenance base of our Air Force in Assam in the wake of the fall-out of the Chinese aggression of 1962 into our north-eastern border and the attendant stand-off, consequent to the continuation of illegal occupation of Indian land by Chinese Army on our north-eastern border.

It was in early 1964, therefore, ie almost an year after I had been posted out of Calcutta, on having been promoted, at a newly-established Air Force maintenance unit in an operational area of Assam, a non-family station of those days, that I had, accidentally, seen that article in print for the first time. An article that I had authored over an year back but had, apparently, forgotten of. And, I had been both surprised and thrilled by that event. The story goes like this. One afternoon, in the late 1963, probably, my Commanding Officer and I were visiting a neighbouring Army forward unit, having been invited by its Commanding Officer for lunch. Since that Army unit, an Engineers construction company, as I recall, and our Air Force maintenance depot were located close to each other, it was natural and customary for us, two field establishments, to exchange informal visits and to get to know each other. Our host for that lunch was then a senior Major of the Corps of Engineers, or the Sappers, as they are popularly known as. Incidentally, I had met the same Engineer officer many years later at the Army Headquarters, New Delhi, too. He had received a number of promotions and become a Brigadier by then and was posted at the headquarters of the Engineer-in-Chief in the Army Headquarters. However, going back, it was at that lunch, hosted by Major Monteiro, then, that I had, also, met one of his young officers, a Captain of the Sappers then, who had, almost accidentally, shown me my article, in print, for the very first time. That young officer had mentioned on the lunch table, as I recall now, that he was then preparing for the entrance examination for the Staff College, and, as we had got talking, had suddenly asked me if I was the same Squadron Leader who had authored an article that had recently been published in the USI journal. Apparently, he had just then come across that article while studying for his staff college entrance examination, an all-India examination that is routinely conducted by our Army/Navy/Air Force every year for selecting candidates for the prestigious Staff College course from amongst the bright and young of the three Services. According to that Captain of the Engineers, that article, in which its author had examined the relevance of the time-honoured Principles of War to future war-fighting, using nuclear and thermo-nuclear weapons, had been an unusual piece, and he had mentioned that he had not come across any other article, so far, on that topic despite his meticulous search of literature in the university and the Army libraries nearby and going through the collection of the USI in New Delhi. In other words, as he had pointed out, that article was, in his opinion, the first of its kind to have been seen by him then, which was written by an Indian author.

As expected of any newly-minted author, I had desperately wanted to believe that I was, indeed, the author of that article and deserved every word of praise that the Captain had showered on that author of that article, especially, his statement that, as a candidate for the Staff College examination, he had found my article an essential reading. But, the reality was that, for a moment, I had actually been unable to, even, recall that, only an year or two back, an article of that kind had been written by me and sent to the USI journal for publication. Probably, it was the circumstances of my having lived in a forward base, away from my family and the usual environment, associated with scholarly activities, for nearly an year by then, that had caused that momentary lapse of my memory. Or, the fact that I had been immersed for many months by then on almost all days of the week in an operational environment, quite unlike that of a peace station, that had caused that momentary lapse of memory. Whatever the reason, however, the fact was that, sitting in that 1000-pounds-tent accommodation that had housed an improvised officers' mess at a forward military base, far away from a city or a centre of learning, I had forgotten for a moment that I had, in fact, written a scholarly article and sent it for publication only an year or more back. I had, therefore, unhesitatingly and emphatically told that sappers Captain that I had never authored such an article nor had I sent one to the USI journal for publication.

However, since that young officer had just then been reading that article he had felt confident that the combination of the three facts, namely that the full name of the author, as it had been printed on that article, was exactly the same as mine, that the Air Force rank which had been printed as the author's rank (ie Flight Lieutenant) was exactly one rank below my present rank, and, finally, that I had been a Flight Lieutenant at my previous unit prior to my elevation to the Squadron Leader's rank at my present, could lead to only one conclusion, namely that none but I had authored the article, published recently in the USI journal. In any event, he had promptly got up from the dining table, as I recall, and fetched the copy of the USI journal from his living quarters and had shown that article to me. It was only then, at that precise moment, that I could suddenly recall, as if in a flash, that I had, while posted at my previous station, Calcutta, indeed, got hold of the materials that I had collected in connection with writing my dissertation for the JCC two years earlier, ie in 1960, and had written that article, using those researched materials, and had then sent it to the USI in New Delhi from my Calcutta office only an year or two back. And, although I had momentarily forgotten all about it, that sudden realization that a scholarly article, authored by me, had, after all, received the approval of an esteemed journal's Editor after it had been received by the USI journal had acted as an instant morale-booster for me, an aspiring 'military' scholar who had been living anonymously, in a manner of speaking, in a forward military base for nearly an year by then! And, when on the following day I had written a letter to the USI, using a free-issue APO (Army Post Office) stationary, requesting that the author's copy of the journal be forwarded to me at my present unit, care of 56 APO, I had received a prompt reply. Not only had the Editor quickly sent me a copy of the relevant issue of the USI journal but he had, also, enclosed a cheque by way of payment of an honourarium, due to me as the author of that article. In fact, as I recall, he had, even, regretted that, not having been able to locate me for almost an year, despite the efforts the USI journal had made, he had, by then, almost, given up any hope of informing me of the fact that my article stood published.

In retrospect, that article represents my first foray into scholarly work in the social sciences or, to be more precise, my debut as an analyst of technology-related issues of international security. And, it was, probably, that singular event, way back in early 1964, probably, more than any other, that had sent me a signal, albeit at an early stage of my service in the Air Force's engineering branch, that post-retirement I could switch from engineering science to a social-science subject which is inevitably impacted by developments in engineering and technology. As I have mentioned, I had done that switch soon after my retirement, ie researching into and writing and delivering occasional lectures at graduate schools on technology related issues of international politics, a subject routinely taught now in political science and international studies departments of many an university in the developed countries and in a few graduate schools in our country, too.

It was, also, in the same USI journal that I had, some three decades later, written my first article, post-retirement, on a technology related issue of international politics and got it published. And, that paper was, probably, also, the first of its kind by an Indian author, because it had managed to diagnose – and discuss in some details – the problems which plague our country's DTIB, even, today. Incidentally, that paper, to my pleasant surprise, had, soon after its publication, attracted the attention of many a scholar in that field and received the accolades of some of those ISS scholars and researchers, too. Most importantly, it had been acknowledged by most of those, whose research interest lies in that particular area of international security studies, as an original piece of work on the functioning of the Indian DTIB, even though there are not many Indian analysts who have given much attention to that subject and written on it. However, the circumstances which had led to my publishing that article in the USI journal, in the first place, were rather interesting. As mentioned, after my early retirement from our Air Force from the position of the Director of TBRL, followed by three years of work as an engineering consultant, I had, in 1993, taken up scholarly work on national and international security issues involving technology. And, it was precisely at that junction, in the late 1993, probably, that I had run into one of my esteemed seniors and an old acquaintance, namely late Major General Samir Sinha, a much-respected former general of our Infantry, whom I had known well but had lost touch with for some years by then. Even though I had heard that he had taken early retirement quite a few years back from the Army for health reasons and then joined one of our border intelligence organizations as its Inspector General I had, also, learnt recently that, having made a superb job of overhauling and running that organization for a few years, he had retired from that appointment, too. In fact, I had lately wondered if he had taken up some other assignment after his retirement from the civil service.

However, as we had run into each other on that chance meeting and had got talking I had been glad to learn that after leaving the government's employment he had joined the esteemed United Service Institution (USI) as its Director. The USI, as known, is an autonomous Indian think-tank of long standing, meant for undertaking and promoting national and international security studies in an independent manner, even though it is managed by our armed forces and largely funded by our MOD. It had, in fact, been established over a hundred and fifty years back by the British Indian Army during the hey-day of the colonial rule and had been run by the British Army in India more or less on the lines of its two-centuries-old parent organization, the venerable Royal United Service Institution (RUSI) of Great Britain, which has its own building and headquarters, located in close proximity to the British MOD in Whitehall, London.

However, as soon as he learnt that I, too, had retired recently and had since then taken to scholarly work in national and international security studies he had asked me, partly in amusement and partly with serious intent, if I had any knowledge of our USI. And, I had happily responded in the positive by stating that, indeed, I have had full knowledge of the USI from my young-officer days and that I had, in fact, written an article, too, as a young Flight Lieutenant, for its esteemed journal, an article that had been published some three decades back. Despite the trend of that conversation, however, it had been a surprise for me, as I recall now, when, suddenly and unexpectedly, General Sinha, who had only accidentally met me on that occasion after a gap of many years, had stated that he would be delighted if I would accept his invitation to deliver a lecture at the USI at my earliest convenience. And, it was thus that I had happened to deliver my first invited lecture at our USI in early 1994, probably. As mentioned in another context earlier, I had chosen for that talk one of the most important topics in my area of research interest, namely the problems and the prospects of the Indian DTIB in relation to the achievement of self-reliance by our country in the field of weapons and equipment.

That invited lecture at the USI, in 1994/1995, had meant my presenting an analysis of our defence R & D and defence industrialisation, the like of which had, probably, never been presented or been seen in print in any journal. My presentation had dealt with the study of the critical differences, in the area of the management structure and the functioning, between India's defence technology and industrial base (DTIB) and those of the developed countries, eg the USA, UK and France, and of the two newly industrialized countries, eg Russia (ie the Former Soviet Union or the FSU) and new China, followed by an analysis of the consequences thereof. As known, the major industrially developed countries have been in the forefront of technology development and arms production for three centuries. France and Great Britain, particularly, had played a pioneering role in the past, ie during the seventeenth to the nineteenth century, in developing military technology and expanding defence production, both in the interest of their own advancement in military power projection and for augmenting national wealth through the export of arms to the industrially undeveloped and less developed countries. Incidentally, that subject of my first lecture at the USI had not only belonged squarely to my own area of scholarly interest but had, also, constituted one of the most appropriate topics for me, as an occasional lecturer, in view of both my two decades-long experience as a military technologist in India and the repeated exposures that I have had to the DTIB management systems of France and Great Britain, particularly, during my work-related visits to those countries. And, since the subject of management practices in industrial organizations in developed countries, in both their private sector and their public, ie the management structures of large industrial organisations in the developed countries, which both develop and manufacture their products, especially, high-technology products, had, also, been well researched by me as an ISS scholar, post-retirement, I had, probably, been one of the few Indian analysts who had had good credentials, as a scholar, to deal with that subject. In short, arguably, I was one the best-placed of ISS scholars in our country to figure out why independent India's efforts at achieving self-reliance in conventional weapons and equipment have failed so spectacularly despite the investments made by successive governments both in the building of infrastructure for the development of military technology and in the development of weapon systems, especially, from 1972 and in setting up a large variety of ordnance factories and public sector defence production units since the mid-1950s.

As was the custom then, that lecture, under the auspices of the USI, had been delivered by me in the large auditorium of our MOD in the South Block. And, that lecture and the article that I had written, following the delivery of that lecture, and got published in 1994/1995 in the USI journal, were both well received. In fact, it was soon after the publication of that article that I had discovered that although there were (and still are) only a few ISS scholars in our country whose research interest focused on the

Indian DTIB, in particular, and military technology-related issues, in general, there were many more in the industrially developed countries, especially the USA, Sweden, the UK and France, who had specialized in that very subject. In fact, when I had noted, for the first time, that there was another scholar with an Indian name who had written a few papers on that subject I had, also, discovered that he was, in fact, an American of Indian origin, whose one research interest, as a professor of political science in an US university, happened to be the same as mine, namely international security issues involving technology. Incidentally, I may mention in this connection that two or three years after my article on the Indian DTIB had been published in the USI journal in 1994/95 that Indian-American professor of political science in a US university had surprised me by tracking me down and speaking to me on telephone, from another city, while I was on a lecture tour in the USA. The reason: He had wanted to have a discussion on the research topic, common to our scholarly interest, namely the DTIB-related issues of international politics, for the reason, as he had explained on that occasion, that he had been invited by a well-known think tank of Sweden to present a paper, on the same subject, at a forthcoming conference in Stockholm. And, that call had surprised me, partly because he and I had never communicated to each other before that, let alone having met in person in India or the USA, and partly because, as he had mentioned then, he had read with great interest my article on the Indian DTIB, which had just then been published our USI journal. Interestingly, on that occasion, the only time we had spoken to each other, albeit on telephone only, he had told me, for whatever reason, that, in his opinion, I, and not he, ought to have been invited to present the paper on that subject by that well-known think-tank on international peace studies, and had speculated on that occasion, as I recall, that the reason why he had been preferred as panelist of and presenter of paper at that international gathering of ISS scholars might have had something to do with the fact he had been better-known as an ISS scholar, having been a life-long professor, by then, in an university in the USA and having started writing and publishing on that subject many, many years before I had done so as an ISS scholar. However, going back to the subject in hand, ie my lecture at the USI, New Delhi, in 1994, although that lecture had been largely attended by many serving and retired senior civilian and military officials, including one recently retired Chief of Naval Staff, and, of course, some young and not-so young professors and researchers of a few of our own universities and think-tanks, it was my article on the same subject, which had been written by me and published by the USI journal a few months later, that had, not surprisingly, received more recognition in the years which had followed, with one honourable exception, however, as I would explain in the this chapter later. As expected, most of that recognition had come from a section of ISS scholars of English-speaking countries, namely the UK and the USA, in particular, whose research interest overlapped mine.

As a new arrival in the ISS community, I had been somewhat surprised, if a little elated, by that success. But, I had, also, noted on that occasion that my article had received more attention from professors and researchers in developed countries than among the scholars in my own country. And, there were understandable reasons for that, I had realized. For one thing, the USI journal had an international readership, especially amongst ISS scholars, eg political science professors and ISS researchers, both in the developed and in the new industrially-developing countries (NIDCs). For another, India had by then started emerging as an economic power, and its ascendancy was being noted the world over, especially the developed world. And, the growth of our military technology and defence production potential were both a concern and of serious scholarly interest to the developed countries, especially, the USA and its NATO allies, factors which had contributed to making my article attract the attention of ISS scholars of those countries. Finally, unlike the new industrially-developing countries, barring one, namely Russia, the developed countries, ie the USA and its allies in the NATO, had recognized that, in the interest of furthering their political goal, they must deliberately promote studies and deliberation by their academic institutions and their political scientists, including the professors and scholars, whose primary research interest was the military technology related issues of international politics. And, most of the well-known US universities, in particular, have always received funding for such research from the federal government and other US institutions which promote research in the ISS. The most reputed universities have, even, constituted special faculties and departments which deal with subjects that they had described as 'Science and National Security' or 'Engineering and Public Affairs' etc. For instance, the MIT (Massachussetts Institute of Technology) had, during those years, a Centre for Engineering and Public Affairs, which was attached to its Dept of Political Science; the Harvard University has a Centre for Science & Public Policy; and the Carnegie Mellon University (CMU) had a Department of Engineering and International Security Studies then, which Dept, as I recall, had, at the beginning, ie in 1995, say, the CMU's esteemed Professor of Computer Science as its Head. In any event, in the first few years following the publication of that article in the USI journal, in early 1995, probably, both the lecture, given at the USI, and the article, that had been published following it, have been cited by a number of scholars and analysts in some of their writings including one or two of their books. Whereas some of those authors were Indians, working in India, there were others who were foreign scholars, eg professors and researchers, who either belonged to departments of political science or international relations in universities abroad or were attached to think-tanks, such as the SIPRI (Swedish International Peace Research Institute). I had, from then on, started receiving invitations for lectures from some of the reputed graduate schools. In two cases, I had, also, received an invitation to write papers, and I have thus had the opportunity, during 1995 to 2000, to contribute a few articles on those subjects to international publications on arms control, such as a monograph, edited by the Swedish International Peace Research Institute (SIPRI) of Stockholm, and an US journal (Comparative Strategy), edited by the National Institute of Public Policy (NIPP) of Washington DC.

But, for me, the most satisfying response to my writing that article for the USI journal had been a letter by a ISS scholar from within our own ISS community. And, that was so because of the following reasons: (a) In developed countries there were many scholars who specialize in technology issues of national and international security and have, therefore, authored books and papers on the Indian DTIB, too, but very few of our own scholars have research interest in technology related issues of international politics, (b) Since my article had constituted a scholarly study of the limitations of the functioning of the Indian DTIB in the light of the experiences of the developed countries, ie the DTIBs of the USA, France and the UK, in particular, I had thought that there might not be anyone, in the Indian ISS community, who would care to read my article critically. The best response, as mentioned, however, had been a response that had come, almost immediately after my article had been published, from a person from within our own ISS community, made up of the very few Indian scholars who had expertise in that subject of the ISS. And, it had come to me in the form of a hand-written letter from that person, namely one Brigadier NP Grant who is now no more but had been an outstanding Indian scholar of national security studies. He had an abiding interest in and in-depth knowledge of our DTIB comprising our defence R & D and our defence production organizations which are held together with an inappropriate management structure. Arguably, he had, also, been an analyst with best of credentials, in his time, for commenting on our DTIB's methods and manners and on its failures in achieving self-reliance in weapons and equipment. He had then been in retirement in Pune for many years but, also, a prolific writer on defence issues during all of that time. As known by many of our ISS scholars of his time, Brigadier Grant had had a distinguished career as a Sapper and, during his retirement, become a regular contributor to the USI journal, although, most unfortunately, I had never known him in person. It goes without saying that he had never known of my professional background. However, I had some knowledge of his work as an ISS scholar, post-retirement, and some idea of his personality through his writings.

I may add that I had, also, gathered from those who knew him well prior to his retirement that, during the last ten years of his Army career, he had served for one term in our department of defence production. However, since I was aware that, in retirement, he used to contribute an article or two to the USI journal every now and then, dealing not only with issues related to the Indian DTIB but, also, with other issues, such as those related to our military operations, I had formed the impression that he had one distinction: He was, probably, the only one of our soldier-scholars then, who, unlike the majority of the retired seniors of our Army/Navy/Air Force's combat branches who had evinced interest only in war-fighting issues or issues related to our foreign policy, he had, also, authored quite a few papers on India's defence production problems. So, it was an altogether pleasant surprise for me when I had, suddenly, received that personal letter from the Brigadier. A letter which he had written in his own hands and written quite a few months before I had had the opportunity to read it. Although I had read that letter as soon as I had returned home from my foreign tour on that occasion, I had noted that he had written that letter almost immediately after my article had been published in the USI journal during my absence abroad. And, more importantly, not having known my home address, he had sent that letter confidently to the Editor of the USI journal in New Delhi, with the request that it be forwarded to my address immediately on receipt. But, because it had taken that letter, sent from Pune by ordinary post, probably, a month or more to reach my locked home in New Delhi via the desk of the Editor of the USI journal in Delhi and, most regrettably, because I had still not returned and did so after another 2 months or so it had taken a total of three or four months, probably, for me to see that letter, written by Brigadier Grant in his own hand.

He had mentioned in that letter that, in his view, my article was the first-ever, informed piece that he had read on what really ails India's DTIB. Coming from one who knew all too well the defects in our management structure, which impeded the functioning of both our defence R and D and our defence production organizations, that unsolicited letter from the late Brigadier Grant, with fulsome praise for my article's critical appraisal of both our military technology enterprise and our defence production set-up, was the best accolade that a newly-minted analyst like me could have received from a critic who had known the subject well. I recall that he had particularly liked the fact that in my analysis of the problems of our DTIB I have not only highlighted the facts pertaining to the management structure of the DTIBs of the industrially developed countries (IDCs), ie France, the UK and the USA, but, also, pin-pointed the reasons why the ills which had prevailed in our DTIB had not found a place in the newly industrializing developing countries (NIDCs), ie the communist or socialist countries China and Russia (ie the Former Soviet Union or the FSU). As I recall, he had, also, commented that by doing so I had shown that our country was unique in one respect, namely that we have failed to acknowledge the 'inherent' defects in our DTIB management structure and to make amends, even, after six decades of our Independence. As I mentioned, that commentary on my scholarly effort by the late Brigadier Grant has, probably, been the most satisfying to me as an analyst, ever. But the sad part is that although I did send a thank-you note to him as soon as I had seen his letter, in 1996, probably, he had not lived long thereafter, having passed away before I could meet him in person . And, I still wonder if my thank-you note had actually been seen by Brig Grant before he had taken ill. It goes without saying that I will always regret the fact that I had not made any effort, even, to speak to him on telephone on seeing his letter, let alone visit him to convey my gratitude, personally, for his taking that unusual initiative to express his views on my article, published in our USI journal. With a heavy heart, I, therefore, take this opportunity to acknowledge in all humility that the receipt of that letter, written in his own hand by Brig Grant, had acted as the best incentive I have ever received for doing scholarly work as an unpaid analyst, post-retirement.

Lectures At Graduate Schools

While I had generally been aware of the fact that in the years following the publication of that (1994-95) article in our USI journal references were often made to it by some of the other scholars in their papers and books it was only recently, in 2005, probably, that I had discovered an interesting fact: One of our reputed scholars of strategic studies, attached to a well-known think-tank in New Delhi, had cited one of my observations as an analyst in his critically acclaimed book on India's nuclear weapons, which had been published in 2004, probably. But, somewhat strangely, while making that citation in the relevant chapter of his book that esteemed Research Professor had referred to the notes that he had taken during the course of a talk on the same subject that I had delivered at the auditorium of the South Block, under the auspices of the USI in 1993-94, probably – and not to the article I had written for its (ie USI's) journal subsequently. Apparently, one of the points that I had made during that talk at the USI had lent support to an observation that the research professor had made in his book of 2005.

However, I had not known that professor personally, not having had an occasion to meet up with him ever, nor had I been aware of the fact that the professor had attended my lecture in the South Block auditorium in the mid-nineteen eighties and taken notes while listening. However, when I found out that the esteemed professor had cited in his book a statement that I had made during my USI lecture earlier, and not referred to my published article, I had felt a little intrigued and wanted to know why he had preferred citing a lecture, delivered by me earlier, to quoting the article that I had authored and got published soon thereafter. And, I had telephoned him and asked about it, soon after I had seen his book and read that citation. That was, probably, some months after his book had been published. More interestingly, however, his reply to my query during that telephone conversation had been forthright, as I recall: He had told me that he had not only attended my lecture, delivered at the invitation of the USI in the South Block auditorium but had, also, taken notes while listening to my lecture, and had preserved those notes for future use and, hence, preferred quoting those notes, taken by him many years before the publication of his book, to citing my article that had been published in the USI journal, an year or so after my lecture.

In any event, as I have mentioned earlier, well before that scholarly book on India's nuclear weapon by one of our country's senior Research Professors of strategic studies had been published that article of mine in the USI journal, which was a follow-up of my lecture, delivered some months earlier, had attracted the attention, also, of other ISS scholars who dealt with issues, pertaining to either South Asia or to military technology and arms control, in general. And, that, in turn, had helped me receive the attention of a few other ISS scholars in our country and abroad and some recognition, I believe, that I was one of the very few of our country's ISS analysts, who dealt, primarily, with technology related issues of international politics. And, the fact that my first analytical paper on the Indian DTIB and related issues, published in our USI journal in 1994/1995, had been taken note of and cited, thereafter, by a few established ISS scholars of industrially developed countries in their scholarly books and papers had a beneficial effect: It had helped me to make up my mind to devote my post-retirement years to scholarly work related, primarily, to technology-related issues of international politics, including the giving of occasional lectures at the invitation of one or two graduate schools in India and many abroad, which teach and research into technology-issues of international politics, eg our own Jawaharlal Nehru University's (JNU) Centre for Intnl Politics, Organisation & Disarmament (CIPOD). In fact, while my writings are now few and far between and published, even, now, in one or two of our own journals, it is, probably, a decade now, ie 2003, that I had given up 'full-time' engagement in scholarly work. Work that had kept me more engaged, in fact, than I had initially expected to be after my retirement. However, one curious fact remains: While a large number of our own country's professors and researchers of think tanks and university departments of political science, international relations and such like and a few of our own retired officers of our three Services and of our Foreign Service etc are engaged in writing and speaking on military affairs, foreign relations and other issues of international politics, a very few of our analysts, however, deal, primarily, with the issues of international politics involving technology, eg a nation's military technology enterprise insofar as it affects national security, eg the impact of missile proliferation on international security, nuclear warhead proliferation etc.

That was one reason why my particular choice of the subject for scholarly work has been, for an Indian analyst, an unusual one, in some ways. In fact, unlike in most of the industrially developed countries, in our country one rarely comes across an ISS scholar who had been an engineer or a technologist by training and earned a living by working as a military technologist or a scientist in engineering discipline but had shown an inclination to read and write on that subject, namely international or national security issues involving technology, even, in his post-retirement years. Therefore, I had not known in the beginning what to expect by way of satisfaction as a newly-minted scholar in our country on technology related ISS.

But, once I had started writing, publishing and delivering invited lectures at graduate schools my work as a scholar and as an analyst had brought more invitations for occasional lectures from some of the reputed universities and think tanks of industrially developed countries, eg the UK, USA and, later, Canada, too, as well as from our own universities and think tanks, eg the JNU, the National Defence College(NDC), the USI and the India International Centre (IIC). Also, on a few occasions, I had been invited by sponsoring universities or think-tanks of international conferences to join the conference as an invited panelist. As known, some of those industrially developed countries, especially, the USA, project both diplomatic and military power to less developed countries, as a matter of their policy. Those countries, therefore, deliberately promoted the undertaking of research and studies on international security issues of current importance by both funding graduate students and research projects that were undertaken by outstanding scholars and professors of

(a) Political Science (as in most universities), or
(b) History (as in Yale University) or
(c) Information Technology studies (as in the Carnegie Mellon University, ie the CMU, where the head of the department of computer science had, at one point of time, chaired the CMU's dept of strategic studies, too, or
(d) Engineering (as in the Massachusetts Institute of Technology (ie the MIT) which had a Centre for Engineering & Public Affairs, attached to the MIT's esteemed department of political science.

It goes without saying that the reason why those developed countries invested their resources in teaching and research in that field is none other than that deriving benefit from such in-depth studies and research in international politics has always been regarded by the developed countries as a pre-requisite for informed policy-making by their government in the area of international politics, including national and international security-related affairs. And, my early exposure to one or two of those universities and graduate schools and think tanks, as an occasional lecturer, had, in turn, made me receive every now and then a few more invitations for lectures at graduate schools and. also, on rare occasions, for joining international conferences as an invited panelist, as mentioned, during that period.

As already mentioned my first scholarly paper, post-retirement, on a national security issue involving technology, namely a critical study of our own DTIB, had been published in our USI journal as early as in late-1994 or early-1995. That was a paper, as I had mentioned earlier, whose publication had been preceded by an invited talk that I had given a few months back at our USI's forum. As it had turned out, that paper had immediately been acknowledged by most ISS analysts of technology-related issues of national security as an unusual contribution by an Indian scholar for the reason that none before had researched that subject enough and been able to go to the bottom of the problem and to suggest a solution. That is, no scholarly work done before my paper was published had characterized our DTIB as an organization whose management structure was inherently defective and needed an overhaul for all of four decades, ie from the inception of independent India. In fact, as I had mentioned earlier, I had been aware of that for many decades, ie from the time I had been a staff officer in our Air Headquarters, once, in Dec 1965, dealing with the indigenous production of air armament, ie the subject of the production of indigenously developed armaments by our ordnance factories and defence public sectors units (PSUs). Later, after I had been inducted into the DRDO and had enthusiastically taken to R & D work as a scientist, fully engaged in developing military technology in our country, my conviction had been strengthened, especially, when my exposure, through studies in the evolution of industrial research and development and the bulk production of very-sophisticated engineering equipment in the developed countries, had shown how defective our defence production organization and its relationship with our R & D organization had been from day one of our Independence.

It was years later, after I had taken to full-time scholarly work post-retirement and done my home work, ie the required research into the management structure of the DTIBs of the industrially developed world, that I had concluded that I had been correct all along in my diagnosis of the problem of our own indigenous defence-equipment production enterprise, generally, and in respect of the reason for the failure of our country and its government to attain self-reliance in weapons and equipment, in particular. And, I had, therefore, found the right and, curiously, the most obvious answer, too, to what many of our own scholars had, for many decades prior to that, viewed as the most important question pertaining to our DTIB, namely why our DTIB had failed to achieve, even, a modicum of success in achieving self-reliance in indigenously developed weapons and equipment, even, after five decades of our independence and despite the making of a substantial investment in our defence production enterprise, in particular. That was and always is an intriguing question, however, in our country in view of our government's rigid hierarchical system. More so, because, unlike in the developed countries, eg the USA, France, the UK etc, and, also, in the new industrially developing countries (NIDC), eg China and Russia (ie the Former Soviet Union or the FSU), we, alone, have failed to achieve self-reliance in almost all of the conventional-weapon systems of the advanced kind.

Although most ISS scholars, here and abroad, who deal with technology-related issues of international politics, had acknowledged the merit of my paper I ought to mention in this connection, however, that, even before I had given my lecture at the USI in 1994 or published my article I had written a couple of articles on two other subjects related to technology, namely technology transfer and management problems, and had got those two articles published in two of our national dailies, the Statesman and the Daily Telegraph. I had, also, given a few talks on guided missile technology on a national TV channel, namely the Calcutta Doordarshan, and the educaional TV channel, run by the University Grants Commission. Those television presentations, made in 1989-1993 ,had been well received, too, because the Iraq-Iran war had just then flared up and kindled a public interest in the role of guided missiles in war-fighting and, particularly, the role of ballistic missiles in chemical weapons, which had been used in that war with devastating effect. All of those scholarly activities had, in a way, prepared me well for my academic work which had followed. And, it was in mid-1993, during my first visit to the UK after my retirement from the IAF that I had received my first two lecture invitations from two well-known graduate schools in the UK, namely the Lancaster University and the University of Hull, both of which had a strong International Security Studies research programme in their respective departments of Politics, and had delivered those lectures. It was, also, probably, during that time that I had given an invited talk at the Royal United Service Institution (RUSI) in London, too. As known, the RUSI of London, founded by the British Army at the heyday of the British Empire, had been the inspiration for the setting up of the USI in New Delhi by the British Indian Army during the colonial rule.

The Lancaster University, The University Of Hull & The RUSI

My lecture at the Lancaster university in 1993 was hosted by a well-known professor in its Dept of Politics, who was, also, then the Director of its Centre for International Security Studies. It was well attended, both by the concerned members of the faculty and the graduate and the undergraduate students of the Dept of Politics, including a few foreign students, I was told, who were then in Lancaster, pursuing graduate studies. During the question-and-answer session that had followed my lecture at Lancaster my responses to some of the questions, which pertained to South Asian security issues and, in particular, the threats posed by Pakistan and China, were somewhat forthright and, therefore, had provoked lively discussions which were, at times, heated, too. In fact, the professor of the department of politics, who had hosted my lecture and presided over it had himself asked quite a few provocative questions and, thereby, very substantively contributed to that discussion. As expected of an old-school British scholar who had his psyche deeply-rooted in the colonialist past of the British empire, he had, on that occasion, disagreed with quite a few of my observations on India's threat perception in relation to Pakistan but had readily agreed with my assessment of threats, posed by communist China.

However, there was a curious turn of events thereafter, and I would like to relate that story here. A few days after I had given my lecture at Lancaster University and returned to London, ie to our daughter's residence, I had received a telephone call from one well-spoken Englishman who had introduced himself as a senior executive of a publishing company and a former Major of the Royal Engineers of the British Army. He had stated that he had done his engineering degree in Cambridge University, as a subaltern of the Royal Engineers, and, after his early retirement from the Army, was at the present time an Associate Member of Lancaster University's Centre for international security studies. He had an abiding interest in South Asian studies, he said, and had planned to attend my lecture but could not do so because of another engagement. He had then stated the reason why he had taken the liberty of obtaining my telephone number from the venerable Professor at Lancaster university and of ringing me up: It was none other than the fact that he would like to meet up with me in London over a cup of tea with a view to getting acquainted and hearing from me, first hand, a gist of the seminar I had presented a few days back at Lancaster university.

Since that gentleman and I seemed to have had a lot in common, eg our engineering education and our military service background, ie our past service in our respective country's Armed Forces's engineering services, and since he had sounded very knowledgeable in international affairs, I had agreed to meet him on a set date. And, when we had met he had turned out to be exactly the kind of person he had seemed to be while he had spoken to me on telephone: A suave person in his early fifties and, as his visiting card had proclaimed, an ex-Major of the Royal Engineers, who had a MA (Cantab) degree, a graduate degree from the famed Cambridge University of England, and a senior position in a publishing company. However, after we had exchanged pleasantries and got down to discussing the political issues that I had discussed during my presentation at the Lancaster university in the previous week, he had expressed a desire for meeting me, once again, this time as a prospective publisher of my forthcoming book. Incidentally, although I had just then begun to write my first book (ie 'Military Technology & Defence Industrialisation: An Indian Experience', which had been published by an Indian publisher a little later, in

2000) I had, at that point of time, not, even, thought about a publisher. Therefore, his eagerness to meet me again for the ostensible purpose of securing a future business, as my prospective publisher, had seemed rather odd to me. And, it had suddenly struck me that his interest lay elsewhere: He was, probably, eager to cultivate me for another reason, and, therefore, there was more to it than met the eyes. In fact, the more he had spoken to me to plead his case for wanting to meet me again the more I had felt that this well-spoken, Cambridge-educated Englishman, who was an ex-Major of the Royal Engineers and had done his undergraduate engineering in Cambridge as a Royal Engineers subaltern, was not what he had appeared to be, namely a well-read senior executive of a publishing house, with scholarly interests in South Asian politics: He was, in all likelihood, a member of the British intelligence service, who used his connection with that professor of Lancaster university only to get an introduction to visitors like me for his own devious purpose.

As known, all developed countries have their own secret services, eg the CIA of the USA and the MI-6 of Great Britain, which routinely recruit a few of their highly-educated and well-placed professionals who would willingly function, also, as spies and informants, while living their own lives as professors, corporate executives and such like. It had seemed certain that the Cambridge-educated ex-Major, with a dubious connection with that professor of Lancaster University, who had an executive position with a dubious book-publishing company in England, had targeted me solely for the purpose of gathering India-related information. Whether the concerned Lancaster university professor, otherwise a reputed scholar of a well known British university, had, also, been functioning as a covert member of his country's intelligence service, the

MI-6, I would never know. But, that seemed likely. In any event, I had not agreed, thereafter, to meet with that senior publishing house executive and ex-Major, nor did I hear from my host, the esteemed professor of Lancaster university, ever again.

My lecture on South Asia related international security issues at the RUSI in London, too, was well attended. Apart from my host, the Director of the RUSI, who had turned out to have been a former Rear Admiral of the Royal Navy, who had chaired my lecture, others present had included a sprinkling of scholars from British think tanks and researchers from graduate schools of universities, in and around London. There were, also, three serving, if distinctly South Asian-looking, Brigadiers, too, in ordinary suits, each then a student of the Royal College of Defence Studies (RCDS) in London, formerly known as the Imperial Defence College (IDC), and they had belonged to Bangladesh, Pakistan and Indian Army, respectively. During the question hour the Brigadier from Pakistan was most vocal, as expected, with his unfriendly questions and hostile comments on my answers and observations on Indo-Pakistan relationship, but the Brigadier from Bangladesh had surprised me. He had referred to a statement that I had made during my presentation, namely that India, alone, among the developing countries of South Asia, was taking big strides in building its economy through the development of science and technology and was, therefore, likely to soon make its presence felt, as a technology empowered country, by developed countries, especially the USA, and had asked me if, therefore, India could pose a threat, in future, to its less-developed neighbour, Bangladesh.

I had promptly given my response by stating that, unlike communist China, which, as an authoritarian state, had invested heavily in its military and its weapon technology base and had developed intercontinental ballistic missiles, multiple-targeted nuclear warheads etc, by diverting most of its resources into its military industrial complexes and utilizing only a small part of its industrial and R & D capability for its economic growth, facts which were well known then, India was a true liberal democracy, which had spent very little so far in developing military technology but invested all of its R & D resources in developing science and technology for economic growth. Consequently, I had pointed out, India never intended to become a hegemony. But the Bangladeshi Brigadier had not looked convinced nor quite satisfied with my answer and assertion, I had felt. In any event, I had added that, while India would never pose a threat to its neighbour, Bangladesh, India had a legitimate expectation that Bangladesh would reciprocate India's well-meaning gesture by maintaining a friendly relation with India and by ensuring that insurgents or agents of foreign powers, inimical to India, were not given refuge in Bangladesh and allowed to set up their bases there for promoting insurgency against and terrorism inside India.

Apart from delivering a few lectures, routinely, every year for the next three years at our own Jawaharlal Nehru University's (JNU's) Centre for Intnl Politics, Organisation & Disarmament (CIPOD), I had, following my first visit to the UK in 1993 – to be with our newly-arrived single, working daughter in London – and the lectures I had delivered on that occasion at the Lancaster University, the University of Hull and the RUSI, delivered invited lectures and presented seminars at a number of other universities in the UK, the USA and Canada during the next decade. In fact, it was my first lecture at Lancaster, which had come to the notice of a few professors and researchers in other British universities, both in the UK and in North America, that had brought in its wake more invitations from graduate schools. Thus it is that I had, in the course of the next ten years and more, delivered invited lectures at some six universities in the UK, many more in the USA and five universities in Canada and one in Germany , some of those lecture-invitations repeated twice or more in the following years. On one occasion, in January, 2003, when I had been invited by a graduate school in Germany, namely the International Studies department of the Christian University in Kiel, a city near Hamburg, there were quite a few interesting exchanges with German students and professors, all of them proficient in English and international politics, during the question hour following my lecture, That had happened at some of the other graduate schools, too, but here I will briefly touch upon only a few of those interesting exchanges with both professors and graduate students .

It was on my very first visit to the University of Hull in the north of England in 1994 that I had met, for the first time, the much-renowned ISS scholar and a thorough gentleman, Professor Colin Gray, who had just then moved back to his home, the UK, from the USA after a long spell in the US academia. As the newly appointed Professor of Intnl Politics in the Department of Politics of the University of Hull, then, he was the first one who had extended an warm invitation to me for presenting a seminar on issues of international security involving space-based weaponry. And, as it had turned out, he had thought well of that presentation, too, especially, the fact that I had tried to give a lucid analysis of the technology of space weaponry and of its likely impact on future war-fighting to a packed house, comprising both the undergraduates and the graduate students of the Dept of Politics in Hull and some members of the faculty. In any event, the Professor had promptly invited me to deliver a lecture the next year, too. I had, therefore, lectured at Hull on two successive years, 1994 and 1995. As mentioned, he himself had then been a new addition to the faculty at Hull,as a senior professor, but I had been surprised to find that he had brought with him a few American graduate students, too, as his students in Hull's political science PhD programme. then Apparently, some of them had worked under his guidance while doing their dissertation for their MA degree in some of the US universities where Colin Gray had taught, albeit as an Adjunct Professor, and they were keen to do their PhD with Professor Colin Gray as their advisor and mentor.

An Englishman by birth, who had earned his doctorate at Oxford University many years back, Professor Gray had, however, been away from the UK for many years and had just then returned to the UK to take up his appointment at Hull. He had, also, told me that the first job that he had taken after finishing his D Phil in Oxford was that of an Asst Professor in the Dept of Political Science at York University in Canada. However, soon thereafter he had moved to the USA to teach and research, but it was as the founder and the Director of a well reputed think tank, the National Institute of Public Policy (NIPP) in Virginia near Washington DC in the USA, that he had made his mark as an outstanding ISS scholar and a policy analyst of international repute. He and his Institute had, over the years, undertaken a series of research projects on foreign policy and national security issues, funded by both the Pentagon and the State Dept, and he had been in demand as an adviser on foreign and defence policy to the governments of a number of other NATO countries, too, besides the USA, eg the UK and Canada. Having recently returned to the UK as the Professor of Intnl Politics at the University of Hull, he was, concurrently, also, the Director of Hull's Centre for Strategic and Defence Studies then.

International Security Studies and Professor Colin Gray

Although, as mentioned, I had, in the following years, received many invitations from graduate schools in the UK, the USA and Canada and, in one instance, in 2003, from an university in Germany, too, it was my meeting up with Professor Colin Gray and getting to know him well during those two visits to the University of Hull in the early years of my taking to scholarly work and my lecturing, again at his invitation, in the University of Reading, later, following his moving to the university of Reading from Hull, that had meant the most to me in the development of my scholarly interest and my expertise in the technology-related issues of international politics. And, his goodwill and encouragement had, also, proved very good for me and my post-retirement career of writing and lecturing at graduate schools: He had not only given me a lot by way of moral support, he had, also, helped me immensely by introducing me to his contemporaries in think tanks and graduate schools in the USA as a competent speaker and researcher on technology issues of international politics. Through that process I had soon reached the point where I had been able to establish my credentials with the International Security Studies (ISS) community and to be known by quite a few scholars of the US academia. That, in turn, had brought me, during the following years, a series of invitations by universities in all three countries, namely the UK, the USA and, later, Canada, as well as the opportunity to be invited as a panelist at international conferences. Incidentally, only those graduate schools of political science and international relations, which had promoted the cause of strategic studies, were obliged to acquire funds for meeting the expenses for inviting guest lecturers, because their graduate students needed to derive the benefit of guest lectures by visiting experts, especially the benefit of the discussions which followed such presentations. In the case of the USA, particularly, a few of those graduate schools would, also, manage to retain on their faculties one or two such guest-scholars as Adjunct Professors, because such scholars who had a great standing with the policy makers of their country and, often, acted as Advisors to their government would be an asset to their faculties. Professor Colin Gray had been one such scholar, and a number of US universities, eg the Southwest Missouri State University's renowned Department of Defence and Strategic Studies then, had managed to retain him as an Adjunct Professor.

In his personal capacity, too, Colin Gray has been very friendly, and I had been very fortunate to have received his invitation as a guest lecturer in his very first year as the Professor of Intnl Politics in the University of Hull. And, it had then occurred to me that it was, probably, my background in science and technology, coupled with my scholarly interest in technology related issues of international security, that had made me, in his eyes, an attractive lecturer on strategic studies. Also, it was, probably, because of my technology related background that he had, for my very first invited lecture at Hull, requested me to give his students an introductory course on international security issues that would likely emerge with the advent of space warfare, involving the use of weapon technology in space and the possible role of space weapons. I had prepared well for that lecture and, even, taken pains to prepare sketches of the concepts of space weaponry for projection on a screen – the only time, in fact, that I had done so – in order to be able to illustrate the concepts of the Star Wars. And, I had been happy to see, as I had entered the lecture hall at Hull on that first occasion, in 1994/1995, that a large body of listeners comprising Colin Gray's graduate students and many other students of the department of political science, the departments of sciences and technology as well as a few members of the political science faculty were already seated. It was then that I had noted that there was one professor among those who had been seated in the first row, who not only looked a person of Indian origin but, also, appeared to have been someone who hailed from my part of India, namely West Bengal.

Inevitably, there was a lively discussion following my lecture, and both Professor Colin Gray and others, ie his colleagues and his graduate students, had participated energetically in the discussions. The only jarring note on that occasion – and a rather embarrassing one for him, if I may put it that way – had been a sudden burst of angry comments that had been made during the question hour by that Indian-looking colleague of Professor Colin Gray, who had sat in the front row. It had been obvious that as a political science scholar that colleague had wished to join issues with me on the foreign policy of my own country. But, it was, also, apparent that he had no knowledge of, or interest in, the technology of space weapons, let alone the subject of my lecture on that occasion, namely international security issues related to space warfare. Apparently, he had attended my lecture for the sole purpose of airing his views as a political science professor of Indian origin, namely that the government of a 'poor' country like ours, as he had put it, had no business to incur expenditure on maintaining a large Army or in equipping it with sophisticated weaponry, and, therefore, needed to be castigated. As I recall, in response to his commentary I had quietly but firmly stated that I was not in a position to respond to his comments, since his observations had no relevance to the subject of my lecture. And, then, Professor Colin Gray had gently rebuked him for disturbing other listeners and the graduate students by trying to engage a guest lecturer in discussions on irrelevant matters and had persuaded him to leave.

As mentioned, I had already started receiving invitations from other graduate schools, in both the UK and the USA. And, when Colin Gray had heard during our discussions on that first occasion at the University of Hull that I was visiting the USA next and had a few lecture engagements at graduate schools there, too, including one at the Massachusetts Institute of Technology, he had wished me well and spoken very supportively of my mission: What he had actually stated to me during that first meeting, the first of my two guest lectures at Hull at his invitation, was that in view of my experience in both technology and national security issues my offer of seminars on issues of international politics involving technology, eg military technology, nuclear non-proliferation, missile proliferation etc issues, would find many takers in US universities and think tanks. And, that, precisely, was what had happened. I had received many more invitations from graduate schools in the USA than in the UK and Canada during the following years. However, as I recall, on the following year I had lecture engagements at three well-reputed graduate schools in the USA, namely the Fletcher School of Law & Diplomacy of Tufts University in Boston, the History Dept of Yale University in Connecticut and the strategic studies programme of the Georgetown University of Washington DC where an adjunct professor, Dr Keith Payne, had hosted my lecture.

I had, also, learnt from Professor Colin Gray during our first meeting at the university of Hull that early in his scholarly career in the USA he had met two interesting ISS scholars of the USA then, namely Professor William Van Cleave, then a professor of Intnl Relations in a reputed university in California, and one of his junior associates, a young scholar called Dr Keith Payne. Apparently, soon after Professor Colin Gray has founded a strategic studies research centre, or a think-tank, of his own, namely the National Institute of Public Policy (NIPP) in Washington DC area, he had invited young Keith Payne to join him as a partner. And, having been remarkably successful in setting up the NIPP on a strong footing and made a name for himself in the next few years, Colin Gray had, also, witnessed the growth of his young colleague, Dr Keith Payne, into an excellent analyst and ISS scholar in his own right. Therefore, when the time came for Colin Gray to return to the UK to accept the offer of the University of Hull to join it as its Professor of Intnl Politics Dr Keith Payne could immediately step into Professor Colin Gray's shoes and take over as the Director of the NIPP. I recall having met Dr Keith Payne for the first time in his office at the NIPP in Alexandria, Virginia, in October, 1994, probably. By then he had already established his own credentials as a competent analyst and advisor on policy issues. And, although the occasion was to discuss some of the issues that would feature in the seminar I was to present, later on the same day, at the renowned Georgetown University's department of defence and strategic studies, of which he was an Adjunct Professor, I had been much impressed both by the depth of his knowledge and by the quality of the work that his team of ISS scholars, working for him in the NIPP, had produced.

I had lectured twice at both the Georgetown University and the Johns Hopkins University, both in Washington DC, during 1994-1998. And, it was there that I had encountered quite a few interesting graduate students, especially among the older ones and, particularly, at the Georgetown's graduate school. As known, it is the practice in the US universities to schedule lectures for graduate students, mostly, in the evenings. It both enables the 'school-funded' students to work for 20 hours a week as a research (RA) or a teaching assistant (TA) in their own department during the daylight hours and makes it possible for the other group of students, the 'older' ones, to undertake graduate studies without giving up their full-time jobs. After all, there are many young executives and office-goers who had done well in their undergraduate studies but cannot undertake graduate studies except by working full-time during the day and joining a graduate school which allows them to attend classes in the evenings. I had noticed that the number of such 'older' students in Georgetown's graduate school for strategic studies was particularly high during the time I had given guest lectures – as high, probably, as the number of the 'young' graduate students. I had been pleasantly surprised, also, to note that quite a few of those 'older' students in my class were very bright and well-read. And, I had ascribed that to two reasons. One, the city of Washington DC has a large number of bright and ambitious undergraduates among the young employees of the federal government and the Congress and the NGOs etc, who, having done well in their undergraduate studies, were both keen and able to secure admission into a reputed graduate school like the Georgetown University's to earn their MA or, even, a PhD degree. Two, Professor Keith Payne, two of whose classes I had taught as a visiting lecturer on two occasions, had been an excellent teacher and had made a name for himself and, therefore, had, attracted more of such mature students than the professors in other schools had been able to do.

The South West Missouri State University

As mentioned, Professor William Van Cleave had been a reputed ISS scholar in the USA and a friend of Professor Colin Gray from long before I had met Colin Gray for the first time in the University of Hull. And, as I had gathered subsequently during my first visit to the SW Missouri State University as an invited lecturer, Professor Van Cleave had made an impact, as a scholar of repute, as early as in the nineteen seventies when he had been in California as a professor of Intnl Politics in a reputed University. Apparently, he had later moved back to his roots, the Missouri State , to establish a defence and strategic studies department, independent of that university's Dept of Political Science, as he had told me, and succeeded in getting funds and endowments for his Department. And, it was because of that reason that he was in a position to incur expenditure for inviting visiting lecturers and, even, appointing a few adjunct professors and thus to enrich his department's teaching and research programme. That was, also, the reason why his department could offer more incentives, ie financial assistance by way of grants and scholarships, to many more undergraduate and graduate students than most other institutions could and thus attract a larger number of meritorious students every year. The net result was that by the time I had received my first invitation, in 1995 or 1996, probably, from that eminent professor for presenting a seminar to his students and research scholars his department had already earned a good reputation for its quality of teaching and research. That had been the first time that we had met, and I had realized right away that it was he who had made that university's Department of Defence & Strategic Studies a big name in strategic studies in the USA. In fact, I had then understood why that Department, which had been established only a few years back by that eminent professor had become a much more reputed Department than its allied department, ie the Department of Political Science, which had been established much earlier. It had become, in fact, one of the best schools for defence and strategic studies in the USA in a rather short span of time, thanks to its founder, Professor Van Cleave. In any event,

I had, also, met, on that occasion, the Chair of the political science department, who had been invited to the dinner that Professor Van Cleave and his associate in his department, an Associate Professor, had given in my honour during that first visit of mine to deliver a guest lecture to the students of Professor Van Cleave's department.

Incidentally, during that first visit to that university I had traveled for the very first time to the state of Missouri, driving some 1200 miles from Washington DC in the company of my wife, and both of us had been pleasantly surprised to find that Springfield, the seat of SW Missouri State University then, was really a small, but a pretty city. Also, the head of the Dept of Political Science of that university, whom Professor Van Cleave had introduced to us at the dinner, had turned out to be one Professor Patel, an American of Indian origin, and he had told me on that occasion that there were only a few families of Indian Americans in that city and that he, Professor Patel, had been the first ethnic Indian to have joined that university as a member of the faculty and that later, only a few years back, one more American of Indian origin joined that university as an Assistant Professor in the department of mathematics or of computer science, probably. I ought to mention here that, Springfield, as a name of a city, is very popular in the USA, and, as known, quite a few other States, also, have a city called Springfield. But our first impression of Springfield in Missouri State, had been very good: It was, essentially, a university town and had all the characteristics of a pretty and a quiet city. Both Professor Van Cleave and his colleagues in his own department, as well as Professor Patel of the Political Science Dept, had impressed me as scholarly and friendly persons.

Since, as mentioned, Professor Van Cleave had a high standing in the International Security Studies community of the US academia then the graduate studies programme of his

Department had been one of the most successful departments in getting federal grants for teaching and research in defence studies. In fact, in those years it had on its rolls a large number of graduate students, and, not so surprisingly, a large number of undergraduate students, also, had opted for defence and strategic studies as their major. Further, I had, also, observed that on both the occasions that I had given invited lectures there it had been a combined class of graduate and undergraduate students that I had addressed. The other specialty of that Professor's department, the one that I had particularly taken note of, was that Professor Van Cleave, while introducing the speaker, would invariably, also, give a brief but lucid introduction to the subject of the lecture to be delivered by the invited lecturer by offering – for the benefit of both undergraduates and graduates of his, probably – his own, excellent, commentary on the issues that the guest lecturer would likely bring up during his presentation. And, although I had always admired him for the quality of that introductory remarks of his, both for their brevity and for their effectiveness, I used to admire him, even, more for the deftness with which he used to encourage his students, during the question hour following the lecture, to ask the right questions and to engage me into a more in-depth discussion than what I had anticipated. Also, I may add here, on both occasions that I had visited the SW Missouri University I had been much impressed by the kind of orderliness that Professor Van Cleave had instilled in his students and the members of his faculty, alike. In fact, on both of those two occasions, while summing up my lecture and throwing the house open for questions and comments, he would, again, do a marvelous job, for the benefit of his students, by highlighting the issues which, according to him, deserve special attention.

Professor Van Cleave had been a registered Republican, ie a member of the Republican Party of the USA, I was aware, and, as known by many Americans, he, having been an important functionary, in his younger days, of that party's intellectual wing, had once taken a break from his job as an academic in order to serve the US government as an Assistant Secretary in the Department of Defence (DOD) for a few years during President Nixon's first tenure. In fact, during my second visit for the guest lecture he had proudly shown me a copy of the former President's memoirs, which had just then been published. That copy, I had noticed, had been the one that had been signed by the author, ie President Nixon, himself and presented as a gift to Professor Van Cleave, a copy in which the former President had fondly referred to the good work that had been done by the young Dr William Van Cleave as an Assistant Secretary of the US DOD. As known, Nixon had gone out of the White House under a thick cloud and is still regarded as one of the wrong-doers of the worst kind among the past Presidents and, therefore, also, as a totally-unethical person, and all of that because of the role he had played, as a serving President of the USA, in the infamous Watergate scandal. Apparently, William Van Cleave, as an young idealist and enthusiastic Republican youth leader, like many others of his time, had, also, been surprised when he had learnt, during the closing years of the Nixon presidency, of that unsavoury side of President Nixon's character. The other interesting thing about Professor Van Cleave that I had learnt during my brief acquaintance with him in those years was that, despite having been a Conservative in his outlook, Profeessor Van Cleave had very high regard for Indian intellectuals and was a great admirer of some of those intellectuals that he had met during his time in the service of the US government. On two or three occasions, I recall, during my two visits there, Professor Van Cleave and I had long and wide-ranging discussions on some of the issues, common to India and the USA, and he had on those occasions spoken of his great admiration for the late Dr Homi Bhabha whom he had apparently met in the USA on several occasions during his days as an US official working in Washington DC, and he had on all those occasions lamented the fact that the life of such an outstanding Indian was so tragically cut short by his untimely death in an air crash so many years back.

Having mentioned the fact that Professor Van Cleave had once served for a short spell, in his early years, as an Assistant Secretary in the department of defence, I would, also, like to mention that most industrially developed countries and the USA, in particular, follow the practice of routinely hiring a few intellectuals from the academia, eg professors of universities, to serve in both the middle and the senior-level positions in the US government for the duration of each presidency. For instance, during every US administration a number of cabinet-level and lesser posts in the State, Defence, Finance, Education, Commere etc departments are routinely filled by bringing in for a few years senior academics of the incumbent President's choice. The same, also, goes for a few of the middle-level appointments in every department of the federal government, eg the Undersecretary and the Assistant Secretary. I was, therefore, not surprised when I noticed a few years after my second visit to the SW Missouri State Univesity that, like Professor Van Cleave in his time, his deputy in his own Department at that point of time, whom I had met as a young Associate Professor with a German-sounding name, as I recall, had been appointed, later, by the Bush administration as an undersecretary of defence. In our country, too, the Prime Ministers in the early years of our independence, notably Jawaharlal Nehru and Indira Gandhi, had followed that practice by bringing one or two eminent intellectuals of his or her choice to join the cabinet as a minister or a senior civil servant. Quite a few posts of senior bureaucrats in many departments and ministries of our country then had, also, been filled by such apolitical intellectuals during those times. Sadly, that practice in the pursuit of excellence has almost been given up in our country now.

It was, also, during my those two visits to the department of strategic studies in SW Missouri State University that I had met, once, a visiting scholar from Europe, an Associate Professor of the famous Christian University in Kiel in Germany, who had joined Professor Van Cleave's department for a short duration then as an adjunct professor. Incidentally, that chance meeting with that young professor from Germany had resulted in my receiving a lecture invitation in the following year from her parent university department in Kiel. Interestingly, the head of the Intnl Relations Department of that university in Germany, at whose invitation I had delivered a lecture in Kiel in January, 2004, probably, had turned out to be the first ISS scholar I had met whose primary research interest had a focus on Terrorism, a topic which since then has attracted the attention of many political science researchers all over the world. In any case, the subject of my lecture in Kiel on that occasion was the threat posed by the rise of the phenomenon of militant Islamism, and a large body of participants comprising both his graduate students and a few students from other departments, too, all of them Germans with proficiency in English language, had attended my lecture that evening. Although that was the first time that I had visited the city of Kiel, the professor himself having received me on my arrival at Hamburg by a flight from London and then having driven me in his car to Kiel, Germany as a country was not new to me. Therefore, I had expected that the German graduate students attending my lecture would be well versed in English. And, that was the case, as mentioned. Therefore, the question hour following my lecture at Kiel had kept me very busy, with a large number of students and the professor, too, participating with their questions and comments throughout the duration. Apart from the fact that, post-9/11, Terrorism as a subject had assumed great importance for most ISS scholars, especially in the West, the Kiel professor's choice of militant Islamic terrorism as the preferred subject for my lecture had, also, been influenced by the fact that ours, ie India, was the first secular and democratic country in the world, which had suffered most by then, pre and post-9/11, from that variety of terror attacks, brought about by cross-border terrorism, promoted by a few of the Islamic states, eg Pakistan in the case of India, particularly, which provided state support for the export of terrorism.

Interestingly, the issue that had been discussed by me most, at the instance of the professor who had hosted my lecture at Kiel, and had attracted greater attention from his graduate students, too, was the classical dilemma that most law-enforcement agencies face in democratic countries in their attempt to prevent terrorism: Whereas the terrorists are not bound by any rules and, therefore, use the most heinous methods to inflict damages on innocent victims, the law-enforcement agency of a democratic country cannot take that liberty. The result is that the law-enforcement agency is, often, unable to prevent terror strikes due to its inability to gather advance information by using lawful methods only. That, as known, is one ethical question which law-enforcement agencies of all democratic countries is yet to find an answer to.

Turning now to my guest lecture invitation by Yale university, the reason why in that case it was their History dept – and not the department of political science or of the international relations – which had invited me for that lecture is interesting: It had its root in the fact that although at that point of time Yale's political science had neither a teaching programme nor any research interest, relevant to my particular area of expertise or research interest in ISS the professor, who had extended that invitation, namely Professor Paul Kennedy, who had by then been an eminent professor of Yale's history dept for many decades, had been an outstanding researcher in military history all his life and, in all likelihood, had, at that point of time, a few graduate students of Yale doing their PhD programme or their MA dissertation on a subject pertaining to either South Asian security issues or international security issues involving technology.

However, the fact that in the case of Yale it was not the graduate school of the political science department that had evinced interest in me and had invited me for giving that seminar on an ISS related issue of my choice had not surprised me, because I had known of the British-born British-educated Professor Paul Kennedy and of his critically acclaimed work on military history when he had been in the UK and had, therefore, deliberately addressed my letter, offering to lecture at Yale, to Professor Paul Kennedy by name. At that point of time I had, in fact, no idea if it was the Political Science or the History Dept of Yale, where Professor Kennedy belonged. As stated, all that I had known had been that, prior to moving to the USA, Paul Kennedy, an Englishman like Professor Colin Gray, had, also, done his D Phil from Oxford University and that, while in the UK, he had been a student and an admirer, in the figurative sense, of the work of the most reputed professor of military history of the first and the second world wars and of the battles in which England had played a major role, namely Professor Liddel Hart. In short, I had known that Professor Paul Kennedy had, in his own right, been an outstanding scholar of British military history from his early years and had authored several books and research papers on military history related subjects well before he had moved to the USA.

Unlike Colin Gray, however, Paul Kennedy had worked more, at least during his early years, on military history than other issues of international security. Presumably, Professor Kennedy had later developed an interest in other issues of international security, and it is, also, possible that, at that particular point of time, he had had a few graduate students in Yale's history department whose subjects of dissertation had less connection with military history than with other issues of national or international security. In any event, he had suggested that, if I wished, I could address the graduate students on WMD (Weapons of Mass Destruction) proliferation.

Unfortunately, however, during that academic session, ie the fall of 1994, probably, I had, after I had completed of my other lecture engagements in the other universities, eg in Georgetown university and the Fletcher School, to urgently return to England on my way back to India, because of an unexpected family commitment. I had, therefore, been compelled to regret, on short notice, my inability to visit Yale on the appointed day. And, consequently, I had to beg out of my lecture commitment at Yale that year, to my own utter disappointment and to the dismay of the concerned graduate students of Yale, probably, if not my esteemed host, the renowned senior scholar of long standing, Professor Paul Kennedy. I regret to this day the fact of that last-minute cancellation of a prior engagement due, entirely, to my own reasons, and I am glad to state that the failure to honour my lecture commitment at Yale university on that occasion had been the only one of its kind in my decade-long experience as a visiting lecturer at graduate schools during my post-retirement years. I had begged out of that lecture engagement, as stated, at the last moment, and I, especially, regret the fact that I had disappointed those graduate students of the history department who had awaited an opportunity, probably, to participate in the discussions that usually followed such presentations by visiting scholars.

The MIT & Its Centre For Engineering and Public Affairs

My invitation for a lecture at the MIT on the missile proliferation issue and the issue of missile defence, in particular, had been extended by the Chair of the Political Science Department. But, on arrival there I had realized that it was the MIT's Centre for Engineering and Public Affairs, which had been attached to the Dept of Political Science, that had selected me as one of their guest lecturers that year. In any event, the lecture theatre of that Centre had turned out to be the venue of my lecture at the MIT. And, it was the senior professor of that Centre for Engineering related public affairs studies, a nuclear physicist by training and with several years of earlier work in the faculty of Physics of another university, who had been accompanied by a young Assistant Professor of Political Science of the Department of Political Science of the MIT, who had received me. And, it was that senior professor of the centre for public affairs studies, who had chaired my lecture session. During those years, it may be recalled, the issue of missile defence, in particular, had heated up the debate on missile proliferation in the USA, because the possibility of an attack on the USA by ballistic missiles, launched from possible enemy territories, eg Iran and North Korea, had seemed real in US perception and had created serious concern. Both the USA and its NATO allies had decided that the best option for instituting an anti-missile defence would be to deploy an adequate network of early warning radars and a system of anti-missile missiles, like the Patriot missile system, the first version of which had by then just been jointly developed by the USA and Israel and, possibly, deployed, too, by

Israel. However, two questions had been uppermost in the minds of the strategic planners and the ISS community in the academia of the USA then, namely (1) the effectiveness of the protection against incoming-missile attacks, that an anti-missile missile system like the Patriot can provide, and (2) the usefulness of the cut-off limits of the speed of the missiles, that have been specified in the regulations of the US-sponsored missile technology control regime (MTCR) as the upper limit of the speed of the 'largest' missile, that a non-US-allied country may possess without contravening the MTCR.

I must, also, mention that by the time I had received the invitation for a lecture at the MIT the US debate on missile defence had received the attention of the US politicians at the highest level, namely the Senators and the Representatives of the House of the US Congress, and a series of open hearings had been held by the appropriate Congressional Committees where the concerned Congressmen from both the parties had heard the expert opinions of a number of scholars and think-tank seniors, who had taken their own positions on either side of that debate, and the so-alled expert witnesses had been cross-examined by the members of the Congressional committees at length. Since all of the details of those US Congressional hearings had been available in the public domain I had read some of those reports in the Indian and other newspapers beforehand and had been generally aware that some of the scientists of the MIT had, also, made it a point to study that issue and made a presentation before the Congressional Committee, in which they had strongly refuted the Pentagon position that a Patriot-like missile defence system would be effective against possible attacks by the prospective enemy's ballistic missiles. But, I was not aware that Dr Keith Payne and the scholars of the NIPP, about whom I had written earlier in this Chapter, had taken an opposite view. However, before I had visited the

MIT I had learnt only that the NIPP had done a study, too, under a project funded by the US government, and, while presenting their findings to the Congressional Committee, had maintained that their study had proved that the Patriot system would be effective as a shield against ballistic missile attacks. However, during my presentation at the MIT I had covered most areas of the missile proliferation problem from my perspective including the recent developments on anti-missile missile but had refrained from referring to the ongoing US debate on the topic of the effectiveness of the proposed missile defence system against ballistic missile attacks by US enemies. Therefore, I had not been surprised by the fact that as soon as I had concluded my lecture the first question that had been asked by some of my listeners, all of them MIT scientists working alongside my host-professor in the that Centre for public affairs studies, had pertained to the ongoing US debate on missile defence. And, it was the Chair himself, the senior professor of that Centre, who had presided over my lecture who had asked the first few of those questions.

That professor had been very interesting as an individual, too, as I recall, who, by the way, had recently visited our country as a scholar. A young but a senior member then, as I had stated, of that MIT Centre for Engineering & Public Affairs, he was much younger than I was, of course, but he was, also, a person with a career background similar to mine, post-retirement, namely a person of science and technology who had, in his early years, pursued a career in scientific research in his own field of physics, namely nulear physics, but had, later, switched to being an analyst of political issues involving technology. A person of Russian origin, he had told me then, who had immigrated to the USA with his parents as a child and, as I recall, had been brilliant as a student of the MIT's physics department, having done both his undergraduate and graduate studies in the MIT, and, after receiving his PhD in nuclear physics, many years back, he had moved away from the MIT to work as a research scientist for some years in another US university before he had returned to the MIT to join that Centre as a policy analyst. In my response to his question, pertaining to the ongoing debate, then, on the effectiveness of the Patriot or a similar missile defence system against ballistic missile threats, I had stated that according to me the probability of achieving a 'kill' with an anti-missile missile, launched by a computerized command post on the basis of the tracking and other data, being fed continuously into a computerized system, was unlikely to be as high as what had then been predicted by some US experts. The reason for my drawing that conclusion, I had, also, mentioned then, was none other than the usual one, namely that some of the assumptions fed into the computational analysis, which constituted the basis of the prediction of the probability of hit, were just that, ie mathematically arrived figures, and may not turn out to be correct always in view of the fact that a number of inputs, ie the estimated values of certain un-measurable variables, fed into the mathematical model for computation, were often based on assumptions of various kinds, which may, therefore, differ from the actual values. However, our discussions had not ended there, and that MIT professor and I had a lot of discussions, later, on other topics, too, in which a few other researchers of that Centre, all equally bright as scientists-turned-ISS-analysts, had enthusiastically participated.

The RMCS at The Shrivenham Campus of Cranfield University

In any event, my experience at the MIT had left a very good taste in my mouth: It is not often that international security issues are researched into by high intellectuals who are, also, eminent men of science. On my way back to India, however, I had given another invited lecture, on arms control and defence industrialization, at the department of political science of the Royal Military College of Science (RMCS) at Shrivenham in the UK. The RMCS is a historically famous teaching institution of the Royal Electrical & Mechanical Engineers (REME) of the British Army, as known, which had for many decades been conducting post-graduate engineering courses in combat vehicles and armament technology for the officers of the British Army and of other Commonwealth countries including ours. However, it had recently been converted into a university college for civilian students-cum-military institution and got itself affiliated to the Cranfield University in Bedford and had, thus, introduced its share of social sciences in its teaching programme to enable civilian students, too, to seek admission for undertaking either undergraduate or graduate studies in some of the social sciences, eg political science and history. Since I was unaware of the changes that had taken place in the intervening years it was only during that visit that I had learnt that the Cranfield Institute of Technology, where I had done my MSc degree in engineering, as a Squadron Leader, way back in 1968-69, was no longer a graduate school for only engineering and business studies but had, also, transformed itself into a full-fledged university which had taken in its fold in recent years two other teaching institutions of England, namely the once-autonomous teaching institution of the EME of the British Army, the RMCS, and a British Agriculture College, each of which had, however, continued to function in its own campus, away from Cranfield.

As known by now, the British government had in the early nineteen nineties undertaken a major reorganization of the university system of Great Britain with a view to expanding the UK's university-level education facility many-fold. For instance, it had through legislations converted, almost overnight, all of the UK's historically-famous technical colleges, namely the polytechnics, into autonomous universities and had thus managed to increase the number of British universities by two to three times. Although in most cases that process had, undoubtedly, resulted in a sudden lowering of the standard of university education in Great Britain and, consequently, the production, for quite a few years thereafter, of a large number of substandard technical graduates there had been a plus point, too: It had, also, ensured that some of their polytechnic colleges, which had developed excellence over the years but had remained under-funded and under-utilised, would henceforth receive due recognition and be put to proper use as full-fledged universities. In the case of the RMCS, for instance, its affiliation with Cranfield university had made it possible to expand its teaching and research programmes. That affiliation, had, also, made it possible for both the military and civilian students of the RMCS to receive university degrees, hereafter, in engineering as well as selected social sciences, as applicable.

At The Fletcher School of Law and Diplomacy

Reverting to my lecture-engagement at the Fletcher School of Law & Diplomacy in Boston in the fall of 1994, it ought to be mentioned that that had come about when I had accepted an invitation from the Tuft University's professor of Intnl Security Studies. And, as is customary, that invitation had been extended to me almost a year back by that professor who, had, also, informed me that he was *ipso facto* a member of the faculty of the Department of Political Science which belonged to an ivy league institution, namely the Fletcher

School of Law & Diplomacy of the Tufts University. While extending the invitation, however, he had made known that later in that year he would be away from the Fletcher School on a year-long teaching assignment at the US Military Academy at the West Point and that a senior colleague of his would host my lecture. That colleague had turned out to be none other than an eminent scholar of international relations of the USA of those days, namely Professor Phaltzgraff, who was a senior professor of political science at Tufts University and, also, a doyen of the conservative-thinking academics of the USA then. He had published extensively on US foreign policy and international relations and had enjoyed great patronage by the Republican administration of the USA at that time. He was, concurrently, also, the Director of the university's Centre for International Relations and, in view of his high standing with the State Dept during the rule of the Republican Presidents, had frequently received research grants from both the department of defence and the State Dept for research and studies on various issues of US foreign policy.

Incidentally, it has always been the practice of the government of the USA, irrespective of the party then in power, to routinely consult eminent professors and scholars on policy issues and to fund research at only those universities and think tanks where the professors belonged to the ruling party. The intention, however, is good in that it enables the academic community to undertake the required research and to render advice to the US Administration, on the basis of research done into various issues, before the government formulated its policies. That practice is sadly lacking in our country where, although token consultation is done in some cases these days, the practice remains notionally important, not having been institutionalized in the real sense. However, the USA is reported to have been well served by such consultations with academics over the years, and some of the other developed countries, too, follow that practice now. And, as mentioned, in the case of the USA it had meant that whenever a Republican President was in the White House, for instance, the professors who promoted conservative thinking would receive more research grants than the liberal-thinking ones, and vice versa. However, since the US Administration in the preceding years had been under a Republican President the standing of Professor Phaltzgraff with the US government had been very high at that point of time. And, having read some of his writings in US journals from time to time, I had, also, been aware that his views on US relationship with the developing world were US-centric and favour policies that promote only the US interests. Hence, I had, while complementing the Professor in my opening remarks for his well-deserved reputation as an outstanding scholar, also, mentioned that my views on world affairs and, particularly, South Asian and nuclear proliferation issues would most likely be at variance with those of the Professor. In fact, I had ventured to state on that occasion that while Professor Phaltzgraff's erudition had justifiably been acknowledged as outstanding by his peers in the USA, scholars from non-aligned countries, eg India, would more often than not disagree with Professor Phaltzgraff on many issues of international relations. In fact, as I had mentioned, some of those scholars would look upon his views as akin to the views of one who held that what was good for the USA was good for the world.

In short, I had made it known that I was aware, while accepting the lecture invitation by the Fletcher School, that my views on South Asian security and non-proliferation issues, as they would unfold during my presentation, would likely be at great variance with those of my eminent host, Professor Phaltzgraff, and that my conclusions would, probably, have a non-aligned-country bias and may cause some consternation among the conservative-thinking scholars among my listeners. And, that was exactly what had transpired on that occasion: At the end of my lecture I was generously complemented for my presentations by all of the faculty members and, especially, Professor Phaltzgraff who had stated in his concluding remarks that he thought very highly of my talk and that it was, probably, one of the best lectures delivered in recent years at the Fletcher School in terms of the quality of its arguments. But it was, also, evident that while students and teachers alike had enjoyed my presentation for its quality and its boldness, my straight talk had, also, ruffled some feathers, both during the presentation and after. Especially, during the question-and-answers session which had followed my talk, when quite a lot of lively discussion and spirited exchanges had taken place between me, on the one hand, and Professor Phaltzgraff, on the other. And, I had gathered later that my presentation, especially my forthright answers to the volleys of provocative questions about the Indo-Pak dispute and nuclear proliferation issues that were put to me by Professor Phaltzgraff and some of his colleagues, had made a good impression on the graduate students. My presentation had been liked better, in fact, as some them had said to me, than the seminars that were given in the previous years by some of the other invited lecturers.

Today, post-2008, after the India-US civil nuclear co-operation has come into force and the western powers had accepted the position that India had emerged as a nuclear-weapon nation in its own right and without contravening any provision of the international laws, it is difficult to envisage how upset those very nations of the western world, especially the USA, had felt with India in those early years. And that situation had continued right up to 2005-2006 when President Bush Jr had initiated the move to reverse the earlier US policy and open a diaogue between India and the USA on civil nuclear co-operation. But, way back then most Indian scholars delivering invited lectures at graduate schools in the USA on nuclear proliferation or, even, other issues would have to respond to a barrage of questions and comments, including hostile remarks at times, put forward by American scholars, comments which sprang from their misconceptions and their widely-held belief that India had clandestinely been engaged in developing nuclear weapons ever since its 1974 peaceful nuclear explosion (PNE). That, in short, had been the situation that I had faced while presenting seminars in the US universities during the nineteen nineties – not only at the Fletcher School in 1994 but, also, at other graduate schools of repute including the Johns Hopkins, the Georgetown, the MIT etc during the following years. It was years later, post-Clinton, with the Republican administration taking over the White House, the US government had slowly changed its course, preparing the ground for, finally, befriending non-aligned India and taking the initiative to start a formal dialogue with our government on civil nuclear co-operation.

As mentioned, all Indian scholars of my generation, who had dealt with the subject of Indo-US relations and/or nuclear non-proliferation issues in their presentations at US universities during those years, would remember the political climate which had prevailed in the US academia during those years. Although our government's response to the US misgivings regarding suspected, ongoing nuclear activities in India had wavered between an outright denial, as in the beginning, and an ambivalence, as in the later years, the US-led western powers were unbelieving of us and had been openly critical. However, the US policy on South Asia had always tilted towards Pakistan and has never been fair to India. On the one hand, there was a total lack of belief in the US elite as regards India's stated position that, despite being technologically capable, our country had abstained from developing nuclear weapons. On the other, the US had always maintained, strongly, that it had no knowledge of any wrong-doing by Pakistan including collusion with China on acquisition of nuclear weapon capability despite the fact that the US intelligence organizations had been collecting enough of incriminating evidence to conclusively prove that Pakistan had been feverishly engaged in making nuclear warheads of its own with China's help, a clandestine but criminal act which made both Pakistan and China culpable of violation of nuclear non-proliferation norms in the most blatant manner.

It ought to be remembered that although, as stated in the foregoing paragraph, the USA had strongly suspected that both India and Pakistan, following different paths, were engaged in activities aimed at acquiring nuclear weapon capability, the US foreign policy on South Asia, because of its decades-long cold-war bias towards Pakistan, had continued to be blatantly partial to Pakistan. In fact, as known, the USA would always favour Pakistan over India wherever the USA had felt obliged to take a position on any issue related to the Indo-Pak dispute, including, even, the issue of Pakistan's promotion of cross-border terrorism. As known, that unconscionable bias against a democratically-governed India and the consequent, utterly-unprincipled tilt towards the military-ruled Pakistan over many decades had totally vitiated the US foreign policy on South Asia during those years. However, there was one silver lining: A few academics, white American professors all, had a more open mind, and while lecturing at some of the US universities during those years I have had the contrary experience too, namely the experience of, also, hearing from the somewhat independent-minded scholars at some of those graduate schools that, in their view, the enhanced threat that the China-Pakistan collusion on nuclear weapons had at that point of time been posing to our country would make it imprudent on the part of the government of India not to take the precaution of developing India's own nuclear weapons capability without further loss of time.

It was in this context – namely the decades-long incorporation of anti-India bias by the USA in the making of its foreign policy for South Asia – that I had taken special care to emphasise in my lectures at the Fletcher School and other universities the following: Although democratic India which, unlike military-ruled, technology-poor Pakistan, possessed the required technological capability to undertake such a task on its own and reserved every right to develop a strategic weapon in the interest of its own national security India, judging from its record, had never indulged in either nuclear or missile proliferation activities nor would it ever do so. In fact, I had pointed out that India had always advocated strongly in favour of universal disarmament and always emphasized the need for the renunciation of nuclear weapons by all nations, a policy which would enjoin upon the USA, the USSR and all of the other nuclear-weapon nations of the world then to give up their nuclear arsenals, too. While India was on a higher moral ground on that account, I had stated, having deliberately abstained from developing a nuclear warhead despite possessing the required technological capability, Pakistan which severely lacked both the technical expertise and the wherewithal had been colluding with China for many years with a view to obtaining the know-how and other assistance in assembling its own nuclear warheads.

Further, unlike India whose record on that account had, also, been scrupulously clean, Pakistan, I had pointed out, had frequently been caught in the act of procuring nuclear components and test equipment from the USA and western Europe in an illegal manner in furtherance of its clandestine activities for acquisition of nuclear weapon capability. Finally, I had, also, pointed out, the fact that the

USA, despite its knowledge of China's ongoing collusion with Pakistan, had, seemingly with deliberation, abstained from taking any action against either Pakistan or China made the USA vulnerable to the charge that it had, in effect, been blatantly violating its own obligations to prevent proliferation under the nuclear non-proliferation treaty. However, in this connection I may state one curious fact: I had learnt from some scholars of both the Fletcher School and a few other graduate schools that it had been that very line of argument of mine on South Asian security and nuclear non-proliferation which had made my seminars at the US universities more interesting despite the fact that my views had, at that point of time, been in direct contradiction of the conventional wisdom of conservative-thinking US scholars. As for the Fletcher School, I must admit that the fact that I had received kudos for my presentation there from my host, Professor Phaltzgraff, too, despite his disagreement with me on many aspects of the US foreign policy then and on the non-proliferation issue, in particular, makes it clear that the qualities of circumspection and objectivity that Professor Phaltzgraff and other scholars of his ilk had displayed while functioning as teachers and mentors in the US academia then have much to commend for.

There were a few other interesting incidents, too, and I would like to recount two of those here. In one case, after I had finished my lecture at the Fletcher School one graduate student, looking every inch a South Asian and, seemingly, a mature student, had strolled over to where I had been seated with a young Assistant Professor. But, as I had noticed, he was dressed more formally than was customary on such occasions in venerable institutions like the Fletcher's. Although my lecture, like those by other visiting scholars, had been preceded by a formal lunch and all those who had attended it, students and professors alike, had been dressed in somewhat formal attires, that mature student, had appeared more distinguished-looking than most other graduate students, partly because of his superior suit of clothes and partly because of the fact that he was in his late-thirties or older, unlike most other students of his batch. As he had approached us smiling, it had appeared that he wanted to speak to me, in particular, and not the young professor who was seated beside me. And, it had turned out to be so. The young Assistant Professor had promptly introduced him to me by his name and added that he was from Pakistan and one of the bright graduate students of his batch and, also, an ex-student of the Fletcher school, having done his undergraduate studies there, some years back. It had turned out that that graduate student was, in fact, an officer of the Pakistan Administrative Service, who had returned to his alma mater the previous year to earn a MA degree by availing of a study leave from his government's service.

When that graduate student had started speaking to me he had instantly made it known that he had come to meet me as much to complement me for the quality of my presentation as to state that he was very pleased with the manner in which I had answered one of the questions that had been put to me during the question hour by a senior professor of his school. That question, he had then helped me recall, had been a tricky one, too: I had been asked by a senior Professor if I was aware of the existence of a rumour that was in circulation then, namely that Pakistan had already acquired nuclear warheads, and, upon my answering that question in the affirmative, whether, in view of the likelihood of that rumour having a ring of truth in it, India was not being foolhardy by abstaining from developing its own nuclear weapon as a deterrent against Pakistan's. Apparently, it had been the answer to that second question that I had given to that professor during the question hour that had pleased that student from Pakistan, namely as follows. I had stated that (a) the Generals who ruled Pakistan were more mature and would not act as hastily and unthinkingly as the leaders of some of the other Islamic countries could, and (b) that the rulers of Pakistan were aware that by ordering a first strike against India they would invite a much harsher retaliatory strike and, thereby, risk the complete destruction of Pakistan itself, for the reason that India, unlike Pakistan, was a vast country, with a large land-mass away from the border, and, therefore, was not likely to be destroyed completely by a first strike by Pakistan.

Now, looking back, however, I think that the real reason why that elite civil servant of Pakistan's Administrative Service had felt pleased with me as a graduate student of the Fletcher School on that occasion was not the reason he had mentioned to me, namely my flattering response to the question whether Pakistan's military rulers could get swayed and order a first strike against India. But, it was most likely my answer to one of the other provocative questions that had been put to me on that occasion concerning Pakistan, namely a question pertaining to the mindset of Pakistan's civil society, that had, probably, pleased that bureaucrat-turned-graduate student of the Pakistan Administrative Service even more. That question had, in fact, been asked by Professor Phaltzgraff himself: He wanted to know why, in my opinion, Pakistan lagged behind India so badly, both as regards economic growth and in terms of educational development, when the two countries had become sovereign nations at the same point of time, ie in August, 1947. My response to Professor Phaltzgraff had been that the basic reason for that disparity in socio-economic development between India and Pakistan was that the civil society of Pakistan had been severely damaged, thanks to a succession of military regimes ruling Pakistan for five decades. In short, although the civil servants working for the government of Pakistan were as competent as their counterparts in a democratically governed country like India, they had, however, been rendered totally ineffective, thanks to the persistent interference by their military overseers and thus made incapable of ensuring that correct policies are formulated and implemented in matters concerning Pakistan's socio-economic development, eg primary education, higher education etc.

It strikes me now that that particular answer of mine, namely the one which had so immensely pleased that graduate student from Pakistan's superior civil service, had, in fact, touched a very sensitive cord, namely the issue of governance of Pakistan: The fact that, as an educated Indian, I had instantly acknowledged, while giving my answer to that question, put by Professor Phaltzgraff, that the civil servants of Pakistan were not at fault but had been rendered ineffective by their military rulers, had proved most reassuring for the reason that I had thereby acknowledged that, but for the interference by their military, the civil servants of Pakistan would have been as effective in planning and implementing correct policies for nation-building as the civil servants of the democratically governed India. As known, Pakistan's conditions have since then deteriorated much more, and, thanks to the decades-long nurture and promotion of the growth of anti-India terrorist organizations inside Pakistan by the government of Pakistan and the consequent rise of the so-called popular support for all types of terrorist organizations within Pakistan and the total break-down of law and order in that country, both USA and other nations of the western world now increasingly view Pakistan as a failed state in every sense of that term.

The other incident had related to an interesting exchange with yet another professor of the Fletcher School, this particular scholar having been younger and of Indian origin. The question that had been put by that young Associate Professor of the History Department of the Tufts University, then, concerned India-Pakistan relations. However, as I write this I am aware that he is no longer at the Tufts, having moved to the Harvard University as a Professor, I gathered. But he had, in fact, been one of the few members of the faculty of the Tufts at that time, who had been invited by Professor Phaltzgraff, the Chair of the lecture session, to seat at the main table of the lunch-meeting on that occasion, ie the table which had been reserved for seating Professor Phaltzgraff, as the host, and my wife and I, as his guests, for the lunch which had preceded my lecture. While introducing that young professor to us Professor Phaltzgraff had remarked that he wondered if I had met that young colleague of his at some other place earlier in view of the fact that the young professor, too, hailed from that part of India where I belonged, namely the West Bengal state or the erstwhile Bengal province of British India. Although that young professor had a familiar name, ie Sugata Bose, I had never seen him before.

However, although I had neither met him before nor, even, known of him and had, therefore, truthfully stated that I had met him then for the very first time I had, later, after my return from Boston the next day, realized that the young Sugata Bose was one of the younger members of an illustrious family of India, namely the family to which the late Subhas Chandra Bose, popularly known in India as the Netaji (ie Leader) for his spectacular role as a leader of India's freedom movement for all of two decades prior to the departure of the British from India. Arguably, one of the two most-effective leaders of the freedom movement in the nineteen thirties and early forties, Subhas Chandra Bose, although much younger than all of the top three leaders of the freedom movement then, had been a trail-blazer and had dealt, probably, the most grievous blow to the British colonial rule in India during it closing years. Incidentally, his eldest brother, Sarat Chandra Bose, a most distinguished lawyer of British India then, had, also, participated in the freedom movement in a big way. Therefore, the ancestry of young Sugata Bose, whose late father had been a trusted nephew of Netaji Subhas Chandra Bose, was very impressive. However, as mentioned, when I had met him at the Fletcher School for the first time, on that occasion, I had no prior knowledge of the antecedents of that young Indian professor or of his family connections in India. All Indians of my generation were aware that the late Subhas Chandra Bose, but for his early demise in a plane crash during the closing days of the second world war, could arguably have been elected India's first prime minister. But, not many Indians would know today that Professor Sugata Bose's worthy father, who later became a reputed doctor of independent India, had, also, in his student-days, played a very important role in India's freedom movement: He had assisted his illustrious uncle, then under house arrest in Calcutta, by helping him escape from Calcutta, under the nose of the British police, and by accompanying him on an epic journey in disguise across the breadth of British India in order that he (Netaji Subhas) could cross the borders of the British India undetected and then fulfill his mission of raising an Indian National Army outside its borders and waging an war of independence against the British.

However, reverting to my guest lecture at the Fletcher School, there had been an interesting exchange, during the question hour, between that young professor and I, which had gone on the following lines. Since only an year or two back, then, a Noble Peace prize had been awarded, jointly, to two leaders of Israel and Palestine, respectively, for their roles in the achievement of what then had been regarded as a lasting settlement of one of history's most fractious disputes, Professor Bose had referred to that big news and had asked me why, if two such bitterly feuding nations of long standing had managed to bury the hatchet in another part of Asia, two other Asian nations, namely India and Pakistan, had not yet managed to reach an amicable settlement of their long-standing border dispute in order that an enduring peace was achieved. I still remember that for a moment, as I had tried to take in the full import of that question, put by that professor, I had felt that a question of that kind had been the least expected by me from someone like Professor Sugata Bose who had been immensely knowledgeable, having been born and brought up in India, and, therefore, well aware of the intricacies of the India-Pakistan relationship. In short, I had wondered why one who was so familiar with the nuances of the history of the British colonial rule and the circumstances that had led to the partitioning of the Indian subcontinent and the emergence of Pakistan as an independent democratic country which would, soon thereafter, emerge as military-ruled dictatorship, would ask that question. I had, even, thought that surely the fact that the Indo-Pakistan dispute was, in many ways, much more deep-rooted and, therefore, more difficult to resolve than, even, the Israel-Palestine discord could not have been missed by that erudite professor. Especially, the fact that no peace could possibly reign in the subcontinent as long as a succession of military dictatorships, which determinedly prevented democracy from taking roots in that country, continued to rule Pakistan, either openly or by proxy.

In short, I had wondered if the professor had not yet thought through the issues involved and not acknowledged that Pakistan's military rulers would always subvert any talk of peaceful settlement with India and, instead, strive for keeping the hostile relationship between India and Pakistan going, since that alone can ensure the continuance of a war-like psychosis inside Pakistan and the consequent acceptance by its people of the military as their rulers. Therefore, I had instantly felt that I ought to point out to the professor that as long as the military ruled Pakistan it would deliberately keep alive the anti-India sentiments in Pakistan and strive to destabilize India by promoting the infiltration into India of Pakistani terrorists and, through it, the growth of secessionist elements on the Indian side of the border. After all, those were the actions that would force India to keep a standing Army on its border and, in turn, enable the Pakistan military to constantly stoke a fear in the Pakistani people of an imaginary attack by India, thus prolonging the condition that would foster military rule in Pakistan. However, I had not verbalized those thoughts in such details but had only given a brief answer.

I had responded by saying the following. First, although while citing the case of the Israel-Palestine peace accord the professor had made an implicit assumption that the Palestine problem had been solved and permanent peace had taken roots in that region, the reality was that it was too early to draw such a conclusion. I had added that only the future events, as they unfolded, would show if real peace had prevailed in that region. Two, as regards the Indo-Pakistan problem, I had told the professor that there had been many twists and turns in the Indian freedom movement during the two centuries of British rule and, especially, during the last two decades of that rule, which had been exploited by the British to perpetuate their occupation of India through the promotion of a policy of divide-and-rule, an action that had, inevitably, vitiated the manner in which power had finally been transferred by the British to India and Pakistan through the partitioning of India in 1947. In short, I had pointed out that the historical misdeeds by the British rulers had sown the seeds of the present ill-will and animosity in the minds of the people of Pakistan and that it would not be possible for them to come out of it till true democracy took roots in Pakistan to enable its people to exercise their own choices.

I had then explained that it was only after true democracy took roots in that country that the democratically elected leaders of Pakistan would acknowledge that the restoration of peace was a pre-requisite for the achievement of economic viability and stability of Pakistan and, thereupon, make a peaceful resolution of the India-Pakistan problem possible. Incidentally, I had recently (2008), again, met that Professor, now teaching in Harvard, at a seminar in New Delhi, which had featured him and a British scholar from Cambridge as speakers. That seminar was, in fact, held in commemoration of the life and work of his illustrious ancestor, late Netaji Subhas Chandra Bose, and, while making an observation in relation to a point, made by him in that seminar, I had reminded the Professor that we two had met on an earlier occasion, too, namely at the Fletcher School of Law & Diplomacy of the Tufts University in Boston. Although I had abstained from mentioning then we had had an interesting encounter during our earlier meeting and a divergent view on an ongoing political development in the middle east, the fact is that, unfortunately, my prediction, on that development, namely the durability of the Palestine-Israel peace accord, has proved right: As known, the Palestine Peace accord of 1994 had neither brought peace in the middle east nor resulted in the abolition of violence thereafter, and, as it stands, both of those two countries would have to strive for peace for many more years before stability and lasting peace reigned in that region.

As already mentioned, I had delivered guest lectures at a large number of graduate schools in the UK, the USA and Canada during the years 1992 to 2005 and, on one occasion, in 2003, at a graduate school at Kiel, near Hamburg, too, namely the well-reputed Christian University of Kiel. In the

UK, apart from the Depts of Politics of the University of Hull and the Lancaster University, I had given invited lectures at the University of Reading, the RCMS (Shrivenham) campus of the Cranfield University and the History Dept of Cambridge University. The reason why Cambridge had invited me was interesting: Two graduate students of Indian origin, a PhD candidate of the History Dept who had come from India on a Nehru Memorial scholarship and a MA student of Politics who was born and brought up in Great Britain, had both opted for dissertations on technology related issues of international security and had apparently read some of my publications and requested their Advisors to invite me as one of the guest speakers that year. It was, however, the research advisor of the doctoral student, a professor of history of Scottish descent, as I recall, who had invited me on that occasion. And, the topic that he had suggested for my seminar at Cambridge was a discussion on South Asian security in relation to India's emergence as a technology empowered nation. It was, therefore, that professor who had presided over my lecture in the History department of Cambridge University on that occasion. A polite don of pleasant personality, he had, however, turned out to be a very competent teacher and strict disciplinarian, too, as I had discovered on that occasion: He had, right at the beginning of my talk, very competently dealt with – and got removed from the lecture hall – an unruly member of the audience, a UK-based Sikh young man, who, it had turned out, was neither a student of Cambridge nor a scholar of any kind anywhere but a 'Khalistani' agitator operating in England, who had come to my seminar with the sole purpose of interrupting the event and drawing attention to the so-called Khalistani (ie the misplaced and transient Sikh-separatist) movement of India in those days. I may, also, mention here that during those years many Indian scholars lecturing at universities abroad had similar experience and that, a few years later while delivering a guest-lecture at the Political Science dept of the University of California at Santa Cruz, too, I had come across a young Sikh of 'Khalistani' persuasion, who had tried to interrupt the question hour following my lecture and had to be disciplined in a similar fashion by the moderator who had presided over my lecture, as I recall.

Lecture On Non-Proliferation at The Stanford University

My lecture at the Stanford University's Dept of Political Science in Nov 1998 under the sponsorship of their Centre for Intnl Security & Co-operation (CISAC) was, probably, one of the most interesting of my graduate school seminars. And, that had been so for two reasons: One, that event was the very first seminar on nuclear non-proliferation that I had presented at an university forum abroad soon after our country had declared itself a member of the select group of nuclear-weapon nations of the world immediately on having successfully carried out a series of underground tests with miniature nuclear and thermonuclear warhead prototypes. Incidentally, the making of that declaration in 1998 had amounted to our shedding the cloak of secrecy and ambiguity which had been the hallmark of our country's declared position on nuclear weapon development till then. Second, that seminar, among all of my guest lectures at graduate schools in India and abroad, had the distinction of having been delivered at one of the most scholarly forums for a debate on that subject, namely a gathering of some of the best-read and most-informed of listeners of the world on that subject. Among the luminaries present at my lecture on that occasion there were three, in particular, whom I would like to mention here, namely my host, Professor Scott Sagan, who was then one of Stanford's best-known professors of political science, the co-Director of the CISAC and, also, an authority on nuclear proliferation studies then; a reputed nuclear physicist of the USA who had just then retired as the Director of the nuclear weapons laboratory in California and joined the CISAC at the Stanford as its co-Director; and a recently retired US Ambassador to Pakistan, who was then a Fellow of the famous Hoover Institution of the Stanford University. While there were many other distinguished scholars in the gathering and, also, all of the graduate students of the political science department and the resident researchers of the CISAC, among the listeners on that occasion, I had found out, later, during the question hour, there were, also, quite a few others who were 'outsiders' in one sense, ie the senior political science scholars and nuclear scientists who were not members of the Stanford community then but were working in or had retired from other research laboratories, software companies, think-tanks or social science organizations which were located in the vicinity of the Stanford University campus.

The Hoover Institution's Fellow cum former Ambassador who had attended my lecture had made it clear at the outset that he was someone who had intimate knowledge of South Asia, because he had introduced himself to me as a former American Ambassador to Pakistan before asking me a series of interesting questions during the question hour. One of his questions had pertained to the reported reactions of the Indian public to the underground nuclear tests that Pakistan had conducted a few days after the Indian tests, and in that connection he had jocularly mentioned that it was quite possible that, despite the secrecy associated with the tests conducted by Pakistan, his successor in Pakistan, ie the next American Ambassador in Pakistan, had been the only outsider who had known of the impending tests by Pakistan in advance, for the reason that the USA had always been in a privileged position in Pakistan and its ambassadors had always enjoyed the confidence of the

President and the government of Pakistan. He had, in fact, also, mentioned that during his time as the Ambassador to Pakistan he had realized that the people of Pakistan had been always in awe of three A(s) whom they had revered, in fact, namely the Allah, the Army and America and in that order! Apparently, when he was in Pakistan he had been in constant touch, almost on a daily basis, with the Pakistani government with a view to keeping his own government in Washington DC abreast of the state of affairs in Pakistan, particularly with regard to Pakistan's suspected activities on making nuclear bombs. He had, also, mentioned that the experience he had gathered before he had left his post in Pakistan had convinced him that China had been actively colluding with Pakistan and assisting it in the making of both the nuclear warhead and the acquisition of ballistic missiles.

Incidentally, as soon as I had finished my own lecture at Stanford I had been told that on the very next day the retired US ambassador was, also, due to deliver a talk on a similar topic at the same forum. I had, therefore, made it a point to attend his presentation before leaving Stanford the next day. And, while listening to his lecture, I had noted with satisfaction that his version of how and why Pakistan had managed to 'develop' nuclear warhead and undertake the underground nuclear tests just then, in 1998, closely following the Indian tests, had largely agreed with what I had stated during my lecture at the same forum on the previous day. Since both he and I had been scheduled to speak at the same venue on consecutive days I had, also, noted with amusement that most scholars who had attended my lecture had, also, been present at the former Ambassador's talk. One of those 'common' listeners, I had noted then, was Dr Wahe Guru Singh Siddhu, the former PhD student of the History Dept of Cambridge University, whom I had first met, as mentioned earlier, while lecturing at Cambridge, England, an year or two back. He was, in fact, the PhD student at whose suggestion the Professor in the Department of History of Cambridge University had extended the lecture invitation to me on that occasion. Apparently he had earned his PhD in Cambridge in due course and then moved from the UK to the USA and was, at that point of time, a post-doctoral Fellow in the Dept of Political Science of Stanford University. Although Dr Siddhu had made a few interesting observations, as I recall, during the question hour following my lecture on the previous day, also, what I had enjoyed more was the comment that he had made during the talk, given by the US Ambassador, on the following day: He had jocularly stated that the reason why Pakistan had taken almost a week to do its tit-for-tat nuclear tests in response to the tests, undertaken by India, may have had something to do with the fact that the Pakistani scientists had to await the arrival of their counterparts from China's nuclear establishment before attempting their tests, for the reason that they (the Pakistani scientists) needed to refer to the relevant technical instructions to make sure that they followed the correct procedure while conducting the tests but had found that they could not read the manual because it had been written in the Chinese language.

During my visits to the USA that year I had, also, to fulfill an engagement at another well-regarded graduate school on the west coast, and I had done that a few days after returning from Stanford. And, since that graduate school, namely the Monterey Institute of Intnl Studies at Monterey, in California, had a great reputation then as a centre of excellence for teaching and research on nuclear proliferation issues, in particular, both the Professor who had invited me and I had anticipated that there would be quite a few graduate students and research associates in Monterey that year – over and above the students and scholars attached to my host professor's department – who would be keen to attend my lecture. In fact, it had turned out to be so, and there were plenty of questions, by both the graduate students and the faculty members, that I had to field during the question hour after my presentation at Monterey. And, among those listeners, I had noted, there was one young scholar of Indian origin, too. And, I had learnt later, as he had come up to meet me after the lecture, that he had done his political science undergraduate degree from the Hindu College of Delhi University and his MA from a US university and intended to join the PhD programme, also, in an US university. Apparently, he had taken a break from his graduate school studies then to do a short stint as a research assistant at the institute in Monterey. However, during the question-hour there had been another surprise for me: While throwing the floor open to my listeners for questions and comments, after I had concluded my presentation, the Professor who had invited me and presided over my lecture had stated with a twinkle in her eyes that some her colleagues at Monterey and she had been aware of the fact that I had given an invited lecture on the same theme, namely nuclear non-proliferation, at Stanford University a week back and that it had been an well-attended lecture event and had generated a lot of discussions including some provocative questions from of my listeners and equally forthright answers by me. So, I had realized that news travels fast and that the Monterey professors, having been aware of the fact that I had been invited to deliver a lecture on the previous week by the Stanford University, too, had actually checked with a faculty member at Stanford how my lecture had gone. Apparently, someone at Stanford, probably a member of the political science department there, had told his or her counterpart at Monterey that I had given a very forthright presentation at Stanford. Incidentally, one of the important points I had made at Stanford while responding to a question that had been put to me by my host, Professor Scott Sagan, had dealt with the western world's puzzlement over one of India's well-known policy declarations on non-proliferation, often referred to as the NFU – or the 'NO FIRST USE' – policy.

The NFU, as known, refers to a nuclear armed nation's self-imposed restraint on the use of nuclear weapons in the conduct of a future war, and that was a policy which, as known, had always characterized India's stance on nuclear non-proliferation and, in India's case, unequivocally emphasized that, unlike its neighbour Pakistan, India will always maintain a non-aggressive posture, even, in the face of Pakistan's continuing threat of a nuclear strike. In short, India's NFU policy was an indication that it stood by its commitment that it would never launch a first strike against any nation. The fact that a question regarding that policy of India had been asked and that it had been asked at a lecture, given by me at the Stanford University, and by no less a scholar than one of the stature of a senior professor of Stanford and one who was then the Chair, ie in other words, by a scholar who had written profusely on nuclear non-proliferation issues and was, in fact, an authority on that subject, and, also, the fact that the Professor had put that question at his earliest opportunity had shown that our country's NFU policy hadn't made any sense to him and to the intellectuals of the USA, which possessed thousands of nuclear and thermo-nuclear warheads but wouldn't dream of adhering to a NFU-like rule. And, the professor who had fired that question had said that in so many words: He had sounded incredulous when he had stated that he had failed to understand why a country like India, which now admittedly possessed nuclear weapons, would willingly take the risk of being devastated by a first strike, launched by another nuclear-armed country in its neighbourhood (and not prevent such a calamity by hitting the enemy first). The reason why he had sounded incredulous was not far to seek, however. It was inconceivable for scholars of his persuasion, namely the deterrence theorists of the nuclear-armed western world, to accept that it was possible for a nuclear-armed nation to willingly take a first strike from an adversary before launching a retaliatory strike of its own.

The answer that I had given to him on that occasion had basically constituted an attempt by me at explaining the underlying logic that had always guided our country's policy on nuclear non-proliferation, namely that as a nation we abhor nuclear weapons, discourage its use by any nation in any form, whatsoever and stand unequivocally committed to the abolition of all types of nuclear weapons and, therefore, would rather take the consequences of a first strike by an unscrupulous enemy before destroying that enemy country by making use of our own nuclear weapons. The discussion that had followed, as I recall, had generated a lot of heat in that august gathering, because most of the others, too, had failed to appreciate the nuances of India's non-proliferation philosophy behind its NFU policy and expressed the same kind of dismay that the Stanford professor did about the logic behind our NFU policy.

It goes without saying that my experience at Monterey, a few days later, had been the same, thanks to the contrast between Indian and western scholars' perceptions on the use of nuclear weapons. I may add that at some of the other centres of learning and, at some of the lecture meetings, such as my lecture to a select group of ISS scholars in and around Washington DC, including academics and analysts of the State Department, which the NIPP had organized, my experience was different: There were many listeners at those events who had been less passionate about the US foreign policy and its aggressive posture and more liberal in their outlook. And, there were less divergence between my views and theirs on many of the issues, relevant to Intnl Security, that I had presented at academic forums. I may add here that some of my other lectures and seminars in US universities, eg at the Southeast Missouri State University at Springfield, Missouri, where the eminent scholar, Professor William Van Cleave, had been the star attraction then on the faculty of its Defence and Strategic Studies department, the California State University at San Bernardino where the Department of Political Science had a well-known scholar of national security studies as its Chair then, the University of California at San Diego and the Georgetown University at Washington DC where the reputed ISS scholar, Professor Keith Payne, had been the mainstay, then, of its staretegic studies faculty, had been more in the nature of teaching assignments at regular classes. And, both the undergraduate and the graduate students of political science and Intnl Relations in those universities had enthusiastically participated in discussions during the question hours. Those were, consequently, a different kind of learning experiences for me.

Social Sciences Graduate Schools In Canada and The Teaching Of International Politics

The graduate schools in Canada where I had delivered invited lectures included the Dalhousie University at Halifax, the University of Manitoba at Winnipeg, the York University in Toronto, the Queens University in Kingston and the Royal Military College, also, in Kingston. The political science faculties and the graduate schools of both the University of Manitoba and the York University were well regarded in Canada then, and I had thoroughly enjoyed the discussions with the graduate students and the members of the faculty at each university's Centre for International studies during the question hours that had followed my lectures at those schools. However, I choose no to go into the details of those discussions here, for lack of space, except to mention two items.

At the university in Winnipeg my host, the Professor of Political Science, had arranged for me to speak at two other forums, following my lecture to the graduate students and the members of the faculty, eg a dinner meeting which had been hosted by a group of Indian professors belonging to other departments of the University of Manitoba, and a town hall meeting of retired professionals, eg retired doctors, engineers, administrators etc of that city, interested in international affairs, too,

At the York University, probably, there was an active participant in the discussions that had followed my lecture there, who had, interestingly, been an Indian who had the distinction of having been a senior fellow of the Centre for Intnl Studies, attached to the university's Department of Political Science then. And, later, when he had formally been introduced to me at the lunch, which was hosted by the Department in my honour, that gentleman had turned out to be one Ambassador Bhargava of India, a former foreign service officer of our country, who had retired from our Foreign Service as the Secretary of the SAARC, he had told me.

As for the Dalhousie University, apparently its Centre for Foreign Policy Studies (CFPS), which had extended the invitation to me, had taken care to select an excellent lecture theatre of that university as the venue of my lecture. And, as I had learnt to my surprise on arrival there, that lecture theatre had been named after the same Lord Dalhousie who, as the British Governor General & Viceroy of India, had once ruled the sub-continent of India, the crown of the British empire then. But what had crossed my mind as a fleeting thought, as I had stood on the podium at the conclusion of my lecture, had been a curious thought: The fact that my just-concluded lecture, a talk that had been delivered by me in the beginning of the twenty first century as an invited scholar from the new India, had been so full of the account of independent India's emergence as a stable democracy and an economically up-and-coming nation and, most of all, as a prospective world power, that it would have, probably, made that ex-Viceroy of India, a colony which had been ruled by him with the unfettered powers of the representative of the British monarch then, turn in his grave. In any event, the arguments and the analysis that had constituted my presentation at the Dalhousie University's graduate school for political science had been nothing short of a complete contradiction of all that the good Lord of the then mighty British empire had, in his conservative world-view and lordly wisdom, held as sacrosanct then, a total contradiction, especially, of his perception of what an India, then horrendously being exploited by its colonial masters, would most likely look like by the turn of the present century.

As for the Queens University at Kingston, where I had been a guest lecturer on two occasions during a span of three years, I had on both occasions traveled from Toronto to Kingston by driving a rented car, covering a distance of only 200 kilometers each way. As often is the case, my host, a senior Professor in the Department of Political Studies at Queens, was then both the Head of the Department and the ex-officio Director of the Centre for Intnl Relations of the Queens University, which had hosted my lecture. Since the Queens is one of the most prestigious universities of Canada, I had assumed that my host was a highly-regarded academic in his field of studies. And, that was the case, indeed. He, a Canadian by birth, had done his MA in the USA and his PhD in London, UK, I had gathered, and had to his credit a number of highly-rated publications. And, yet I had found him to be a very pleasant person on both the occasions. And, despite the fact that at that juncture, sadly enough, he had had some personal problems at home, the professor had been very kind and courteous. Although the subjects of my presentation on both of those occasions were equally interesting in that both the topics were issues of international politics, then, involving technology, namely Military Technology and Arms Control on one occasion and WMD Proliferation on the second, and although the attendance was very large on both occasions and had comprised both the graduate students and senior scholars, attached to the Centre for Intnl Relations, it was my lecture on the second occasion which had proved more eventful in a rather unexpected way.

On that second occasion at the Queens the total number of participants who had attended my lecture had been slightly less, but one component of that gathering, namely the group of senior scholars who had consisted of a few faculty members, a couple of emeritus professors, and a few Senior Fellows and the Fellows of the Centre, had been distinctly large. They had belonged to two age groups, however. There were a few who were senior in age and had, probably, joined the Centre as Senior Fellows after having retired from their respective service, eg a former Canadian diplomat, a Canadian technocrat who had retired from the UN, a retired General of the Canadian Forces and the few emeritus professors. But, there were others, too, who were much younger and were either the members of the faculty or serving middle to senior-ranking officers of the Canadian and the American armed forces, who were, at that point of time, attached to the Queens as Fellows. Consequently, the discussions during the question-hour, that had followed my lecture on that occasion, had been quite informed and, even, animated at times. All of the younger Fellows of the Centre, as mentioned, had obviously been selected with care and been on deputation from their respective Service then, ie Lieutenant Colonels of the Canadian Forces or of the US Army or the US Air Force or the Marine Corps, who had proficiency in academics, too. Those participants had seemed to be an energetic lot, while the older participants, including the Senior Fellows of the Centre, had appeared more quiet and had, in fact, a little less enthusiasm for asking questions.

Since many issues pertaining to technology empowerment and economic development of both the developed and the developing countries of the world had figured in my lecture on that occasion, two aspects of the current situation prevailing in the world had figured prominently in my presentation, namely (a) the emergence of China and India as fast-rising economic powers and the consequent closing of the gap between the developed countries, led by the USA, and the newly industrialized developing countries, ie Russia, China, India and Brazil, and (b) the contrast in the sphere of technology capability between the leading developing countries of the world, eg Brazil/India/China/Russia, on the one hand, and the rest of the world's developing countries, on the other. Consequently, the current status of India as an increasingly technology-proficient nation had come up for discussion during the question hour. And, it had turned out that while the younger participants, ie the Fellows of the Centre, were totally in agreement with what I had stated on that issue, one member of the older set, particularly, the one who had been an Ambassador of Canada during the closing years of his service, had serious reservations about some of the points I had made in my analysis. I had immediately sensed, therefore, that the ex-Ambassador of Canada, who had, probably, retired many years back from a position held in Europe or the USA, had not been in touch with the current developments in China and India and had great difficulty in acknowledging the fact that India, too, had made phenomenal progress since the departure of the British rulers and, particularly, during the last two decades. And, although he had kept to himself throughout my lecture and had listened quietly he had suddenly stirred himself up at the very end of the question hour and had indicated that he wished to speak. Therefore, just when my host, the professor, had got up to give his concluding remarks, it was the Ambassador who had interrupted him and started to speak. He had stated that, having visited India some years back and seen for himself the conditions on the ground then, he had difficulty in accepting what I had stated in my presentation in relation to India's current position in the spheres of economic progress and technology development activities.

Since it was getting late, however, I had instantly decided not to engage him in a long discussion but to give a brief response to the comments made by that ex-Ambassador. I had, therefore, politely pointed out that all of the facts pertaining to India and China that I had quoted in my presentation, especially the economic data, had been reported by experts and analysts in the developed countries, too, eg the USA, the UK, and, even, Canada, in the books or articles which were published in reputed journals, eg the Economist of London and American dailies like the Wall Street Journal and the New York Times etc. But, before the discussion could go further it had, mercifully, taken a turn which had made it unnecessary for my having to argue my case for long. It was the others of the group of listeners and participants, ie the young Fellows of the Centre, who had come forward and had stated, almost in one voice, that the former Ambassador had not kept in touch with the developments in the world at large and ought to check the facts pertaining to India for himself. One amusing example of how Indian technologists had in recent years reached an important position in the IT industry of the world had been given on that occasion by one of those young participants, a Fellow of the Centre, who was a Colonel of the US Air Force then: He had quoted a few recent cases of young American enterpreuners of Indian origin in the Silicon Valley displacing white Americans as owners of software start-up companies and doing well, too, in some cases displacing the native-born American start-up enterpreuners. He had added with a chuckle that he knew that fact well, because his brother, who had his own IT business in the Silicon Valley earlier, is unemployed now.

As mentioned, on both the occasions that I had visited the Queens University I had traveled by a rented a car from Toronto to Kingston and back. In the UK, too, I had done the same, eg to deliver guest lectures at the Lancaster University, University of Hull, Reading University, Cambridge University, RMCS etc. But those journeys were much shorter than the distances I had covered, in rented cars, in the USA during my visits to universities for guest lectures. While for most lectures in the USA I would make use of air travel, I had, for the first of my two visits to the SW Missouri State University, driven some 1200 miles to Springfield, Missouri, the seat then of the SW Missouri State University. I had, also, undertaken similar road journeys for my lectures at a number of other universities in the USA, eg the Fletcher School of Law & Diplomacy of the Tufts University in Boston, the MIT in Cambridge, Massachusetts, the University of Maine, in Orono, Maine, on the east coast, and the Stanford University and the Monterey Institute of Intnl Studies on the west. I could do this, ie use a rented car, because the universities there, as known, have a system in place for promptly reimbursing the expenditure, actually incurred by an invited lecturer for road journeys. However, in my home-town, New Delhi, I had gladly driven my own car for giving an occasional guest lecture at a think tank, for instance, without getting a reimbursement of any kind, thanks to the red-tapes of our administrative system. That had happened on several occasions, in fact, when I had given invited lectures, during 1994-98, at the Centre for

Intnl Politics, Organisation & Disarmament (CIPOD), one of the graduate schools of the Jawaharlal Nehru University (JNU) in New Delhi. However, I had done that with great pleasure, because on most of those occasions I had received the invitations for giving guest lectures from a brilliant young scholar of the JNU of those years, now Professor Kanti Bajpai, who was then an Associate Professor at the CIPOD. He had met me for the first time at the CIPOD at a seminar, given by me at some other Professor's invitation. That was a a joint meeting of the graduate students and the members of the faculty of the CIPOD in December, 1995, probably, and, while exchanging pleasantries after my lecture, he had mentioned that the CIPOD lacked scholars in my particular interest-area and asked if I would like to volunteer to give an introductory course on technology related issues of national and international security for the benefit of his graduate students.

As known, the USA has the maximum number of universities, and those are of two kinds, namely the privately-financed universities and those owned by the State governments. While quite a few of the most famous of US universities are privately-owned, eg the Harvard, the Princeton, the Yale, the Stanford etc, there are many other equally good universities which are State-owned, eg the University of Maryland in College Park in Maryland State, the University of California at Berkeley (UCB) in California State, the University of California at Los Angeles (UCLA) in California State etc. In fact, California is one large State of the USA, which has quite a few state-owned universities, of which the UCB and the UCLA are the most reputed, probably. I had, once, been invited to deliver a lecture by one such State-owned university of California, namely the California State University at San Bernerdino (CSUSB) which had a strong and well-funded graduate studies programme in defence and national security studies in its political science department. And, a large part of that funding for the security studies programme used to come from the federal government, eg the Department of Defence, in the form of assistance or scholarships for graduate students who joined the Master's degree course or the doctoral programme in defence studies.

The Professor who had invited me and chaired my lecture on that occasion was an erudite person, but he was, also, an unique person in one way, I had found. He had in his young days served a full term of engagement in the Marine Corps of the USA, he had told me. And, he had looked the part, too, having possessed a good physique like an ex-Marine. Apparently, after finishing the stipulated period of service in the Marine Corps he had availed of the veterans' scholarship scheme, like many in the USA but, unlike most veterans, had, in due course, ended up with a good PhD in strategic studies from a reputed university and joined the US academia many years back. Obviously, he had done very well as an academic in that he had risen to the position of a full Professor in a short time, with good publications to his credit. A very polite individual with good manners, too, he had, also, told me that he and his wife enjoyed hiking and living outdoors during their holidays. We had got on very well, in fact, during that brief visit to his department. However, I had, also, noted that he was an arch conservative in his political belief and thought poorly of the liberals of his own country. Of course, while accepting that lecture invitation I had known of his political persuasion. But, that had not deterred me from doing a good job of analyzing the US foreign policy, including its shortcomings during my presentation. I had been critical of his government's policies on a number of issues on that occasion, eg its infamous technology control regime and, particularly, one of its off-shoots, the missile technology control regime. In all honesty I must admit, however, that despite that divergence in our views he had praised me sky-high, while making his concluding remarks, for the quality of the talk that I had given to his students.

Lectures At The CIPOD Of The JNU and The NDC

The Centre for Intnl Politics, Organisation and Disarmament (CIPOD), was the first graduate school in our country, with emphasis on teaching and research on ISS. It was, therefore, inevitable that I had got in touch with the CIPOD in the very beginning of my joining the community of ISS scholars. The Director of the CIPOD then, a professor who had just then returned to the JNU's main campus in South Delhi, as I recall, after doing a stint in the JNU campus in the North East of our country, had readily extended an invitation to me to present a seminar to a joint meeting of the faculty and the graduate students of the CIPOD. And, it had turned out to have been a very interesting occasion for me, because my lecture was very well attended in the sense that every member of the faculty of the CIPOD then and quite a few others from other Centres of the SIS, apart from all of the graduate students on the CIPOD's roll were present. The discussions that had followed my lecture during the question hour was, in a way, even more interesting. More so, because the discussions were dominated by only one personality, the senior-most professor in the CIPOD of those days, a founder member, in fact, who is no more but had been well known in his time because of his diplomat-politician-professor background. He had been an early entrant to our Foreign Service but had tendered his resignation as a Joint Secretary to get elected as a young member of our Lok Sabha for one term and had made a name then as as a rising star of the Bharatiya Janata Party (BJP) before he had given up politics to join the JNU as a professor. He had disagreed with me on many issues of intnl politics during the question hour and had a comment to make on practically each of my responses, irrespective of whether he or someone else had asked the question. However, he was totally polite throughout the session, if at times a little sarcastic in his comments, especially in his comments in relation to the USA. But, it was an amusing experience for someone like me who had not met him before nor had much knowledge, at that point of time, of his past.

My invitation to speak to the students of our National Defence College (NDC) as an invited panelist had been a surprise, too. That had happened a few years after my now-acclaimed article on the subject of the Indian DTIB had been published in the USI journal but soon after, probably, my first book, entitled 'Military Technology & Defence Industrialisation: The Indian Experience' had been published. I had received that invitation in the form of a telephone call from one of the four members of the NDC's Senior Directing Staff in New Delhi then. The caller, an Air Vice Marshal of our flying branch, a fighter pilot whom I had never met before, had stated that, having read my article and my book, he was very keen to have me give a talk to the current batch of the NDC students as a panelist on that year's panel for 'technology and national security' issues. He had explained that my research and writing on our persistent failure to achieve the goal of our DTIB, namely a reasonable degree of self-reliance in weapons and equipment, had thrown a new light and that the students of the three wings of the military Services and of our civil services, all of Brigadier/Captain/Air Commodore/ equivalent ranks, currently undertaking the NDC Course, would benefit from my talk and my participation in the panel discussion. I had readily agreed to accept the invitation, on one condition, however, namely that I would join the panel if I knew the antecedents of the other two members of the panel. He had responded by mentioning the names the NDC had tentatively selected as panelists that year. And, as I recall, I had only one suggestion, and that was immediately accepted. In the event, the panel that year had consisted of the Chairman of the Ordnance Factories Board then, a gentleman from Kerala state whom I had not known of earlier, and a senior DRDO scientist who had been nominated by the then Scientific Advisor, Dr Abdul Kalam.

As customary, the session had started with the three of us covering three aspects of the subject of our panel discussion, and that had been followed by a open house, in which questions and comments are invited from the floor, consisting of seventy senior officers from our military and our Civil Services and about ten foreign students, ie senior military officers from other countries. I was the first one to give the talk, and the aspect that I had covered was Governance and DTIB management. I could see how my talk dealing with our DTIB management structure had somewhat surprised our own students, both from our military and our civil services. And, as I had expected, most of the questions and comments had been directed to me, later, ie during the question hour. After the other two panelists had given their presentations all of us, both students and panelists, had gone for the scheduled tea break. During that interval a few students had come over to me and had complemented two senior directing staff members of the NDC, who were speaking to me, for having invited me as a panelist. Those few, also, congratulated me for the originality of my presentation. And, as soon as we had reassembled I had known I had proved right: All of the questions had been addressed to me.

Since my analysis of the defective management structure of our DTIB had pointed to one major problem, namely the lack of an integrated management, consequent to a division of responsibility, at the apex, for Development-cum-Manufacture, between the Scientific Advisor who heads the Development function only and the Secretary (Defence Production & Supply) who, as the controller of our Ordnance Factories, heads the Manufacture function, most questioners had asked how things were done in the industrially developed countries and why our government had not made amends and brought both Development and Manufacture under one unified management etc. And, I had been kept very busy throughout, responding to those questions and comments. A straightforward answer to most of those questions was that an overhaul of the management structure at the top of our DTIB was overdue. And that meant that our system of governance, inherited from our colonial past, had not been reformed and, therefore, remained totally different from the system that prevailed in the developed countries, including Great Britain itself. In fact, there were lots of laughter when, in response to a question on the peculiarity of our DTIB management system, put by an officer-student, a lady, who had belonged to our Audit & Accounts Service (IA&AS), I had pointed out that, even, in her own organization things were no longer the same: Unlike in the early years of our independence when the position of the Comptroller & Auditor General (CAAG), had always been filled by an officer of the IA&AS cadre, it was a senior officer of the IAS cadre, often someone who had just then retired as a Secretary to the Government, who nowadays filled that position. All in all, our panel discussions had been very lively on that occasion.

The Fourth Intnl Conefernce On Controlling Arms

During those years I had, also, attended a few international conferences as an invited panelist. Although all of those conferences had as their theme one or the other of the several issues of international security, then in the forefront, there were two conferences, in particular, which had proved most interesting. The first one, called the Fourth Intnl Conference on Controlling Arms, had been held in Philadelphia, USA, in the summer of 1996, probably, and was, as its name suggests, the fourth conference in that particular series of 'arms control' conferences. The reason why I had been invited was interesting, too. Only an year or so back I had met at one of my lecture events in Washington DC an ISS scholar who was a senior partner of a think- tank which traditionally sponsored that particular arms control conference once in two years, using financial grants given by the US State Dept among others. The event where I had met that gentleman was a lecture of mine, organized by another think-tank, namely the NIPP, at a venue close to the NIPP office in Alexandria. And on that occasion the subject of my lecture had been a very important issue of international security of that time, namely the future of India-USA relations. That lecture was apparently very well received, probably, because I had tread a new ground: I had predicted that in view of the disintegration of the former USSR a few years back, ie during 1988-93, and the consequent cessation of the decades-long cold war, the USA would very soon be obliged to change the direction of its foreign policy on South Asia, a policy which it had severely tilted towards Pakistan for short-term gains, and enter into a new strategic partnership and economic cooperation with democratic India, and that by continuing to delay that action the USA was only harming itself in many ways and, most importantly, it was promoting the cause of the Taliban in Afghanistan and the growth of terrorist organiations inside Pakistan in the aftermath of the with-drawl of the Soviets from Afghanistan.

Although, as mentioned, that lecture had been well received by that assembly of scholars and analysts, which had included a few, even, from the policy research divisions of the State Dept, the CIA etc, and although many of them had come up to the rostrum after my lecture and congratulated me on the quality of my presentation it was only one individual in that gathering, namely that senior partner of the concerned think-tank, who had, unbeknown to me, been impressed enough by my lecture to have taken the initiative to meet me separately, after my lecture, and to have asked if I would like to be invited to an international conference on arms control in the USA the next year and take part in one of its panel's deliberations as an invited panelist and speaker. That impromptu invitation had both pleased and surprised me, more so when he had mentioned in the same breath that in the past only one Indian ISS scholar had been invited to their conference a few years back as a panelist and that the Indian invitee on that occasion was none other than General Sunderji, the former Chief of the Indian Army, who had, I learnt then, attended the Second Intnl Conference on Controlling Arms as an invited panelist.

About six months after receiving that oral invitation from that senior academic of the think-tank and well after my return to India, I had received a telephone call from him, followed by a letter, stating that the fourth international conference on controlling arms would be held in Philadelphia a month hence and that the organising committee extended their invitation to me to join that four-day conference as an invited panelist on the panel on Non-nuclear WMD (Weapon of Mass Destruction). And, I had gladly accepted that honour. That intnl conference had been a major event then, and yet I had been surprised to see, as I had arrived at the hotel lobby for checking in, that there were nearly a hundred participants who had already arrived and checked in and were greeting each other. The arrangements made for receiving the few invited participants were perfect, too. And, all delegates had soon been ushered into the first event of that 4-day conference, which was a get-together, designed to welcome all of the participants. As expected, it was during that event that I had met the other members of my panel for the first time. I found that besides India, five other countries, namely Great Britain, Germany, Australia, Japan and China, had been selected for representation on the panel on Proliferation of Non-nuclear WMD, but that there was one absentee, however, namely China, whose relationship with the USA had, at that point of time, suddenly deteriorated, as I recall. Also, although a civilian senior scientist of Great Britain had earlier been nominated by the organizing committee to represent his country on that Panel and to chair the Panel discussions on the following day he had been unable to come and, at the last moment, another senior British ISS analyst, a retired Admiral of the Royal Navy who was then the Director of the Chatham House, a prestigious think-tank of the UK, had been requested to fill his place.

The Admiral had been altogether an engaging person, and although he was the senior-most in age amongst us and a person who had been accustomed to receiving special deference in his own country, having been awarded a knighthood, too, he had got on famously with the two of the members of our WMD panel who were fluent in English, namely the Australian, who was a senior bio-technologist of the Australian Defence R & D organization, and myself. However, at the Panel discussion the next day, after each one of us had given a presentation on his or her perceptions on the likely nature of a future WMD threat and the best possible measures for its prevention, and after the discussions had been thrown open to the floor, it was the

Admiral, a co-panelist sitting next to me, who had asked the first question. And, his question had been addressed to me in a voice slightly tinged with exasperation. He had singled out one of the points that I had made in my presentation, namely that our country's enormous technology capability notwithstanding, our country had scrupulously adhered to the principles of non-proliferation of both nuclear and non-nuclear weapons of mass destruction and that our record in that respect had been better than those of the developed countries and of the former Soviet Union (FSU). He had then stated that he did not believe that India was as technology-capable as the developed countries and that many in the developed countries suspected that India's technologists were proficient in 'copying' products, already developed by a developed country. He had cited India's drug manufacturing industry as an example and stated that India had been making certain drugs in infringement of patent rights, held by companies in the developed countries.

In my response I had strongly refuted the Admiral's statement regarding the alleged violation of intellectual property rights by our country and, also, upheld the factual position that, thanks to the leap-frog advancement in science and technology in post-colonial India, our scientists had been able to develop many generic drugs by independently undertaking research and development activities. I had, also, added that India had fully observed all cannons of intellectual property rights while developing those generic drugs. I had, also, mentioned in that connection that, as an emerging economic power of the world, India would always honour the rights of other countries but would make full use of the World Trade Organisation (WTO), then in the making, to uphold its unfettered right to independently develop new technologies. To my pleasant surprise, a number of participants from the floor had, then, come out in support of my point of view and had openly refuted the point that my British co-panelist had tried to make. As an aside I would, also, like to mention here that in the evening of the same day I had met an US delegate who had attended our WMD panel discussion in the morning and had witnessed the exchange that the British panelist had had with me. He was an ISS analyst and a retired US Ambassador, who had served the US Army in his early days. He said that, while undergoing one of the US Army's command and staff courses as an infantry Major in his early days, he had known General Sunderji, when Sunderji, as a Major of the Indian Army, was doing the same course. He had mentioned to me that a situation, similar to the one I had experienced in the panel discussion earlier in the day, had arisen a few years back, too, at an earlier conference, ie the Second Intnl Conference on Controlling Arms, where retired Gen Sunderji had been an invited panelist on the proliferation of nuclear WMD. He said that on that occasion a US delegate had tried to refute a point, made by the Indian panelist, retired Gen Sunderji, and Gen Sunderji had strongly defended his position supporting India's right to develop its own nuclear weapon in defence of its own security and sovereignty and characterized the US delegate's observation as one smacking of racism.

The other example of an interesting conference that I had attended as a panelist, among the few I had attended as a panelist, had been an international conference on an issue related to militarization of Space, which was held in Southampton University in Great Britain in 2002, probably. Although it was held in Great Britain in collaboration with the Mountbatten Centre for Peace Studies of the Southampton University, that conference had, in fact, been an American initiative and sponsored by the Monterey Institute of Intnl Studies where, it will be recalled, I had delivered an invited lecture a few years prior to that. My having been able to attend that conference as an invited panelist had been a sudden affair in that I had no inkling earlier that a conference of that kind was being organized by a professor in the US academia nor of the facts that the papers had been invited months back and the list of panelists finalized. Interestingly, it was a professor of another graduate school in the USA, where I was then on a visit to deliver an invited lecture, who had brought the news of that forthcoming conference to my notice by asking me if I intended to attend that conference in England on my way back to India. As mentioned, I had no knowledge of that conference till then. However, soon thereafter, when I was still in the USA, I had got a cordial invitation to attend that conference as a panelist from the concerned professor of Monterey at whose initiative the conference was being held.

The Conference On Weaponisation Of Space And International Politics In Southampton

Although I had once, a few years prior to that visit to England, met that professor of Monterey when I had delivered a seminar at the graduate school in the Monterey Institute of Intnl Studies in California, at the invitation of another professor of the same institute, a lecture on nuclear non-proliferation by me that he, too, had attended and although I was aware of the fact that he had known of my research interest in Space Warfare and related issues of international security I had been surprised to get that invitation. More so, because he had taken considerable trouble in order to be able to invite me to that conference, I had later discovered: He had kept my invitation on hold for a day or two and then confirmed it, because, as he had told me later, in the absence of the knowledge of my whereabouts he couldn't contact me and include me on time in the list of invited panelists but had managed, eventually, to get hold of the required funds for my travel from London to Southampton and back and for my stay in the hotel in Southampton. In short, it was only because of my having contacted him, almost, at the eleventh hour before the commencement of that conference, when I was about to leave the USA for England, en route India, he had managed to locate me in the USA and thus to learn that I was, in any case, stopping over London, England, on my way back from the USA to India that I had been able to avail of a perfect opportunity to participate in that conference in Southampton on Space and International Security. And, I had been very glad to attend it.

I ought to mention here that, unlike in the Reagan era, during the presidency of the senior President Bush the subject of space weaponry had gone much out-of-style in international security studies, consequent to the cessation of the cold war. It was, therefore, only during the first term of junior Bush as the President of the USA that a few Republican power-brokers had successfully lobbied for the revival of the US interest in Space for perpetuating the US domination of Space-related trade and commerce. And, as I recall, it was precisely at that juncture that a section of the ISS scholars of the USA had taken the initiative to organize that Conference.

Immediately on my arrival from London at the conference venue in Southampton by train, I had met a number of participants, as I recall, many of them from the USA but, also, from other countries including France, Canada, the UK, Pakistan, China etc. That was, also, precisely when I had realized that, apart from scholars and analysts working in developed countries, a large number of the participants were officials and diplomats who had been nominated by their respective governments. However, a majority of the

US delegates had consisted of individual scholars belonging to universities, think-tanks and NGOs (Non Governmental Organisations), but there were representatives from the US federal government, too, eg a few delegates from the State Department and the Department of Defence. The two delegates from Pakistan, both serving Brigadiers of the general staff from two different directorates of the Army Headquarters of Pakistan then, had arrived at about the same time as I. And, they had been the first two delegates I had been introduced to by an official of the Conference. Both were very polite and had greeted me warmly, but it had seemed to me that they had been aware of the fact that an Indian had been selected by the Conference committee as one of their few invited panelists and that the Indian panelist was none other than a retired senior of the Indian Air Force, to boot. What had been surprising, however, was that the next morning I had discovered that there was a second Indian participant, too, and that he had come to attend that conference as an official delegate of our government. The manner of my getting to meet up with that only-other Indian participant attending that conference had, however, been interesting, too, since I had no prior knowledge that our government had, like some of the others, also, sent an official delegate, by nominating a senior diplomat, posted then as a Minister in our High Commission in Lonodon, to attend the Southampton conference as either a delegate or an observer or an invitee.

That chance meeting had taken place the next morning, about an hour or so before our conference had formally assembled. And, I had met him at the hotel's dining room as I had come in for breakfast on my way to the first session of the conference. As I had entered that room for my breakfast I had noticed that almost all seats were taken and that there was one vacant chair, next to the one occupied by an

Indian-looking gentleman. I had, therefore, joined him at that table and occupied that chair, but as we had introduced ourselves to each other he, too, had seemed surprised to see another Indian participating in that conference. However, after I had told him that I had come to attend that conference as an invitee, ie an invited panelist, ie in my individual capacity, he had explained that he belonged to our Foreign Service and had been nominated to attend that conference as a representative of our government. He had added that he had, also, traveled from London where he was then the Minister in charge of political affairs in our High Commission. However, it had turned out that he had, also, been a student in Calcutta and a man of science, a BSc (Honours) from the St Xavier's College and a MSc in physics of the Calcutta University, as I recall, before he had competed for and secured a place in our foreign service. As the only two Indians, at that two-day conference in Southampton, both of us with some form of science education under our respective belts, we had, therefore, something in common. However, he had told me that he had no expert knowledge in the subject of that conference nor had he dealt with any of it so far in an official capacity during his career as a senior in our foreign service. Apparently, he had been a senior joint secretary in our External Affairs ministry in New Delhi before he had moved to London, and he had mentioned that his wife, who was, also, a senior officer in our foreign service, was then posted in Geneva. However, thereafter, during the next two days, it was only once or twice that we had met each other, and that, too, very briefly, such as hailing each other from a distance during the tea break. He had mostly kept to himself and, during the breaks, had kept the company of one or two foreigners, probably, diplomats of other countries. In any case, he had remained a silent observer while attending presentations and discussions throughout the conference.

There were three sessions, out of the six or so, which were of particular interest to me as an Indian analyst, because our country, the only developing country which had invested heavily in its own space programme right from the beginning of our Independence, had made notable progress, as known, in developing and making communication satellites and, more importantly, the satellite launch vehicles (SLVs), building indigenous SLVs for various ranges/heights and launching indigenous satellites for educational programmes and for communication generally. India has its own rocket-launching facility, too, as known, and was, by then, well on the way to making it a success in the international commerce pertaining to satellite-launching, and, in that sense, we had a bigger stake in the proceedings of that conference than, even, some of the world's developed countries. And, I had occasions to offer many of the pertinent comments and suggestions at each of those three sessions. In fact, I had made quite a few interesting points in relation to the papers, presented by authors and scholars who belonged to several countries of Europe, eg France, the USA and the UK, and a few of the other countries. And, some of my observations were well received by both the authors and the respective panel chairmen. For instance, in one case a senior specialist, a French delegate, had missed mentioning an important point, an omission that had amounted to his ignoring one of the important concerns of our country in relation to the continuation of the international space cooperation programme in its present form, and I had raised the issue during the question hour. In fact, at the request of the panel chairman, I had then given a detailed commentary on what had been missed out by the author of that paper. And, both the presenter and the panel's chair had thanked me for my contribution.

Incidentally, I had, also, on that occasion, joined an issue with another scholar, a delegate from Great Britain, who was the director of a London-based NGO, it had turned out. And, that intervention by me had yielded an acknowledgement by that scholar of quite a few other omissions that had been made by her in her paper, including one that had amounted to her failure to acknowledge that the NGO movement in our country had been strong and effective, too. Finally, although our country's official delegate at that conference, a senior diplomat who had then been a minister in our High Commission in London then but was, some years hence, our Ambassador to Italy, had not presented any paper at that conference nor participated in any discussion in any one of its seven or eight sessions, he had made it a point to congratulate me once, during a coffee break, on the contributions that I had made, as an invited panelist, by articulating our country's deep concern about the ongoing militarization of space by both the USA and Russia, and, more importantly, about the likely threat of 'occupation' of space by the other military-empowered nations of the world, too, including our neighbour, China. I would, also, like to mention that, unlike our country's official delegate to that conference, the delegates of quite a few other nations, diplomats all, had been very active at that conference. And, that had included the official delegates of the USA, France, China and, even, Canada, a country which has, to my knowledge, made but token investments so far in Space-related ventures but had been very active at that conference and presented two papers on that nation's viewpoints in relation to the utilization of Space. I ought, also, like, again, to mention that, to my utter surprise, our neighbour, Pakistan, too, had been officially represented at that conference and by no less than two delegates, both of them Brigadiers of the Pakistani Army, then serving with two different directorates of their General Staff headquarters, as they had told me.

Chapter 4

Entering The Portals – The Indian Military and Its Defence Technology and Industrial Base

In September, 1968, in the fourteenth year of my Air Force service, I had been selected by our government as one of the three officers of the engineering branch of our Air Force for undertaking post-graduate studies at the Cranfield Institute of Technology in the UK, now renamed Cranfield University. That year, as I recall, a total of five young engineering specialists from our Army, Navy and Air Force had been selected for advanced studies in selected branches of engineering disciplines, relevant to military technology. And, that had been done in pursuance of an ad-hoc policy of our government, then in force, a policy which had enabled our Armed Forces, like those of other industrially developed and developing countries, to select and depute, for higher studies, a few of the university-educated engineers of the military to universities in developed counties. Incidentally, a few years later, in early 1970s, our government had done away with that ad-hoc-ism, and instituted a long-term policy which had allowed, for a few years, the selection every year of some fifty or more young officers of the engineering branches of our Army/Navy/Air Force for post-graduate studies in engineering in Indian universities. And, while most of those candidates, duly selected by a selection Board chaired by the Scientific Advisor then, were sent to universities in India including the Indian Institutes of Technology, a very few of those selected candidates, probably the ones who had topped the merit list during the selection process for candidates for training in our IITs, were, on some of the years, deputed for advanced studies in universities in the UK or the USA, instead.

That selection for advanced studies in Cranfield had proved to be an excellent news for me then for two important reasons: (a) I had twice earlier been left out of the selection process itself for the reason that I had had the dubious distinction of having done a technical staff course in our own MOD's Institute of Armament Technology a few years back and (b) in my case that particular post-graduate course, for which I had been selected, would give me an opportunity to earn a MSc degree in Rocket technology by research, as opposed to most Master's degree in engineering, since that course, at Cranfield, had been specifically designed as a MSc-level research degree course. I had been aware that, as a student joining that course, I was expected to be proficient enough to be able to undertake successfully a piece of research work of an acceptable standard in one year's duration, the criterion of acceptability being the 'originality' of the research done by the student, as judged by a committee of examiners. Incidentally, in my case that committee of examiners had included one professor, namely the one who was designated by the university as the advisor for my studies, and he was the one who would decide if my research work had met the criterion of originality and possessed a certain degree of excellence before my thesis would be sent up to the committee of examiners. However, since at that point of time, at the end of October, 1968, I had done my previous course and had done well in it, too, only three years back, ie a post-graduate-level technical staff course at our defence ministry's Institute of Armament Technology (IAT) in Pune, I had felt confident that I was in a good shape for taking a crack at that research-based MSc degree course at Cranfield, for which I had been selected.

That technical staff course which I had completed with some distinction in Oct, 1965, by securing the first place in the merit list, had been called the sixth advanced air armament staff course and had come up in the ninth year of my Air Force service, ie in April, 1964, when, while I was serving at a forward Air Force base in Assam, I had been subjected to a selection process and, incidentally, had been given the first place during that selection process, too. I may mention here that the Advanced Air Armament Course was being offered by the IAT for many years, both before and after I had done that course, as its only post-graduate-level course then. However, that institute, which had, probably, earlier been affiliated with Pune University for some years, is now an autonomous teaching and research institution of our government, empowered to award undergraduate as well as post-graduate engineering degrees including the PhD.

Coming back to the story of my studies in Cranfield, the fact that I had done a post-graduate-level engineering course only three years prior to my joining the MSc degree course at Cranfield had given me an important advantage, as I have mentioned: It had provided me with an opportunity to brush up on my academics, especially, my knowledge of higher mathematics, after a lapse of some 11/12 years from the time I had completed my undergraduate engineering degree in the university in Jadavpur, Calcutta, in 1953. For instance, during my stint in the IAT, only about three years prior to my proceeding to Cranfield, I had acquired some of the much-needed knowledge in partial differential equations. And, since my research work at Cranfield had, in fact, called for a good bit of the knowledge in partial differential equations I had had no problem in Cranfield and had thus been able to earn a commendation from the Board of Examiners for the quality of my research work and had acquired a good MSc degree-by-research in November, 1969. And, all of that had been possible only because I had been able to set up a mathematical model representing my research problem, namely the heat transfer process associated with the enhancement of the burning rate of a metal-fibre-incorporated solid propellant rocket engine, with the characteristics of the metal fibre as well as the geometry of its incorporation in the propellant grain varying from one configuration to another and to then to solve those equations successfully, all using partial differential equations.

However, as soon as I had returned to India I had found that there was a surprise waiting for me. The Air Headquarters, following its usual routine, had finalized its plan for my next posting. But this time it had not, in its wisdom, posted me at an Air Force formation but had deputed me to work as a mid-level scientist in a civilian scientific organisation of our MOD, namely a DRDO laboratory in Hyderabad, an unit which was within the preserve of the Scientific Adviser to our Defence Minister, who was ipso facto, also, the Director General of the DRDO. It was only then that I had learnt that during my absence in England our Air Force headquarters had received a request from the headquarters of the then-fledgling DRDO in our MOD and had agreed to make my service available, on my return, to its laboratory for guided missiles, located in Hyderabad. As it had turned out, the nucleus of that laboratory had been established nearly a decade back in Delhi, in the form of a Special Weapons Development Team (SWDT). But, it had yet to deal with any project for hardware development for our military, except for one, namely a competence building activity, albeit poorly-funded, for developing an indigenous version of an obsolescent ATM. It had, in fact, never received any kind of meaningful resources from our government right from its inception and done very little, therefore, either by way of building its R & D infrastructure or developing technologies for guided missiles. In any case, like most others in our Air Force then, I had no prior knowledge of the activities of that laboratory. And, the surprise was all the more in my case, because I had some familiarity with the DRDO, having dealt a little with both its headquarters and some of its better-known laboratories, eg the ARDE & ERDL, during my recent tenure at the Air Headquarters before I had left for Cranfield but had no knowledge, yet, of the work of that laboratory in Hyderabad.

However, soon after joining the laboratory I had understood why it was that, prior to my joining that institution as a scientist in December, 1969, I had not been aware, even, of the kind of work that that particular laboratory of the DRDO had been engaged in. That DRDO laboratory, in Hyderabad, ie the DRDL, had, in fact, since its founding, neither received any funds for its build-up nor, unlike some of the other laboratories and establishments of the DRDO, been given any kind of work or project for the development of technologies of guided missiles over the years, far less an indication on when, exactly, our government planned to allocate to that laboratory some minimal funds for letting its scientists, some 15 of them on its payroll then, take up some amount of technology development activities.

That, then, was the position of that guided missile laboratory, the DRDL, when I had joined it in December, 1969 on completion of my MSc degee at Cranfield university. In short, the position was that during all of the preceding years the handful of civilian defence scientists that were posted at that laboratory had neither done any meaningful work towards the building up of some, at least, of the meaningful facilities that were required for commencing R & D work on either missile-propulsion or guidance and control devices etc. It goes without saying, therefore, that the then SA-cum-DG DRDO himself had been in no position to tell the scientists in the DRDL as to when, in the future, their services would likely be sought by their laboratory's potential customers, ie our Army/Navy/Air Force.

And, as for the reason for my having been posted by our Air Force at that near-non-functioning laboratory, on completion of my studies in rocket propulsion, I had soon gathered that it was a combination of the following circumstances that had brought it about. (a) Since my post-graduate research degree from Cranfield had Rocket Technology as its specialization it had stood to reason that the best utilization of my service ought to be made by a guided missile laboratory, and (b) The Chief Controller of R & D (CCR&D) at the DRDO headquarters during those years, ie Maj Gen J R Samson, ie the deputy to the Scientific Adviser then, had specifically requested our Air Force for my services to be made available to that guided missiles laboratory on my return from the UK. Also, as is often the case in such matters, there was, also, a reason why Gen Samson had taken that initiative: He had personally known me and had formed some opinion on my suitability, because, as mentioned, before going away to Cranfield I had been the Air Force staff person at Air Headquarters who had often been seen and heard by General Samson as a young participant in meetings and discussions between the Air Force and the DRDO.

In fact, as the Secretary of the joint Air Force/DRDO standing committee on indigenous weapon development projects then, I had been, particularly visible in the Air Force/DRDO review meetings, some of them informal and jointly chaired by Air Marshal (later Air Chief Marshal) O P Mehra, then our Air Officer in charge Maintenance (AOM) and Major General Samson, the Chief Controller Research & Development (CCR&D) of those days. Interestingly, I would, also, be seen by the CCR&D in some of the other meetings, held in the MOD, eg the Production Review Meeting in the Department of Defence Production & Supply. That is because the AOM, who was known for his preference for consulting directly with the staff who dealt with the subject, would ask me to accompany him to those meetings where General Samson would represent the DRDO. Interestingly, although most of the time, during those meetings, I would be engaged in briefing the AOM in whispers or taking notes, I would, at times be asked to speak aloud, too. That is because the AOM would ask me to speak aloud in the meeting to provide clarity, whenever the subject of discussion involved .important technical issues. Thus, General Samson had often seen evidence that I had the trust of the AOM. In short, I had made a good impression on Gen Samson during my tenure at the Air Headquarters, and when he had found out later that I had left the Air Headquarters and gone to England for doing a post-graduate degree in Rocket Technology in Cranfield University he had made up his mind to ask our Air Force to post me, on my return, at the guided missile laboratory, ie the DRDL. And, just before my return, he had just done that, ie personally requested Air Marshal OP Mehra, who had by then shifted from the post of the AOM to take over charge as the Deputy Chief of Air Staff (DCAS). In short, unknown to me, I had been earmarked for being posted at the DRDL, the guided missile laboratory, on my return from the UK.

Graduate Studies And A Future In Military Technology

Some comments on what is described in our country as the post-graduate engineering studies that I had done at the Cranfield University, then called the Cranfield Institute of Technology, may be of interest here. Designed as an advanced course with its focus on developing research capability in a post-graduate student, that course had, also, entailed my taking post-graduate level instructional courses in aerospace and propulsion related subjects, such as advanced fluid dynamics, heat transfer and jet propulsion engines. Interestingly, those were the early days of computer science and of the main frame computer, and I had been obliged, also, to study – on my own and for the first time – the basics of computer science, too, namely programming using the most advanced language of those times, namely the Fortran 4. That self-tutoring was necessary because computer science had not, even, been developed in the nineteen fifties, when I had done my undergraduate engineering degree, and it was only in the nineteen sixties that its development had made rapid strides in the USA and a few other developed countries. Like my contemporaries, I had no knowledge of computer science or of programming, because neither the IAT in Pune, India, where I had done my first post-graduate engineering course during 1963-64 nor the other university colleges of engineering in our country then, with the exception of the two IITs and the IISc, had possessed main-frame computers. In short, I had to learn the basics and the Fortran language enough to write computation programmes in order to be able to make use of the latest-design main-frame computer, IC-1904, of our university, the Cranfield Computer Centre, for undertaking the computations pertaining to my research work. Here, a word about my research Adviser, the late Professor Ian Smith of the Dept of Aircraft Propulsion (later re-named the School of Mechanical Engineering), will be in order. In the beginning he had, probably, been anxious about the choice of my research subject, a piece of analytical work which required the use of advanced mathematics, but had yet never made it known. Since, however, I had been obliged to consult him, in the beginning, almost on a daily basis, because selecting the topic of my research project had posed an unexpected problem for both him and me.

Since I had joined the course in end-October 1968, a month or so later than the date of its formal commencement in September, thanks to the delay which had occurred in getting our MOD to issue the sanction for our joining the course and, consequently, for our deputation to the UK, none of the 'easier' or more 'student-friendly' topics of research, eg topics which primarily called for doing experimental work, as opposed to undertaking mathematical analysis, were available to me. Consequently, I had to accept, for my research, a piece of analytical work, ie work in mathematical modeling. Interestingly, the reason why most graduate students preferred experimental research to analytical work was none other than the fact that the latter called for some knowledge of advanced mathematics of one kind or the other.

Here, as a tribute to my Advisor, who is no more, I would like to mention one incident which illustrates the objectivity and the fairness that Professor Ian Smith had shown during his stewardship of my research studies at Cranfield: When he had found out, soon after my arrival in Cranfield, that, having been late by a month to join my Course, I had lost the opportunity to select a piece of experimental work as the topic of my research project and was, therefore, compelled to take on an analytical piece of work, Dr Smith had taken particular care to make me aware that he would not be of much help if I got stuck: He had frankly told me that he had essentially been an experimental researcher from his early days, eg when he had done his PhD at the Imperial College of Science of London University, and, not having had a particularly strong background in mathematics, he had done all of his subsequent research, too, using experimental methods. In other words, while he had, out of compulsion, suggested that I select a piece of analytical research work he had, also, made it known that unless I was strong in differential equations I would not be able to tackle my work and that, as far that went, he would not be of much help, either. About a month later, when I had done my own home work and concluded that I needed to use partial differential equations for dealing with my problem, my Adviser agreed that the knowledge of ordinary differential equation, of which he had some, wouldn't be enough for me. That was when I had, again, recognized that Professor Ian Smith had acted very honourably when he had warned me in the beginning itself that, in certain circumstances, he would not be of much help and that I would have to entirely depend on my own ability to master enough of the required knowledge of mathematics in order to be able to tackle my research problem.

Incidentally, my home work had led me to the conclusion that, as mentioned, I needed to use partial differential equations to develop the required model for solving my problem, namely the development of a mathematical model for studying theoretically the enhancement, or otherwise, of the burning rate of a solid propellant of a rocket engine by incorporating metallic fibres of various kinds, ie a theoretically-derived model which will enable me to predict burning rates as a function of such independent variables as the type of the metal/alloy, the dimensional characteristics of the metal-fibres (eg its cross-sectional shapes, size), its spacing etc. The objective of the study, of course, was directly related to the attainment of substantially higher impulse of solid propellant rocket engine. It may be recalled that the attainment of that objective had been of great importance, then, in the real world, only because during the early to mid-nineteen sixties the missile propulsion designers of the USA were set to replace, for their intercontinental ballistic missiles, the inherently less-suitable liquid propellant rocket engines with large-size solid rocket engines and have, in fact, already done so in the case of some of the older-model ballistic missiles. In short, it was generally known by most propulsion scientists in the academia by then that although enough experimental data have been obtained in the USA under classified research funded by the US DOD, it would be interesting to make an attempt to predict theoretically the influence of metallic fibres, incorporated in higher-impulse composite propellant, on propellant burning rate. Incidentally, in my case, that analytical problem had been suggested by my Advisor as the topic of research for my MSc degree as soon as he had realized, in early November 1968, that all of the experimental research topics that were made available to Cranfield's MSc class of 1968-69 had been taken by other students, who had arrived weeks before I had, I must mention here that in doing so Professor Ian Smith had picked up one of the best and most topical of analytical research-problems on rocket propulsion that an Adviser could have selected for his student at that particular point of time. However, when I had convinced him that my research-topic cannot be successfully tackled with the knowledge of only ordinary differential equations he was, even, more forthcoming: In that case, he had told me, he would likely be, even, less of a help except in the final stage, while giving me a go-ahead for writing my thesis and presenting it to the other members of the committee who would examine my thesis. However, at that point of time I had no idea why my advisor had repeatedly cautioned me that unless I had felt confident that I had the required mathematical skill I wouldn't be able to meet the required standard, expected of a student who was a candidate for a MSC-by-research, ie the criterion of an original piece of work. But later, well after I had returned to India with a good degree and had received the commendation of my examiners for the quality of my research work, it had suddenly struck me that the reason why my advisor had made me doubly aware that I might not be able to attain the required standard unless I was good enough in mathematics was this: There were one or two students before me, ie in the previous two years, who had, also, taken analytical problems as their research topics but had failed to satisfy the required criteria for originality of work and had ended up receiving a low-class degree.

Although I had a lot of hard work to do in Cranfield – and lots of worry, too, regarding my ability to master adequate knowledge in partial differential equations with two or more independent variables etc – I had, finally, managed to digest the relevant mathematics adequately to develop an appropriate model with appropriate boundary conditions with a view to solving those and predicting the enhanced burning rates of a given composite propellant incorporating different types of metallic fibres. I had researched and then come across an earlier (1930s) attempt at finding an analytical solution to a set of equations, similar in some respects to mine, and had successfully modified that, by setting up appropriate equations to suit the reality of the propellant-combustion boundary conditions, and arrived at the correct solution. Incidentally, the equations which defined the two boundary conditions of my particular differential equation were, also, complex in nature. And, I had ended up by producing a good thesis. That is to say that the theoretical model, proposed by me for predicting the enhancement of burning rate as a function of the relevant parameters of the metallic fibres, had proved correct. And, even if somewhat fortuitously and unexpectedly, I had, also, towards the end of my research work, succeeded in finding published evidences of very relevant, experimentally-derived, hitherto-confidential, metallic-fibre-incorporated, solid propellant burning-rate enhancement data. And, happily, those data had shown how well those experimentally-derived data in a laboratory in an US university, under a then-classified research, had agreed with the results, obtained by me theoretically. I had thus managed to provide an excellent proof of the validity of my mathematical model and of the quality of my piece of work.

However, I would like to mention that I had not found it easy to get hold of those experimental data, and I could, finally, do so only after lots of efforts on my part and on the part of the Chief Librarian of Cranfield University and, that too, at the nick of time. That is because during my year-long search of literature I had drawn a blank, and it was at the last moment that I had come across an unclassified paper which had hinted that some classified experimental research work had, in fact, just then (during mid-1969) been completed by an university in the USA under a research grant, given by the US Department of Defence (DOD). Apparently, the results of that classified research project had been presented by the researchers only recently at a classified meeting of the American Institute of Aeronautics and Astronautics (AAIA). In fact, it was through sheer luck and towards the end of my search that I had chanced upon that unclassified paper where the fact regarding that classified research work had been mentioned in a Note. And, it was my energetic pursuit of that last-minute lead, that had, finally, yielded the experimental results of that classified research of the USA in the form an unclassified Patent document, which, to my good luck, had been published by the US Patent Office in September 1969, as I recall. It was the availability of that unclassified document that had enabled me to reproduce those data in my thesis as a proof of the validity of my theoretical work, much to the satisfaction of the examiners of my thesis. Both the external members of my Board of examiners and my own Advisor had taken my oral examination for my thesis towards the end of August 1969, as I recall, and had been very pleased with my work. And, that had earned me the recognition that I had done a good piece of analytical research. That recognition had felt good, indeed. More so, because notwithstanding the fact that both my Advisor and I had suspected that in the USA the researchers had been engaged in classified experimental work on the enhancement of burning rate by incorporation of metallic fibres, as early as in the early to mid-nineteen sixties I had not succeeded till then in locating any kind of reference, even, to those experimentally derived results in any of the published papers on the high-burning-rate solid propellants of the latest variety, namely sophisticated composite propellant. And, but for my last-minute success in the continuous efforts at finding, even, an oblique reference to that classified-research-generated data in a published paper, that I had continued to make energetically till the end, my thesis would not have made the impact that it had.

The story of that last-minute success in getting those experimentally-derived data is interesting, too, and, probably, worth recounting. During my year-long search for publications on solid propellant rocket research, for writing the chapter on literature review in my thesis, one thing had led to another, and I had nearly given up all hopes of finding the information that I was looking for, namely some experimentally derived data on enhancement of solid propellant burning rate. It was at that juncture that I had suddenly come across an unclassified paper, published in an US journal, which had made a claim that US researchers, under a classified research project, had achieved spectacular results on the enhancement of burning rate of a solid propellant by incorporation of metallic fibres of copper, silver etc. Although no other details pertaining to that classified work had been mentioned in that unclassified paper, published in a 1969 issue of the AIAA journal, the authors had hinted that some results of those experiments had recently been presented at a classified session of the Propulsion panel of the AIAA. On seeing that claim I had promptly requested the Editor of the journal of the AIAA if I could get any other information pertaining to the reported presentation of those experimental results. Although, as expected, my request for 'additional' information had been turned down, the Editor of the AIIA journal had, however, stated that two patents had just then been granted to the US department of defence by the US Patent Office on the basis of that work and had quoted the Patent numbers, too. It was thus that I could obtain copies of those two US patents at the last moment and show-case my analytical research as a good piece of work by quoting the experimentally-derived data, mentioned in those two patents, as a proof that the data derived by experiments were in agreement with the results obtained by me analytically.

Renewal Of Our Defence Research And Its Guided Missile Work

Going back to my joining that laboratory in Hyderabad, I must confess that that 'routine' posting by Air Headquarters at the end of December 1969 to an ill-equipped R & D institution had not, in the beginning, felt good at all. It had almost seemed like a problem, in fact, mostly because I had perceived soon after joining that laboratory that a feeling of gloom and a sense of hopelessness had pervaded the minds of the handful of missile scientists who were then posted there. And, that uncertainty as regards the future of that ill-equipped laboratory had brought in its wake an all-round apathy in those scientists who had then numbered a meager fifteen or so. Even the three or four post-graduate qualified engineering officers of the Air Force and the Army, who were posted as scientists in that laboratory then, were despondent, too. Since that perception of gloom had gradually grown in strength and had increasingly made me alarmed, the thought uppermost in my mind was that in the prime of my career as an engineer of our Air Force, then, I could not afford to remain long in that environment and thereby risk impairing my ability to work well and enthusiastically. Fortunately, it was precisely at that point of time that, all of a sudden, the news broke that the previous SA had retired on superannuation and that a new incumbent had taken charge of the DRDO. And, with that, things had suddenly changed, as I recall, and the future of all DRDO laboratories had looked promising almost overnight. Further, it became soon evident that a few, selected laboratories, namely those dealing with high technology weapon systems including ours, had been hand-picked by the new SA for an instant overhaul. In short, we had suddenly received the much-awaited green signal for commencing meaningful work by starting to build our infrastructure and facilities, including our scientist manpower, on the highest priority.

It had become evident that that infusion of funds and resources in the DRDO – after nearly three decades of neglect – was being done with a view to reviving, primarily, the guided missile laboratory, the DRDL, but, also, the other high technology Laboratories. As far as the DRDL was concerned, that had meant undertaking, without loss of time, the development of the much-needed infrastructure, facilities and technologies, related to guided missiles, and, soon thereafter, the development of one complete missile system, a tactical guided missile itself. In short, we had then suddenly found ourselves launched into a career path of high-technology development activities, activities which, in retrospect, ought to be seen as the launching of a planned drive by our government, the first of its kind, towards the establishment of self-reliance in military technology. That drive, it ought to be restated, was taking place after two decades of neglect of the DRDO but, happily, before the complete undoing of the excellent work that had been done by its visionary-founder, Professor Kothari of Delhi University. As the first incumbent to the post of Scientific Advisor (SA) to the Defence Minister at Prime Minister Nehru's request, Professor Kothari, who had started the Defence Science Organisation (DSO), had excelled in his work and made history when he had declined to join the ranks of the salaried bureaucrats but had served our government, albeit on only a professor's pay, with full dedication and great enthusiasm during his short stint as the SA before reverting to the academia. Although Professor Kothari's stewardship of the defence science organization during Nehru's time had lasted for only three or four years, probably, it had firmly laid the foundations of a national R & D organization, solely dedicated to the development of military technology in India. And, despite a lack of clarity in our government's policy on the role of science and technology in national security in those early years, Professor Kothari's work had served the most important purpose. It had ensured that the miniscule DSO of his making would eventually lead to the formation and, later, the buid-up of the DRDO, with self-reliance in military technology, in general, and advanced weapon systems, in particular, as its goal.

The fact that the much-awaited revival of the DRDO in 1971-72 had appeared so sudden is important, too, because it says a lot about our government's way of working then. It shows that it was only at that point of time that our government had, finally, woken up and decided to make amends to its incredible failure to acknowledge the role of military technology in the preservation of India's security and sovereignty. And, by triggering that change and kick-starting the process for attaining, at least, a semblance of self-reliance in weapons and equipment on a fast track and, through it, the development of two critically important weapon systems for our military, namely guided missiles and strategic weapons, our Prime Minister had managed to send a message down the line that self-reliance in weapon systems cannot be attained by establishing a defence industry which relies primarily on the indigenous manufacture of imported weapons under license agreements.

In short, it was at that point of time that our political leadership had decided to usher in the much-awaited change in its perception of the role of military technology in national security, in particular, and in our science and technology build-up, in general. Since our earlier policy of investing exclusively in the development of technologies for civilian-industrial applications, to the exclusion of military technologies, had been the hall mark of India's science policy till that point of time, it had meant a sudden departure from that earlier policy that, under Prime Minister Nehru's stewardship, had laid emphasis only on the promotion of those institutions whose work contributed to our socio-economic development directly. And, by investing only in such institutions as the Indian Agricultural Research Institute (IARI), the national laboratories of the Council of Scientific & Industrial Research (CSIR) and the Atomic Energy and the Space Research Organization, our government had in those years, unwittingly discouraged the development of dual-use technologies, too. Inevitably, that sudden making of amends by our government to its earlier policy had triggered an instant overhaul of the management and functioning of India's DRDO and of our laboratory in Hyderabad, particularly, but had benefited a few other laboratories, too, namely those involved with the development of a few other weapon systems and their platforms, eg the Aeronautical Development Establishment (ADE), the Gas Turbine Research Establishment (GTRE), the Combat Vehicle Research & Development Establishment (CVRDE), the Electronics & Radar Development Establishment (LRDE), the Naval Science & Technology Laboratory (NSTL) and some of their supporting laboratories.

What is interesting, however, is that the long-awaited change had, in fact, been brought about, almost exclusively, at the instance of our then prime minister herself, namely Mrs Indira Gandhi, the same Prime Minister who had been responsible for initiating, soon thereafter, two other, equally-unusual changes in India's foreign and defence policies. The first of those two moves, unusually bold in terms of a nation's power-projection enterprise, was the giving of concurrence to our Army's strategizing a spectacular defeat of Pakistan, in response to its unprovoked attack, by engaging its Army on two widely-dispersed fronts and bringing about the total defeat of the military of Pakistan in its eastern wing, namely the East Pakistan, and the consequent birth of a new nation, Bangladesh. Her second move was, even, more striking from the perspective of the two super-powers then, namely the USA and the Soviet Union. She had motivated a selected section each of our defence scientists and our civilian-use, nuclear-research scientists to work in tandem to successfully develop in secrecy a nuclear explosion device, culminating in the undertaking of an underground peaceful nuclear explosion (PNE) by our country as early as in 1974, an occurrence which had signaled India's entry into the highest echelons of science and technology capability. The suddenness of that PNE, as known, had startled the developed world, and it had jolted the USA, particularly, by its daring and long-term technology implications.

The PNE had signaled that despite her economic backwardness non-aligned India had technology capability and cannot be taken for granted. And, although by doing so India had openly defied the writ of nuclear-armed nations and thereby had earned the opprobrium of the developed countries for seemingly all time, post-1974, it was not long before India had overcome that hurdle. Thanks to the foresight of that brilliant Prime Minister, Indira Gandhi, India under another Prime Minister some two decades later, in 1998, had successfully tested underground its own nuclear and thermonuclear warhead devices and declared itself a nuclear weapon nation with a difference: Despite developing its nuclear weapon capability in defiance of the unjust provisions of the US-mandated nuclear non-proliferation regime India remained totally committed to the principles of nuclear non-proliferation. As known, India has since then been accepted by the USA and its allies as a legitimate member of the select group of nuclear weapon nations of the world and has, even, signed a civil nuclear cooperation agreement with the USA. Recently, in 2010, the USA has, also, lifted the technology control related embargo, it had imposed on India consequent to India having undertaken nuclear warhead tests in 1998. And, the withdrawl of that restriction has now made it possible for India to acquire dual-use technology related equipment, also, from the USA and its allies.

However, as far as our laboratory in Hyderabad was concerned, that much-awaited change – soon after my entering the portals of the DRDO in December 1969 – had been brought about by a combination of three factors, namely: (a) The advent of an eminent scientist as the first SA-cum-chief-of-DRDO with the powers of a Secretary had sent a signal to all wings of our government that the country's Prime Minister had, finally, accorded due recognition to the need for achieving self-reliance in military technology, (b) The vision and energy of our new SA, then, were phenomenal, and, lastly, (c) With the induction of an empowered SA by our Prime Minister the realization had dawned on the Chiefs of our three Services that our military's weapons requirements ought, in future, to be increasingly met by taking recourse to the 'make' method, as opposed to the age-old 'buy' method, which our military and, more to the point, their 'masters' in the corridors of power had been used to all of our earlier years post-independence.

Admittedly, there is no indication yet that the goal of self-reliance is likely to be achieved by our country in the immediate future. But, there is a sense of urgency now, never seen in our country before, to do the right thing and to make sure that indigenously developed systems were no longer brushed aside as distractions and left out of our military's weapons acquisition programme hereafter. That is precisely why a number of weapon systems, developed by our DRDO, are now in our military's inventory and are increasingly being deployed, too, by our Army/Navy/Air Force for actual war-fighting. In short, it was at that point of time that the realization that our military cannot afford to perpetually depend on the import of weapons from developed countries had, all of a sudden, dawned upon our country.

In short, the immediate consequence of that change in our government's policy on military technology at that point of time was the dawning of realization that the work of the DRDO was a serious business, too, and as important in the long run, probably, as the war-fighting by our military.

That, in its turn, had triggered a one-time change in our Air Force's personnel policy then. And, it was that change in their policy on the transfers of personnel in exceptional cases, at the behest of our government, that had made it possible for the DRDO to retain me on a long term basis, along with a selected few other post-graduate qualified engineers of our Army/Navy/Air Force, who, too, had been working as scientists on tenure postings at that point of time but had proved their mettle. However, the process culminating in the issue of a government letter spelling out that decision had taken its own time, and it was only in the beginning of the fourth year of my tenure with the DRDL that I was formally informed that our Air Force had agreed that my services could be utilised by the DRDO on a long term basis while I continued to remain on the active list of our Air Force.

The IAF and Its Engineering Branch

To get to the beginning, however, namely the story of my entering the portals of the Indian Air Force after having acquired an undergraduate degree in engineering at the College of Engineering & Technology in Jadavpur, Calcutta, I ought to mention that in those early years one had to have a good Bachelor's degree in Engineering or a Master of Science in Physics, with Electronics, by way of eligibility for entering the selection process for our Army/Navy/Air Force as a direct-entry permanent commissioned officer of one of its several Engineering branches. Once short-listed on that basis, the applicants were called in groups of thirty to forty and had to undergo a four-day testing process comprising physical fitness tests and a few tests pertaining to mental faculties. And, a few in each group who would qualify had to undergo a medical examination by a Central Medical Establishment. In my particular case, ie in the case of the selection of candidates for the 1955 batch of engineering officers, the Air Headquarters had short-listed some one hundred fifty young engineering degree-holder applicants and sent them up in batches to the Air Force Selection Board at Dehradun. In my batch of thirty such candidates only four had been selected by the selection board in Dehradun and sent for medical examination by the Air Force central medical board in New Delhi. Although three of us, out of those four, had been declared fit only two of us had, finally, joined the Air Force's technical training college, along with thirty two others who had been selected from the other batches of candidates that year.

During the medical examination we had a surprise: Although all four of us had looked fit and although I was the only one who was underweight then and, therefore, had looked less fit, I thought, it was our tall and well-built batch-mate during the selection process, one of the four that had been selected by the selection board out of a batch of thirty candidates, who had, however, been rejected by the medical board on account of some problem with his eyes. He was a bright metallurgy graduate from the Banaras Hindu University, as I recall, who had belonged to a family, settled in Banaras, too. Although I had lost track of him for three decades I had suddenly met him once in 1987 or 1988 at a lunch in the IIT, Kanpur. He, Dr Malik, it had turned out, had pursued a scholarly a career after giving up his earlier plan to join the Air Force's engineering branch, and, after a long stint as a professor of metallurgy at the IIT Bombay, had moved recently to the IIT, Kanpur, as its Director. We were both on our fifties when we had met at that lunch hosted by his institution, and he was much surprised when I had recognized him despite the changes in our respective appearances due to the passage of so many decades. But, the fact is that I had some prior knowledge that it was most likely that the current Director of that IIT was no other than the person whom I had met all of three decades back at the Air Force Selection Board in Dehradun. That knowledge had come about only because a few months prior to that lunch at the IIT I had briefly met one professor of the same institution, who had mentioned to me that the Kanpur IIT had recently received a new Director, one Dr Malik, who was a former professor of metallurgy at the IIT, Bombay. Therefore, when I had met that gentleman, Dr Malik, at that lunch in IIT, Kanpur, my hunch that he was the same young metallurgy-graduate, Mr Malik, of my youth had proved correct: The moment I had met him at that lunch and mentioned that he and I had known and met each other in our youth three decades back at the Air Force Selection Board in Dehradun, he had been much surprised and delighted, as he, too, could recall that we had, indeed, met three decades back.

The other candidate of my batch, who had been selected by the selection board and, even, found fit by the medical board but had yet opted out, was some one from my engineering college, who had been an year junior to me and both a good sportsman and one of the bright students of his batch. He, however, had misgivings about going in for an Air Force career, having had no stomach, it had turned out, for the kind of regimentation that was an integral part of the life in the Air Force, and I, too, had agreed with him on that. That friend of mine, BR Chaudhuri, had, thereafter, joined a newly formed PSU, called the India Refineries Ltd then, as an engineer, That PSU, as known, had later flourished as the Indian Oil Corporation (IOC), and he had, in due course, held senior positions in the same field in his later years, Now a retired petroleum technologist of the World Bank, he, too, had done very well in the mainstream of India's engineering profession.

After my selection for our Air Force in December, 1954, it was in April, 1955, that I had joined the tenth direct-entry engineering officers' course at the Technical Training College (TTC) of our Air Force in Bangalore along with some thirty four other newly commissioned officers, all of us good engineering degree-holders from some of the most reputed institutions of our country then, eg the IISc Bangalore, and the university colleges of engineering at Banaras, Jadavpur, Shibpur, Jabalpur, Delhi, Roorkee, Bangalore, Guindy etc. Incidentally, during those early years of independent India only a few autonomous engineering colleges, eg Jadavpur, Beneras, and the IISc – out of the fifteen reputed engineering colleges of our country then – had, unlike the state government-owned engineering colleges like Shibpur, a sizeable quota of seats, earmarked for other States of India and, therefore, an all-India character like that of the IITs which had not existed then but had started soon thereafter.

Now, consider this. Back then, way back in 1955, most of us, engineering graduates all – and, somewhat surprisingly, even, most of those young engineering graduates who had joined the Army/Navy/Air Force well after us, till the mid-sixties, in fact – had not been aware that by opting for the Armed Forces we were taking a great risk as far as our future careers went. Because of the paucity of vacancies, even, in the middle ranks, a disproportionately large number of direct-entry engineering officers in the military had, even then, a bleak prospect as far as reaching, even, the middle-senior ranks is concerned. But, we had learnt of that only after joining the Air Force. And, it was then that the knowledge had dawned on me that, even, the most competent amongst us cannot be assured of promotion to, even, the rank of a selection-grade Wing Commander, let alone of going higher up the ladder to senior positions. In short, most of us had realized later that those engineering graduates who were good scholars and wished to join a government service ought to make the correct choice right at the very beginning, namely opt for the Civil Services entrance examination rather than the selection board for the military's engineering branches.

Since during those early years the competition for selection-grade promotions to Wing Commender rank in our Air Force had depended both on the availability of vacancies and the relative merit, as viewed by a selection board that process of elimination of officers from the selection process had continued right up to the highest rank. Most officers of the engineering branches of our Army, Navy and Air Force, then, could not be promoted, even, to a selection-grade Wing Commander's rank and had, therefore, been obliged to retire early either as Squadron Leaders or, after serving for some ten more years as superseded Squadron Leaders, as a time-scale Wing Commanders. When one considers that most of us, who had joined the Air Force's direct-entry engineering officers batch in April, 1955, had happened to have had good academic records and, therefore, had had reasonably good prospects for securing competitive vacancies at the civil services entrance examinations, too, one will conclude that most of us, especially, those who had excelled in our Board-level examinations and our university examinations, ought not to have taken the career-risk by joining the engineering branches of our Air Force.

As it had turned out, our batch, eventually, had a little more success in promotions than most other batches of Air Force officers of the engineering branches had had. But, even, that had merely meant that as much as sixty percent of our batch – instead of the usual seventy five – got superseded during the first cut-off for promotion from the rank of Squadron Leader to the rank of selection-grade Wing Commander. That had resulted in most amongst us, with good engineering degrees from reputed universities, having been superseded at the first stage of the selection for promotion. Further, years later, at the final stage of my Air Force service, a total of only five of us, which, however, had amounted to a 'whopping' twenty per cent of our batch, as opposed to the usual two percent, had managed to clear all of the promotion barriers for selection-grade promotions from Squadron Leader to Air Vice Marshal or, as in the case of two of our younger batch-mates, to the rank of Air Marshal. But the fact that the relatively higher success rate in the case of our batch of Air Force engineering officers had still meant that most of my batch-mates had been superseded at the very first cut-off for selection-grade promotion to Wing Commander and had, therefore, been compulsorily retired much too early as Squadron Leaders, in some cases, and as time-scale Wing Commanders, in others, despite our having acquired bachelor of engineering degrees from some of the best institutions of our country then is, indeed, a sad commentary on our military's and our government's career planning efforts of those times. More so when one took into account the contrast between our promotions and our civil services promotions then. Even the most incompetent ones, including some who were known as indifferent or, more importantly, marked as corrupt officials, also, climb to the top of the ladder of the civil services routinely, as known.

There has been a little improvement in our military's career planning, lately. The selection-grade promotions now start with the rank of Colonel (and Group Captain and Captain in the case of the Air Force and the Navy respectively). However, in our times and for most of us, the young engineers of our country in the early years of our independence, the Armed Forces had their charm, and, unbelievable as it may seem now, we had worked happily as young officers. In the case of our particular batch, in fact, there were two, both engineers from the most reputed college, who had received the opportunity to join the Civil Services cadres but had declined the offer. Those two –

both had retired as Air Vice Marshals – had, unlike most of us, done a BSc (Honours) degree first- and a good one at that (First Class in Physics from the St Stephens College of Delhi University, both) – prior to joining their electrical engineering course at the Indian Institute of Science. But, both had, also, appeared at the civil services examination before getting selected by the Air Force selection board for the engineering branch and had, as they had found soon after joining the Air Force, done well enough in the written examination to have received calls for interview for selection for the Indian Police Service (IPS). Further, although their interview calls had come a little before they had joined the Air Force's Technical Training College (TTC) they had weighed the implications of a career away from their roots in engineering and then declined the opportunity. Both of those batch-mates of mine, Late Air Vice Marshal Krishnaswamy and Late Air Vice Marshal Khurana, had done well in our Air Force, too, having been selected for advanced courses in aviation electronics at a reputed university in the UK in their early years and filling important positions as they had gone up the promotion ladder. But, as in the case of the others, in their cases, too, there was no knowing at any stage of their careers if there would be enough of vacancies in the senior positions for their promotion to the next selection-grade rank.

As known, the position in respect of jobs for engineering graduates in our country had drastically changed about a decade after we joined our Air Force's engineering branch. In fact, the change – for the better – had totally transformed the employment scenario by the early nineteen seventies, when good engineering graduates from reputed institutions had started receiving opportunities to join managerial cadres in the public and the private sector, thanks to a spurt, finally, in the growth of commerce and industry in our country. Not surprisingly, therefore, the awareness since then, among the engineering graduates from the better known universities of our country, of the career hurdles in our Armed Forces has grown, and, but for a few honourable exceptions, the engineering graduates of well-reputed institutions and universities of our country no longer consider joining the Armed Forces as a career option, alas.

Chapter 5

The Guided Missile Laboratory and Its Build-Up

As mentioned, when I had joined the DRDL in Hyderabad in December, 1969, it had lacked the basic infrastructure, a semblance of the required scientist manpower and budgetary allocation of any kind for undertaking the development of complex weapon systems like the guided missile. Worse, it had no plan, either, for equipping itself, given the absence of any hope for a change in our government's prioroties. Of course, it had had a long history of nearly two decades of existence as a designated centre for R & D in guided missiles, with half of that history having been enacted in that very location itself, namely Chandrayanagutta, on the fringe of the old city of Hyderabad.

In its technical area, which comprised only one two-storied non-descript building, a few temporary structures, ie sheds, built in the nineteen fifties or thereabout, and a vast un-built area. The building, which passed for an improvised laboratory for both guidance and control systems, had however, some rooms earmarked for the sitting of eight or nine scientists, who between them covered as many as six or seven missile related technologies and accounted for two-thirds of the total number of scientists of the DRDL at that juncture. The balance of the rooms of that building had been put to use for installing a few obsolete and obsolescent electronic test equipment that were meant to be deployed for the testing of either components or assemblies of guidance and control systems or the checking the serviceability of recording instruments that were used for the static testing of both types of rocket engines, solid propellant and liquid propellant. As for the accommodation in the sheds, the most important one had an obsolete (IBM-1600 class) main-frame computer installed in it. Another two had housed two improvised static testing facilities, one each for testing small-size solid propellant rockets and the specially-rigged rocket-test-hardware, meant for the simulated testing of a bipropellant liquid rocket engine. The instruments that were used for measuring the combustion chamber pressure and the thrust parameters of each type of rocket engine were common, however, and were housed in a partitioned portion of the larger of the two sheds, ie the shed for liquid propellant rockets.

The handful of qualified scientists, numbering fourteen or so, as mentioned, had been patiently waiting for nearly a decade, probably, by the time I had joined the DRDL, for commencing their first task, namely the build-up of the Laboratory's infrastructure for the development of technologies that together constitute what is known as missile technology and, thereafter, for taking on meaningful technology development activities. I had noted then that those 12 or more scientists and their deputies, who were known as scientific assistants, were traveling everyday to the laboratory at its far-flung location, outside the outskirts of the old city of Hyderabad, but had become frustrated, thanks to the endless waiting for, first, the sanctioning of funds by our government for building appropriate buildings and other structures, a sanction for an expenditure that would amount to a very large sum of money, indeed, and, then, the initiation of many other actions by other authorities for providing adequate power and water to that distant location before the actual work of construction could commence. But, strangely enough and most shockingly, there were no signs then – even after nearly a decade of the moving of that nucleus of that guided missile R & D unit from its earlier location in old Delhi to that undeveloped tract of land, well outside the old city of Hyderabad – that the sanctioning of funds by the government for building the DRDL or the actions for persuading the State government or the City government to initiate immediate action for developing the required infrastructure for the supply of adequate electric power and water to that particular location outside the old city would be taken in the near future.

There were, in addition, another two old and dilapidated buildings at another location, about a mile away from the technical area of the laboratory, bearing the names, Ahmed Manzil and Mohammed Manzil, which housed the administrative sections of the DRDL. Apparently, those two derelict buildings, built nearly a century back, probably, were the abandoned residences of two erstwhile 'noble' families of the Nizam era, and those were being used by the Laboratory for housing its administrative offices including the Director's office and as sitting accommodation for a few other scientists then. As mentioned, the buildings in the so-called technical area had been in a slightly better shape, even if their location, a large piece of undeveloped land about a kilometer away from the Manzils, had posed logistical problems. However, both those 'better' buildings and the nearby sheds were equally bereft of any fittings or fixtures that were appropriate for any accommodation meant for scientific experiments-related activities. In short, barring those few so-called 'laboratories', meant for the use of missile control and guidance-related work and the two static test beds for the work of the rocket propulsion scientists and an obsolete main-frame computer plus an ill-equipped and a very-small workshop, with no more than a few simple machine-tools, our Laboratory then had no infrastructure, far less the appropriate test and fabrication facilities, that were required for undertaking design studies, the fabrication and testing of materials, components and subsystems of a guided missile and a host of related activities. As for the civilian-cadre scientists, some twelve of them, as mentioned, at the time, December 1969, I had joined the DRDL, as mentioned, they had ranged from the then Junior Scientific Officer to the Deputy Chief Scientific Officer (DCSO), of which there was only one, namely Shri S L Bansal, a brilliant undergraduate engineering degree-holder of the Banaras Hindu University, an early post-graduate diploma holder of Cranfield University in advanced Electronics and, probably, the first recruit of the Defence Science Service (DSS), which was conceived and launched by the first Scientific Advisor, Dr DS Kothari. Incidentally, Mr Bansal who had, some years later, become my boss for a few years, had become a Distinguished Scientist before his retirenent. The Defence Science Service (DSS) of the then Defence Science Organisation (DSO) had been renamed the Defence R & D Service (DRDS) when, a few years later, the DSO had been named the DRDO. There were, also, in the DRDL then three or four scientists who, as in my case, were officers of the engineering branches of either our Air Force or our Army or our Navy, all of whom having been deputed to the DRDL by our government after having acquired post-graduate engineering qualifications.

If one keeps in mind the number of people, with adequate skill in diverse branches of technologies that are required for addressing the tasks involved in designing and building the required infrastructure for fabrication and testing and for developing the prototypes of the components and subsystems of a guided missile, one would appreciate that, apart from the absence of infrastructure and test facilities for guided missiles, the gross inadequacy then of scientific manpower had ruled out any meaningful activity being undertaken by our Laboratory, the DRDL, then. For instance, the exercise of undertaking, even, the preliminary design of a guided missile necessitates, among other things, undertaking performance estimation and associated calculations with reference to the integrated system and its subsystems and, also, optimizing the design by fine-tuning the variables, all of which had called for the use of state-of-the-art computing machines, ie the advanced versions of the mainframe computer of that period. But, our laboratory had only been equipped with an obsolete IBM machine of the 1600 series which was presumably given to our laboratory as a gift under a US-sponsored technical assistance programme for our newly independent country, as I had been given to understand then. Therefore, the undertaking of the design of a missile system and its subsystems and components, which together constitute an integrated system, and the fabrication and testing and flight-testing of those components and subsystems, ie the task of developing a complete missile system's propulsion, guidance, control, structure, ground equipment etc and integrating them – which required the services of a host of specialists covering a wide variety of technologies and a vast infrastructure of technological facilities – seemed a far-fetched task.

One would, therefore, instantly recognize the hopelessness of the state of affairs that had prevailed in the DRDL, our country's nascent guided missile laboratory then, when I had joined that institution in December 1969. Neither the missile propulsion division, which I had been assigned and which, between its solid and liquid propulsion rocket groups, had six or seven scientists then, each of them with either an undergraduate engineering degree or, as in two cases, a MSc degree, nor the other divisions, eg the Aerodynamics or the Structures, each of which had only one or two scientists, or the Control and Guidance divisions or the Instrumentation division or the Systems Studies group or the Workshop, had the required infrastructure of tests and fabrication facilities nor the wherewithal by way of scientist manpower for doing meaningful work. And, the reason for that had not been far to seek: Our laboratory, the DRDL, which had owed its origin to a Special Weapons Development Team (SWDT) that had been conceived and set up in the early fifties by the first Scientific Advisor, the legendary Professor Kothari, had been located, initially, in a hutment in old Delhi. And, although it had subsequently been shifted from the city of old Delhi to the outskirts of the old city of Hyderabad and renamed the DRDL it had not grown at all, in a manner of speaking, despite its nearly two decade-long existence by then as the SWDT/DRDL. However, once Professor BD Nag Chaudhuri had been inducted as the Scientific Advisor in 1971-72, a sudden change had emerged, as mentioned earlier, and the affairs of our laboratory had undergone a sea change, starting with the installation of a new Director.

That sea-change had happened, an year or so after I had joined the DRDL, as, also, mentioned earlier, because of two reasons, namely (a) our government had, at that point of time, suddenly reversed its earlier policy on military technology development and had accorded the development of military technology its much-deserved and much-awaited priority and had, therefore, empowered the SA-cum-DG DRDO with the financial and administrative powers of a Secretary to the government, and (b) the choice of the incumbent for that newly empowered SA's post, by our visionary Prime Minister, Indira Gandhi, had been an excellent one. Professor BD Nag Chaudhuri, formerly an eminent professor of nuclear physics, had by then been well prepared for his new job, having functioned as a Member of our Planning Commission for a while prior to that and, thereby, acquired enough skill in navigating through the maze of our bureaucracy and getting things done on a fast track. In short, a visionary scientist and a dynamic individual had suddenly been empowered by our Prime Minister, for the very first time, to build the DRDO and to kick-start the development of military technology in our country without further loss of time. And, in fact, it had soon become evident that the Prime Minister's choice had proved right: The induction of that new SA, the third in the history of the DRDO, had soon made a world of difference to the future of the DRDO and the build-up of military technology in our country. Curiously, it was within a few days of his installation as the new SA – before he had, even, visited our laboratory – that I, as a member of a delegation of four heads of disciplines of the DRDL then, had my first opportunity to visit the only other R & D centre of our country, which dealt with guided missile-related technologies then, namely the Space Science & Technology Centre (SSTC), later renamed Vikram Sarabhai Space Centre (VSSC), of the Indian Space Research Organisation (ISRO).

DRDL Delegation's First Visit To The VSSC: The Undoing of a Long-Standing Disconnect

That institution, as mentioned, dealt with most of the technologies that constitute the common ground between a Guided Missile and a Space Launch Vehicle (SLV). And, that Centre for the development of SLVs by our space research organization had already grown into one of the largest R & D Centres of our country by then. For instance, it already possessed a number of sophisticated development facilities for the prototype manufacture of a wide variety of subsystems and components of the SLV, eg a high-energy, composite propellant production facility incorporating the facilities for the casting of large-size, composite propellant grain, a series of elaborately instrumented static testing facilities for small to large-impulse solid rocket engines, a nearly completed state-of-the-art static test facility for liquid propellant rocket engine, two wind tunnels etc. There were, in fact, a plethora of prototype production and test facilities of all kinds, eg a solid rocket hardware fabrication facility, well-equipped electronics test facilities, a laboratory for control and guidance equipment, a structures and materials testing laboratory, a laboratory for pyrotechnic devices etc, to name a few. Some of those facilities, eg the composite propellant manufacturing facility, had, in fact, been set up by the ISRO under a programme for international co-operation in space technology and utilizing the technical assistance provided by a few developed countries like France, in particular, which had laid the foundation for international cooperation on Space and had eagerly cooperated with our country as an important member of the Space Programme. We had, also, noted with pleasure that all of those facilities were being manned by a very large pool of qualified scientists and technologists recruited by the ISRO in its early days. The SSTC/VSSC had a beautiful location, too, comprising hundreds of acres of developed land, overlooking the sea but close to the city of Thiruvantapuram. Not far from that R & D Centre there was, also, another ISRO facility, namely our country's first and the only instrumented range then for the launching rockets carrying satellites of small sizes, eg miniature weather-forecasting satellites. That rocket launching range had, also, been built a few years back by the ISRO with the technical assistance of France under the then ongoing international co-operation programme for space technology.

That visit of ours had turned out to be an eye-opener and an exceptionally satisfying learning experience for all four of us from the DRDL. In my case that visit had been, even, more of an ennobling experience, because, as an Indian who had just then returned home after doing graduate studies in aerospace in a British university, I had known of some of the advances that had been made in rocket technology by developed countries but had very little knowledge of the progress that our own country had made by then. I had, therefore, felt both proud of our country's achievements and concerned for our own Laboratory, the DRDL: Proud, because it had become suddenly evident to me that, as the prime centre for the development of India's space launch vehicles, the SSTC had already made phenomenal progress in most of the technologies which were common between Space Launch Vehicles and Guided Missiles, and concerned, because I had realised that the ISRO and its SSTC had already built and put into use most of the facilities of interest to the DRDL whereas the DRDO and, particularly, its guided missile laboratory, the DRDL, had continued to remain starved of resources for, at least, a decade by then. I had, also, noted with alarm that all three of my own colleagues in that delegation, namely seniors, all of whom were much older hands in missile technology, had, also, seemed to have been surprised by that evidence, namely that, unlike the DRDO and its DRDL, the ISRO and its SSTC/VSSC had made phenomenal progress during the last one decade under the leadership of the Chairman of the ISRO, the legendary scientist and visionary, Vikram Sarabhai. More importantly and, also, shockingly, however, I had been struck by the incongruity of the situation, namely that until that visit those colleagues of mine had, despite their having been part of the DRDO's missile development activity since the mid-nineteen fifties, been as ignorant of the existence of that vast array of missile/space technology-related R & D facilities of the ISRO, as a new comer like I had been.

In short, while feeling proud of the achievements of our Space Research Organisation, I had, also, felt somewhat apprehensive. That was because our delegation's visit to the SSTC/VSSC in 1971, the first of its kind, had, also, brought into focus another fact, namely a disquieting aspect of the DRDO's style of functioning during the preceding years: While the DRDL had continued to exist notionally as our country's guided missile development laboratory for nearly a decade by then it had, in reality continued to remain ill-equipped and unfit to undertake such work, primarily for the reason that the DRDL and the DRDO had either failed or done very little, by way of making serious efforts, to persuade our government to provide the required resources for developing infrastructure and technologies of guided missile. In short, that visit had suddenly opened my eyes. I had suddenly realized that the DRDO under the dispensation of the second SA, who had just then left the scene after nearly a decade in that office, namely Dr Bhagavantam, the distinguished physicist who had succeeded the illustrious first SA, Professor Kothari, had been either unwilling or unable to force the issue and to persuade our government to see the obvious, namely that unless the kind of resources which the ISRO had received from our government for enabling the SSTC/VSSC to develop our own SLVs were, also, sanctioned for the DRDO to let its guided missile laboratory, the DRDL, to build its infrastructure for developing guided missiles, no meaningful work on indigenous guided missiles can, even, commence in our country.

Further, it had, also, dawned on me then that my colleagues in that delegation, all veterans of India's guided missiles enterprise, had, probably, known of the reality that, unlike the DRDO, the ISRO had continued to receive funds and had made phenomenal progress in letting its research centre, the SSTC/VSSC, to build precisely the kind of technologies and infrastructure which were relevant to both SLVs and Guided Missiles. However, it was, also, evident that despite having built those facilities the SSTC/VSSC had never been in a position to – either on its own or in response to the DRDO's request for such assistance – extend a helping hand to the DRDL so far. I had, therefore, also, concluded that, in any case, there had been a lack of goodwill between the DRDO and the ISRO during the preceding years which had coincided with tenure of the second SA. In short, there had been a lack of rapport between the second SA and his counterpart, the eminent physicist, Dr Vikram Sarabhai, who had been the Chairman of the ISRO, and it was only the advent the new SA, Dr Nag Chaudhuri, that had, finally, triggered a change and brought about the normalization of relationship between the DRDO and the ISRO. A development that had evidently made it possible at that point of time for our delegation to visit the SSTC/VSSC for the first time ever.

Incidentally, that conclusion that I had drawn regarding the apparently-in-explainable disconnect between the ISRO and the DRDO during the preceding one decade had, also, found support from a few other pieces of circumstantial evidence. One, since the DRDL – and its earlier avatar, the SWDT – had existed for many years by then, with two or three of my four colleagues in that delegation, then, having been on its roll as missile scientists from its very inception, it would be reasonable to conclude that those colleagues of mine had all been well aware, over the years, of the phenomenal growth of the SSTC in Trivandrum, a location close to Hyderabad. Two, the same three colleagues of mine in that delegation had, I had, also, found then, had known that in the recent years a few of their own young scientist-colleagues in the DRDL had left the DRDL to join the SSTC/VSSC for better career prospects. In short, those colleagues had been fully aware of the reality that the SSTC had grown enormously in a matter of a few years and, yet, been reluctant – or so it seemed to me – to acknowledge the fact that the ISRO, unlike the DRDO, had enjoyed the confidence of our government from its very inception and been successful where the DRDL, ie the DRDO, had failed, namely in obtaining adequate resources for the DRDL. The SSTC, it was evident to all of us during that visit, had already managed to build most of the facilities which it had needed, including some important ones which the DRDL had, also, needed but had failed to acquire so far. I may mention here that the DRDL's annual budget then, ie before the advent of Dr B D Nag Chaudhuri as our new SA, had only been a negligible fraction of the SSTC's and that the paucity of resources had prevented the growth and the functioning of the DRDL all of those preceding years.

As known, two of our national-level R & D organizations, the Atomic Energy Organization (AEO) and the ISRO, had commanded the full attention of our government right from the beginning. Consequently, apart from infrastructure and facilities, both of those organizations, unlike the DRDO, had managed to build a large pool of scientist manpower, too. It was during that visit that we had, also, seen that the ISRO had spread its net far and wide to recruit a large number of fresh graduates in science and engineering both from Indian institutions and, in the cases of some of the SSTC's mid-level and senior positions, from universities and research institutions abroad. In fact, as I had, also, noted, all of those seniors, with work experience in advanced technologies, had been recruited abroad. And, those were the Indians who had done their post-graduate studies in universities in the USA or other developed countries and then had worked successfully in reputed R & D institutions there. As mentioned, the ISRO recruiters had poached on the DRDL, too, and I had noticed that one or two among the younger scientists of the SSTC/VSSC had greeted my DRDL colleagues as old acquaintances, having worked in our laboratory under those very colleagues of mine during their earlier years.

The only conclusion one could have drawn from all of this was that the DRDO had failed do what the ISRO had done by way of building infrastructure and facilities during the preceding decade. In short, the second SA had, for some reason, been ineffective while leading the DRDO. In contrast, the contributions of the first SA, Professor Kothari, who had served in that appointment only for two or three years, albeit in an honourary capacity, had been outstanding. He had not only laid the foundations of the DSO/DRDO most methodically but, having planned for and set up the first few of its Laboratories and Establishments, had, also, inducted the very first crop of bright and young scientists and a few seniors, too.

It must, however, be pointed out in defence of the lack-lustre performance of the second SA that during his tenure as the SA our government had not given him the powers commensurate with his responsibility. In other words, as in the case of the first SA, the second SA, too, had lacked the 'status' to be able to persuade our government, ie the Prime Minister, the Defence Minister and the Finance Minister, to provide the wherewithal required to develop military technology in our country. He had not been accorded the status of, even, a Secretary to our government, for instance, and, also, not been given, even, the limited powers, exercised by a joint secretary to the government at our Centre, even though his salary had matched that of a joint secretary. Not surprisingly, therefore, it was the Defence Secretary in the early years of our Independence who had devised an ad hoc arrangement, in which a joint secretary in the Department of Defence Production & Supply of the MOD had been asked to take care of the process of according formal sanctions for such of the DSO/DRDO's project expenditures as were within his powers. And, that was how the functioning of both the first and the second SA as the head of the DSO/ DRDO had been facilitated. Evidently, that position had been most inappropriate for building the defence R & D enterprise of a sovereign nation like ours: An organization like the DSO/DRDO from its inception had, to be effective, needed a chief with, at the least, the administrative and the financial powers of a Secretary to our government. However, it must, also, be said in all fairness to the second SA that, given the offer of a job like that of the SA, very few of our senior scientists and professors then would have been spirited enough to forego that offer for the reason that the conditions associated with the job were inappropriate. I must, also, point out that his predecessor, Professor Kothari, the first SA, had been fully aware of this shortcoming in our government's policy on military technology then. In fact, though he had enthusiastically accepted the position of the SA at the request of our first Prime Minister, Pandit Nehru, and although he had done a magnificent job as a pioneer on an uncharted sea he had made it known at the very beginning, while accepting the job of the SA, that he would function only for a term and in an honourary capacity: During his tenure as the SA he would not give up his position as a Professor of Physics of the Delhi University and would continue to draw only the salary, due to him as an university professor. He had thus ensured that, despite his having to depend on the Secretary in the Dept of Defence

Production & Supply of the MOD for getting approvals and sanctions for the work of the DRDO, he would not be regarded as someone subordinate to a Secretary to the government but, on the other hand, be held in high esteem by all concerned including his immediate superior, the Minister for Defence. However, that arrangement had worked well for the first SA only because the DSO/DRDO, at its formative stage, had primarily been required to make a beginning in the development of know-how pertaining to simpler weapons and systems and to establish only the first few of its laboratories. During those early years the DSO/DRDO had neither been in a position to undertake costly projects nor had felt the necessity for the incurring of large expenditures.

As mentioned, the first SA had excelled in rapidly establishing and enlarging the boundaries of the future work of the DRDO and, simultaneously, setting up the first two or three of its laboratories for applied research and inducting, thereby, an excellent core of young but inspired scientists and engineers who would, soon after induction, also, undergo training in the design of weapon systems. In short, the DSO/DRDO at that stage had not reached a position which called for undertaking the actual task of developing high-technology systems nor been faced with the problem of obtaining funds for building costly test facilities and acquiring sophisticated test equipment etc. But, the second SA had, soon after assuming the responsibility of the office, been required to implement those plans. And, by not putting his all into trying to pressure our government to take the decision to invest in military technology and setting up the required laboratories without further loss of time, he had let invaluable years to be lost and had thereby defaulted. However, as already mentioned, the position of our government had suddenly changed in 1971 with the induction of the third SA, Dr Nag Chaudhuri. From then on the SA to the Raksha Mantri had not only been accorded the financial powers of a Secretary but had, also, in some significant respects, been given a few additional powers over and above those which the heads of our administrative ministries and departments exercised.

I recall in this connection that it was, also, during that first visit to the SSTC/VSSC as a member of the DRDO delegation that I had suddenly realized that what had earlier seemed to have been an act of shortsightedness on the part of our government, namely its failure to invest adequately in military technology during the first two decades of our Independence, had, in fact, not been a failure in the true sense. It had, in fact, been an act of deliberation from the first day of our Independence, borne out of a deeply-held conviction of our first Prime Minister, Jawaharlal Nehru, and most of his colleagues in the cabinet then, namely that in view of India's dire economic straits and the paucity of our resources to develop the economy of our country the build-up of our military and, especially, of our military technology enterprise did not deserve the kind of priority that our other nation-building enterprises had deserved including such science and technology missions as, even, our Space research programme, our Atomic Energy and our Scientific and Industrial Research organizations. However, there was, also, another factor which had, arguably, contributed substantially to our government's indifference towards the DSO/DRDO from its inception and, thus, to its reluctance to invest in India's military technology.

That factor was our political leadership's perception, formed during the long years of our non-violent struggle for independence against the British-led security forces, that a newly liberated non-aligned country like ours ought not to accord the same importance to its military and military technology enterprise as to its other imperatives of nation building. In short, the fact that the DSO/DRDO during the first two decades of its existence had never been regarded by our government as an enterprise, meant to take its charter of developing self-reliance in weapons and equipment as a serious business. An unfortunate outcome of our political leadership's wrongly-held perception at the dawn of our Independence of the role of our armed forces and of our need to achieve self-reliance in weapons and equipment in the preservation of national security and sovereignty. It is not a surprise, therefore, that the R & D component of our defence technology and industrial base had never before 1971 been called upon to function as a meaningful organ of the nation's system of governance or held, even, remotely accountable.

It was, also, during that visit to the SSTC/VSSC that our delegation had met Dr Brahm Prakash, a reputed professor and metallurgist, who had then been the Director of the SSTC. We were aware, however, that it was Dr Vikram Sarabhai, the eminent physicist and a great visionary, who, as the Chairman of the ISRO, had been the real force behind the spectacular growth of the SSTC/VSSC. Very unfortunately for our country, however, a tragedy had, overtaken the ISRO only a few months thereafter, because Dr Sarabhai, who had so very successfully led the ISRO from its inception through its spectacular growth to its present eminence and had, also, been leading our Atomic Energy Organisation most effectively after the equally-sudden and untimely demise of the genius of a physicist and institution-builder, Dr Homi Bhaba, had, also, passed on due to fatal heart attack. Incidentally, it was after that sad event that the SSTC was rightly renamed the Vikram Sarabhai Space Centre (VSSC). Although I had not known it then I had been destined to visit the VSSC many a time during the next decade and more, and, as it had turned out, my second visit had taken place very soon after the demise of Dr Sarabhai. And, it was during that second visit, in fact, that I had got the opportunity to see the SSTC/VSSC in greater details and, therefore, had the opportunity, also, to meet up with most of the heads of its research divisions and to study in depth how our own Laboratory's technology development activities, eg in the field of missile propulsion of various kinds, could benefit from seeking a closer association with the VSSC in terms of (a) enabling our scientists to both make use of the VSSC's test and fabrication facilities in the interim and access its expertise in composite propellant technology, (b) obtaining prototype propellant supplies from their prototype production plant and (c) taking advantage of their experience in getting solid rocket engine's hardware fabricated by appropriately-equipped manufacturing facilities in our private and our public sector industries etc. And, it was then that I had seen from close quarters how profoundly the SSTC/VSSC had benefited from the vision of the founder-Chairman of the ISRO, Dr Vikram Sarabhai, and understood the true dimensions of the role he had played in the planning and the successful execution of our country's Space programme, a success that had made the SSTC/VSSC a centre of such excellence. If one recalled that, beside the VSSC, the R & D centre for the development of its SLVs, the ISRO had four or five other R & D centres in Bangalore and elsewhere going full stream before its visionary leader, the inestimable Vikram Sarabhai, had passed away. Some of those are its satellite design and development centre in Bangalore, its liquid propellant rocket (LPR) engine fabrication and test facilities in Tamilnadu and its world-famous SLV-launching station and experimental range at Sriharikota. Legacies which will forever remind every Indian how large the contributions of Vikram Sarabhai had been to the success of India's Space Programme.

The development work I had undertaken in the DRDL – and, later, my subsequent work in other fields of rockets and missiles R & D programmes – had rapidly grown during the next decade and resulted into my having to undertake many more of such visits to the SSTC/VSSC, especially, during the next five years. However, I ought to state here that when I had visited the SSTC/VSSC for the first time itself – as a member of the first-ever DRDO delegation – I had clearly sensed that it would be in the DRDO's best interest to promote co-operation between the DRDO and the ISRO at the earliest and, especially, between our laboratory, the DRDL, and the VSSC. It had, also, struck me during that first visit to the SSTC/VSSC that, in view of the advances that had already been made by the ISRO, our new SA, Dr Nag Chaudhuri, had foreseen correctly that the onus of making a start in that direction lay entirely with us and that he had been a true visionary in dispatching our delegation to the SSTC/VSSC as early as possible for laying the ground for future co-operation and collaboration.

As already stated, I had become well acquainted with my counterparts in the VSSC during the next one or two years. That, in turn, had made it feasible for me to initiate a few collaborative development projects in the fields of rocket propulsion and solid rocket propellant. That first visit by me was, therefore, followed by many more, both by me and by others in my discipline, during the remaining years of my tenure in the DRDL. In my particular case, some of those visits were occasioned, also, by having to attend meetings of a few of the VSSC's expert committees and selection boards for scientists, while the purpose of the others had been to monitor collaborative R & D projects, eg one between the Solid Propulsion Division of our Laboratory and the Propellant Division of the VSSC and another between our Solid Propulsion and the VSSC's Composite Propellant Manufacturing Facility. Those were the two projects, in particular, which had made me come into close contact with two interesting senior scientists of the ISRO, each then the head of a technology division of the VSSC. Both had later become stalwarts of the SSTC/VSSC, namely Dr Vasant Gowarikar and Mr Kurup. One of those projects was aimed at developing technology for cast double base (CDB) propellant and its inhibition technique, while the other concerned the prototype manufacture of a composite propellant grain for a large-thrust, solid rocket engine for a typical surface-to-surface guided missile. Both projects had been defined by us keeping in view the potential use of those two technologies in our future missile propulsion systems. For instance, the cast double base propellant grain in a long-burning configuration had emerged as the best option for the sustainer rocket engine of an ATM, and therefore, its technology needed to be developed at the earliest. That, in turn, had called for efforts to be put in by two agencies in parallel, one within the DRDO (ie ERDL) and the other outside (ie SSTC). The other project concerned the development of high-energy composite propellant based solid rocket engines which were the preferred booster propulsion systems for some of the surface-to-air missiles (SAMs) and, also, for long-range surface-to-surface missiles (SSMs), eg ballistic missiles. Due both to the circumstances associated with my work in solid rocket and the consequent greater interactions with the solid propellant scientists and manufacturing specialists of the VSSC I had, probably, been instrumental in strengthening a spirit of professional camaraderie between our laboratory's scientists and those of the VSSC during those early years. In fact, I had, also, become more instrumental in some ways, later, in fostering this kind of co-operation between our two organizations than some of my other colleagues had been.

In later years there has been a much greater synergy between the DRDO and the ISRO, particularly, in the field of composite propellant rockets, than in any other area of missile/space technology. The reason for that is that composite propellant and rocket propulsion are disciplines in which guided missiles, on the one hand, and space launch vehicles, on the other, have a large stake. However, during that visit by our delegation we had not lost sight of the truth that, as in the case of most other collective endeavours, a research and development centre (ie a laboratory) is only as good as the leaders of its technology divisions are. Our delegation had, therefore, taken particular care, also, to get acquainted with the SSTC/VSSC's senior scientists and technology managers who, between them, had represented the full spectrum of the disciplines which were common between Space Vehicles and Guided Missiles. In fact, that was the only occasion when all four of us, the heads of four divisions of the miniscule DRDL of those early years, had received an opportunity to meet with all of the senior scientists of the SSTC/VSSC and to have a discussion with their Director, too. I may mention here that while some of the NRI senior scientists of the SSTC/VSSC whom we had met then had stayed back and had settled in India there were a few who, too, had been outstanding in their fields and had served the SSTC/VSSC with great distinction, as pioneers, for the first few years but had later returned to the USA.

Of those NRI senior scientists of the SSTC/VSSC who had stayed back there was one, in particular, namely Dr Mukherjee, who had stood out among the rest. He, too, had done brilliantly as a research scientist in the USA before joining the SSTC as the head of its Materials & Metallurgy division, but, as an individual, he had an unusually interesting personality, with a deep-rooted attachment to our country. An ascetic bachelor and a selfless person, he was much above the fray of the office politics of the SSTC or the battle for the turf. Not unexpectedly, therefore, he was later, also, made the head of the VSSC's administration division. And, as expected, he had proved a success there, too. Most notably, he had turned out to be the best and the most acceptable person for arbitrating over disputes between the various technology divisions of the SSTC/VSSC then over the allocation of funds and manpower resources. The fact that he was known for his impartiality in all such matters had helped him run the administrative affairs of the VSSC smoothly. During one of my subsequent visits to the SSTC/VSSC I had learnt that, as a deeply religious person and a life-long devotee of Shri Ramakrishna and Swami Vivekananda, he had been encouraged by the Ramakrishna Mission's establishment in Trivandrum to serve that institution as a devotee who could reside within the precincts of that math. Apparently, he, unlike the rest of his colleagues in the SSTC/VSSC then, had chosen not to buy any residential property for himself but had, instead, been contributing most of his salary and savings to the charitable causes, espoused by the Ramakrishna Mission.

Scientists of The VSSC In Its Early Years

Many of those senior scientists of the ISRO had, in due course, risen in stature both within and outside the VSSC and the ISRO. One or two had done very well, both for themselves and for our country by subsequently moving on to other departments of science and technology of our government. Among the senior scientists of the SSTC/VSSC with whom I had more association during those years there were one or two whom I readily recall. One of them, Mr Kurup, had been the founder of their composite propellant manufacturing facility, having been a chemical engineer by profession and been trained in France, subsequently, at the manufacturing facilities for propellants and explosives of the French government's explosives development and manufacturing company, the SNPE (Societie Nationale Poudre et Explosifs), which was then the licensor for the ISRO's composite propellant plant. The SNPE was and, probably, is a singular and an unique government-owned explosives R & D and manufacturing enterprise of France, and it was the enterprise which had developed solid propellants for both the launch vehicles of the European space programme and the solid rocket engines of the French ballistic missiles. Although in the beginning that facility, an integrated composite propellant manufacturing unit, headed by Mr Kurup, had not been formally designated a research division of the SSTC/VSSC despite its falling within the purview of the functional control of the Director of the SSTC/VSSC, Mr Kurup had proved to have been a good manager for innovation, too. And, his propellant manufacturing facility had eventually been formally inducted into the VSSC's R & D set-up. As known by the propellant scientists and, even, the other senior scientists of the VSSC community then, it was Mr Kurup and his team of chemical engineers, which had, in due course, successfully developed the in-situ casting technique for the SLV's large-size, composite propellant booster rocket motors, whose propellant composition had been developed by the VSSC's propellant R & D division. That team under Mr Kurup had, also, contributed a lot to the development of the manufacturing techniques for the fabrication of all types of solid rocket booster motors for the ISRO's SLVs, using the VSSC-developed composite propellant compositions. As known, some of those solid propellant booster rocket engines, developed by the VSSC, had, later, been used by us, too.

All in all, Mr Kurup and the next senior member of his team, Mr Uttam, who had later stepped into Mr Kurup's shoes, had proved to be excellent managers and innovators.

Both of them had, also, come out as very sincere and transparent individuals who had proved to have been great team leaders, I had noted then. Although Mr Kurup had most likely counted many of his colleagues in the other R & D divisions of the SSTC/VSSC as his personal friends then, there was one, in particular, whom he had been close to and whom I had often met in his company in those early days of the SSTC/VSSC, I recall. I had, no doubt, met that gentleman earlier, too, namely a young engineer called Mr Abdul Kalam, when I had visited all of the technology development divisions of the SSTC for the first time, in 1971, probably, as a member of the first-ever DRDL/DRDO scientists' delegation, comprising four or five scientists of the DRDL. But the briefness of those first-time meetings with each of the SSTC/VSSC senior scientists, during that 4-day visit by our delegation, and the fact that we had met too many scientists in quick succession then had made it difficult for me to remember that I had met that friend of Mr Kurup earlier, too, in the Pyrotechnic Division of the SSTC, of which Mr Kalam had then been the head. Therefore, it was only when I had got the opportunity to meet that young scientist, Mr Abdul Kalam, in the company of Mr Kurup several times thereafter – usually over working lunches in Mr Kurup's office during my work visits to the composite propellant manufacturing division of Mr Kurup – that I had been able to get properly acquainted with that unassuming scientist, the now-famous Dr Abdul Kalam, the former President of our country.

Incidentally, the office of Mr Kurup had been one of the few divisions of the SSTC, which I had visited on many occasions during my interactions, as our Laboratory's (ie DRDL's) solid propellant rocket scientist, with the composite propellant scientists of the SSTC/VSSC in those early years. However, its adjacent Division had happened to be that of another explosives-related R & D division, namely the Pyrotechnic division, which, as mentioned, was then presided over by Mr Abdul Kalam. As mentioned, Dr Kalam, was then the head of the SSTC/VSSC's Pyrotechnic division, and his work on the development of many kinds of explosives-actuated devices for application in the the SLVs, eg the devices for stage-separation, had made him earn a good reputation as a young scientist already, as I remember. During my subsequent visits to the VSSC's composite propellant manufacturing facility I had realized that Mr Kalam, whose office had been located close to Mr Kurup's, was a friend of Mr Kurup. And, in those early days of the SSTC/VSSC's pioneering work on the development of indigenous space launch vehicle (SLV), both Mr Kalam and Mr Kurup had made a mark as two of the good scientists of the SSTC.

Another scientist of the SSTC/VSSC then, a senior one, namely Dr Vasant Gowarikar, who had headed the VSSC's propellant development division, and had, some years later, become the Director of the VSSC, is, probably, remembered now by many in our country as one of our senior scientists, who would later be appointed the Secretary to our government in the Dept of Science & Technology (DST) and had often been seen in the late nineteen eighties on our Doordarshan (TV channel), speaking on what he had termed as a new and improved mathematical model for Indian weather forecasting and its success. That was, probably, because his reach as our Secretary (DST) had provided Dr Vasant Gowarikar the opportunity to work with the physicists of our meteorology department on our long-term weather forecasting techniques. As I recall, the results of that effort, put in by Dr Gowarikar then, had looked promising. However, the weather gods being as temperamental as they usually were, that model had its pitfalls, too, and had, later, proved not so infallible, after all.

Infrastructure Build-Up Post-SSTC-Visit

Soon after the return of our delegation from its visit to the SSTC/VSSC our Laboratory had submitted a report to the SA, in which we had highlighted the fact that the SSTC/VSSC already possessed a vast array of infrastructure comprising quite a few of the types of test and fabrication facilities which our Laboratory, too, had badly needed for its own work on guided missiles during the past decades but had sorely lacked. Since our report had, also, mentioned that the SSTC/VSSC had, even, acquired a large complement of junior to senior scientists in record time, some of the latter sourced mostly from NRI professionals, by resorting to extra-ordinary methods for selection and appointment of scientists we had strongly recommended that the DRDO, too, ought to commence building up of the DRDL without further loss of time by inducting, on the one hand, a majority of the required number of young scientists in various disciplines through the process of holding interviews at the campuses of our universities and Institutes and by simultaneously undertaking, on the other, the design and construction of a selected number of test and fabrication facilities within our Laboratory's estate. As for the balance of facilities which were either essential-but-costly-to-build or not-so-costly-but-less-urgently-required (eg a range of wind tunnels, a variety of environmental test facilities for the full-scale testing of some of the subsystems or its components etc), our recommendation had been that we proceed with caution. That is, we ought not, in those cases, to rush in but take a stock of similar facilities, available with other institutions in our country and, therefore, accessible to us for occasional use, eg the test facilities of either government-owned R & D laboratories or of our Universities and Institutes of technology, before we take a view on making investment decisions for the acquisition of similar facilities for our own use. Some examples of such national-level R & D institutions, besides the SSTC/VSSC, which had facilities of this kind were the CSIR laboratories (eg the National Aeronautical Laboratory), the laboratories of the Indian Institute of Science in Bangalore, the facilities of the Indian Institutes Technology in Kharagpur, Mumbai, Madras and Delhi and the laboratories of some of our other centres of excellence in university colleges of science or of engineering and technology, eg the Computer Science department of the College of Engg & Technology of the Jadavpur University etc.

In short, we had tried to emphasize in our report that (a) the DRDO and the ISRO ought to pool together their resources for component-testing and prototype-making to the extent feasible in order that our laboratory, the DRDL, can take full advantage of the investments, already made by our country in the ISRO's SSTC/VSSC, and that (b) in view of the lead already taken by the VSSC/ISRO in this regard, it behooves on the DRDO and on our Laboratory and, especially, on the heads of its technology divisions, to build good relations with the senior scientists of the SSTC/VSSC and to make use of their facilities, wherever feasible. The same went, also, for the technological resources available in the other centres of excellence in our country, eg the laboratories of the CSIR, the sophisticated production and engineering test facilities, built by some of the corporations in our public and our private sectors, eg the Bharat Plates & Vessels Ltd (BHPV) at Vishakhapatnam, the Larsen & Toubro Ltd (L & T) of Mumbai etc. In short, our objective had been to save the country's precious resources, wherever possible, while building cur test facilities and prototype-making units.

As I recall, our delegation had returned to our laboratory from that 4-day visit to the SSTC/VSSC, full of energy and enthusiasm for commencing work on guided missiles without further loss of time. All of us had felt that the new SA, by sending our delegation to the SSTC/VSSC as soon as he had taken over the DRDO and, equally importantly, for the first time in the history of the DRDO, for a fact-finding mission and for discussions with our counterparts in that premier R & D centre of the ISRO on our common areas of technology, had given us a signal that he had meant business. A signal which had become loud and clear when he had taken further action immediately thereafter by initiating measures to revitalize the DRDL and, indeed, the DRDO itself. The facts that within a day or two of his arrival on the scene and taking his brief from the Defence Minister and the Prime Minister he had summoned our Laboratory's Director for a frank discussion on our Laboratory and that he had, also, obtained the concurrence of the Chairman of the ISRO and, then, immediately, sent our delegation to the SSTC/VSSC for that fact-finding mission had spoken volumes for the new SA's determination and leadership. He had, no doubt, guessed that the SSTC/VSSC, having been the only other R & D institution of our country which dealt with technologies, common to space launch vehicles and guided missiles, had by then been fully developed and equipped itself for its job. And, he had instinctively understood that the need for initiating measures to build up the DRDL in co-operation with the SSTC/VSSC and thus to launch our country's much-delayed guided missile development programme was paramount. Interestingly, to us in the DRDL that sudden upsurge in activities involving the development of guided missiles by a hitherto-fore moribund Laboratory had, also, meant that the new SA had been fully aware of the sorry state of affairs in our country's missile development enterprise and, equally, of the decades-long neglect of the DRDL, the nodal laboratory for guided missiles, by our government. As mentioned, we had, therefore, lost no time in preparing our report on our delegation's visit to the SSTC and on our discussions with the heads of its technology divisions and its Director and sending it to the DRDO headquarters. However, since we were, also, aware that the implementation of any decisions that the SA would eventually take after due deliberations on the recommendations, made by our delegation, would, unavoidably, mean the incurring of large expenditures on the build-up of facilities in the DRDL and some of the associated laboratories we had, at that stage, felt somewhat apprehensive and wondered, as I recall now, how exactly the new SA would go about taking his decisions on the build-up of the required facilities in our Laboratory and implementing those decisions.

We were, therefore, pleasantly surprised when, soon after our delegation's visit to the SSTC/VSSC and the submission of our report and recommendations, the new SA had landed in our midst in Hyderabad. We had, obviously, been right in concluding that he had meant business, as history now shows. Apparently, having read our report and recommendations after our delegation's visit to the SSTC/VSSC and after holding discussions with our Director and his other advisers, the SA had come fully prepared to spend enough time in our Laboratory for exchanging notes with each one of us, ie the heads of the technology divisions of our miniscule guided missile laboratory then, as well as some of our other senior scientists. He had talked to us over long hours, on all of the issues, and questioned each one of us on our combined recommendations. And, that long discussion had given us enough opportunity to interact with our new SA, both collectively and individually, on that occasion. A phenomenon which ought to have been a routine in any healthy R & D organization of any country but one which, I was given to understand by the older colleagues in the Laboratory then, had never occurred during the years following the departure of the visionary first SA, Professor

DS Kothari. Surprisingly for a person with the kind of busy work-schedule that Dr Nag Chaudhuri had had then as a newly-inducted SA – or, not so surprisingly, probably, considering how enormously capable he was – the new SA had visited us, again, on a similar mission soon thereafter. On that second occasion he had taken particular care to get a more complete picture of each aspect of our laboratory's problems in relation to both the facilities that were required to be built for development of technologies and the courses of action that it would be possible for our Laboratory to take in the next two to three years under the prevailing circumstances, especially our resources constraint. As a future historian of the DRDO would show, the new SA had assimilated the facts in the least possible time and had given his decisions on the sanctioning of funds almost as soon as each of our technology divisions had got around to formulating its cases for the facilities build-up and convinced him of their necessity. Even in the cases of those proposals which had been costly and, therefore, necessitated the obtaining of sanctions at the level of the cabinet committee he had succeeded in obtaining approvals and sanctions of our government in record time, thanks to the foresight and the hard work that had characterized his endeavours.

As known, irrespective of whether a proposal for sanctioning of expenditure involved making use of the financial powers of only the SA or invoking the powers of the appropriate cabinet committee, which in those days had meant the approval by the CCPA (Cabinet Committee for Political Affairs), each case for sanctioning of expenditures had invariably meant for the concerned technology division's scientists the undertaking of extensive design studies and cost benefit analyses prior to drafting the proposals. It had, also, often meant for some of our scientists the walking of the corridors of offices in the South and, on some occasions, the North Block and attending meetings and presentations with a view to convincing some of our departments' financial advisers and other mandarins of the merits of each case and of the necessity for according sanctions. That had been the case, unfortunately, even for some of senior designers who, necessarily and sadly, had to put in hours of work at overcoming the bureaucratic red tapes and ensuring that the forward movement of the relevant files is not interrupted. In some of the high-value or otherwise-sensitive cases, which had necessitated the making of presentations by our scientists, led by the SA, to either the Defence or the Finance Minister our new SA had put in additional efforts and managed to get those cases sanctioned expeditiously, too. In most cases, however, the obtaining of approval of our proposals – because those involved convincing the SA and the financial advisors to the SA – had never suffered any delay, thanks to the home work done by us and the spirited answering by our scientists of the questions raised by the SA on the technology implications of each of those proposals. We had, also, noted then that his ability to deal expeditiously with any superfluous objection that may have been raised by his financial advisor but that did not actually stand scrutiny had been phenomenal, and that feature had proved a great blessing for our scientists and our Laboratory. As known, if any one of the three senior officials dealing with DRDO's proposals involving major expenditures, ie the Joint Financial Advisor (JFA) and the Financial Advisor (Defence Services) of the MOD and the Finance Ministry's Secretary (Expenditure), raised objections or made un-favourable observations, even, in cases where such expenditures had to be incurred in the interest of the advancement of technology or of the development of an advance-technology weapon system our first-ever empowered SA, in his capacity as the DG DRDO-cum-Secretary (Defence R & D), would himself join the debate to convince them of the need for incurring that expenditure. Otherwise no progress in the development of military technology in our country from a scratch could have been made in Nag Chaudhuri's time. In some instances, however, it had been possible for our scientists to logically divide a large, consolidated work proposal into two or three smaller projects in order to get each one of those sanctioned more expeditiously and thus to avoid the delay involved in having to get a consolidated case approved. The speed at which our scientists, in those years, had been able to cut short delay and commence their development work had contrasted sharply with the record of the earlier period. And, since prior to putting up any proposal for sanctioning of funds the scientists had to undertake detailed design studies and cost analyses they had, understandably, to work harder and put in more of that kind of analytical work in the case of those proposals which involved technology development or facilities build-up than in the case of the staff project proposals, ie proposals for the development of user-sponsored hardware.

Evidently, the new SA had managed to boost the morale of our scientists to a very high level in order to be able to create an environment which facilitated the putting in of such intensive work by our scientists in a sustained manner. All in all, it was a big change for the scientists of our laboratory, who had never before been seen or heard by anyone of authority in the corridors of power. And that sudden change in the work culture of the DRDL and, indeed, of the DRDO itself, which had been brought about by our new SA, had impressed all branches of our government including the Finance Ministry. And, that, in turn, had made it possible for the DRDO to secure larger investments towards the development of military technology, in general, and the build-up of guided missile technology, in particular. Obviously, the new SA had driven us hard and pushed himself hard, too. And that, despite the fact that he, as the

SA to the Defence Minister, had other responsibilities, too, ie responsibilities over and above those that were connected with his duties as the DG DRDO. However, it was evident that Dr Nag Chaudhuri, while having to shoulder both of those responsibilities, had stretched himself to the limit. Probably, that was the reason why he had managed to achieve within a span of only two to three years what had seemed, then, to many as unachievable in a lifetime. Just as Professor Kothari, our first SA, had shown outstanding capability as a visionary founder of military technology in India despite his short tenure and the limited nature of his mandate during the early days of our first Prime Minister, Jawaharlal Nehru, Professor Nag Chaudhuri, the third SA, had scored an outstanding success in building military technology in India in a short span of only three years during the early part of the tenure of our fourth Prime Minister, Mrs Indira Gandhi. A success which many in his shoes would, probably, have taken much longer to achieve.

Chapter 6

Military Technology and Governance: The Early Years

An overview of the state of affairs prevailing in our government during the early years of our Independence, and, especially, as regards our higher defence management, which, as known, is, for all practical purposes, run by men of our country's civil services, who often depute for their masters, namely the leaders of our political parties in power, would, probably, make one understand why the induction, for the very first time, of an 'empowered' senior scientist of our country as our third SA-cum-Secretary-cum-DG DRDO, in 1971, had made all the difference to the DRDO's functioning and, especially, the functioning of our guided missile laboratory, the DRDL. The fact was that the occurrence of a combination of circumstances, for the very first time, namely the selection of a competent scientist as the SA-cum-DG DRDO and empowering that person with the financial and administrative powers of a Secretary to our government for the very first time had lifted a veil over our country's military technology enterprise. In fact, all of us, scientists, in the DRDL, then, which comprised a dozen or so mostly junior, a few middle-level and one or two senior scientists, had felt that a morass of inaction and apathy, that had, for no fault of our scientists, seriously disabled the DRDO and its guided missile laboratory, the DRDL, in particular, for all of two decades by then, and that veil had suddenly been swept aside. The net result: The state of affairs that had earlier so demoralized the DRDL and, especially, its young scientists, in particular, had suddenly given way to an environment of robust optimism for the future of military technology in our country.

The circumstances that had led to that change were interesting, too. Having left the academia a few years back at the invitation of our government, the new SA, Professor B D Nag Chaudhuri, had, initially, served our government for a few years as a Member of our Planning Commission and had then shifted to the MOD as the SA. Therefore, he had already been exposed to our government's way of working, including the hurdles posed by the red tape of our system. And, although he had entered the service of our government at the highest echelon of our bureaucracy as a Member of our Planning Commission and had then the status of a minister of state, too, he had been fully aware of the difficulties that one had to surmount if delays in decision-making and in the implementation of those decisions were to be avoided or, at the least, minimized. Also, since, as already mentioned, his arrival in the MOD as the SA had been accompanied by the conferment to him of the powers of a Secretary to the government the scientists of all laboratories of the DRDO had, indeed, experienced a sudden change in the style of functioning of their own headquarters, ie the DRDO headquarters in New Delhi. Apart from the fact that the SA himself could now function as the sanctioning authority for those competence-building projects whose cost did not exceed the financial power of a Secretary to the government, there was, also, another advantage: The attitude of some of the other ministries which needed to be consulted along the route that a major-project proposal would have to travel to reach the cabinet, ie the sanctioning authority, and, especially, the attitude of the Ministry of Finance, while dealing with a DRDO laboratory's proposals for sanctioning of funds, had undergone a sudden change for the better. Interestingly, whether the action which had brought about that that change, namely the sudden empowerment of the job of the SA by our Prime Minister then, had been an act of deliberation by our Prime Minister to set the matters related to our country's military technology enterprise right and, through it, to transform the hitherto-ineffective DRDO into an effective tool for the development of military technology in India, or it was no more than a measure that had necessarily to be taken by our government then in order to accommodate in the office of the SA-cum-DG DRDO an already-empowered official, ie Professor Nag Chaudhuri, a Member of our Planning Commission till then, will never be known. But, that measure, ie the selection of an already empowered official of Nag Chaudhuri's capability as our country's third SA, had made all the difference, as mentioned. One would justifiably believe, therefore, that in this particular case it is the foresight of an unusually-gifted and popular Prime Minister, Late Mrs Indira Gandhi, which had led, finally, to the discarding of our past policy on military technology, a policy which, as mentioned, had done incalculable damage to a newly independent country's national security infrastructure from its inception, and to the setting of matters right.

Although that belated mending of our government's earlier policy on military technology, in the beginning of the nineteen seventies, had, probably, resulted from a change in our Prime Minister's perception on the need for attaining self-reliance in weapons and equipment the full benefit of that change has, even, now not been realized by our country despite the passage of over four decades since then. For instance, while the integrated guided missiles development programme (IGMDP), covering a range of our military's missile related requirements from the tactical guided missiles to the ballistic missiles for strategic application, has had a reasonable success, some of the other major projects, each one of those aimed at developing equally important conventional weapon systems, eg the main battle tank (MBT), the advanced light helicopter (ALH) and the light combat aircraft (LCA), had not met the desired goal, namely the establishment of large-scale, free-flow production within a reasonable time-frame. Similarly, although a few other state-of-the-art weapon related systems, eg special-application radars and a multi-barrel rocket launcher system, have been successfully developed, admittedly all of those achievements, put together, have so far touched only the fringe of our military's total procurement programme for weapons and equipment. However, as we will show later, the reason for that short-fall in achieving self-reliance in conventional weapons of the sophisticated kind is the result of yet another wrong-doing in policy-making, namely our opting for the continuation of an un-integrated management system of our DTIB by retaining an inappropriate higher defence management structure in our MOD. There was one redeeming feature in this otherwise gloomy picture, however, namely our success in achieving self-reliance in guided missiles and strategic weapons. A success which has almost single-handedly ensured the inviolability our nation's security and sovereignty.

Like his two predecessors in the post of the SA, Dr Nag Chaudhuri, was, also, a physicist. But, having been a member of the faculty of the one-and-only well-equipped Department of Nuclear Physics of our country during those early years, ie the Calcutta University's College of Science's

Department of Nuclear Physics, he had a slight edge as a new incumbent to the post of the SA-cum-Secretary (Defence R & D). Having started his career as a nuclear physicist many years earlier under the world-renowned Indian physicist, Professor Meghnad Saha, he had been held in high esteem by our first Prime Minister, the legendary Indira Gandhi. Although any comparison between his predecessors and Dr Nag Chaudhuri would not be fair, because Nag Chaudhuri had been the first SA to have wielded the powers of a Secretary to our government and, therefore, the very first 'empowered' Director General of the DRDO, it would be fair to say that both the first and the third incumbents to the post of the SA were equally brilliant, namely Professor Kothari, our country's first pick for the post of the SA, who, however, had remained un-empowered, and Professor Nag Chaudhuri, our third SA.

Since its inception the DRDO (then called DSO, as explained) had never been thought of by the leaders of our freedom movement, led by the legendary Jawaharlal Nehru who had formed the first government of independent India, as an important organ of new India's government establishment. In their view the head of the DSO/DRDO of independent India had not deserved to be given the financial powers of, even, a Secretary to our government. This is because the making of a self-reliant Military, equipped largely with indigenously developed weapons and equipment, had not figured as a priority in our government's plan of actions, ie as an essential pre-requirement for building and enhancing our national security infrastructure. Therefore, the development of military technology, in a proper and an effective manner, had not, even, made a start in our country before the arrival of Dr Nag Chaudhuri, as the third SA-cum-DG DRDO in 1971. As planned by the mandarins, insofar as the DRDO's administrative and finance-related work was concerned, the first two SAs had technically functioned as senior but 'un-empowered' officials within the jurisdiction of the Secretary (Defence) of the MOD or, as later, of the Secretary (Defence Production & Supplies). In fact, a Joint Secretary of either of those two departments of the MOD had been, from the beginning, earmarked for dealing, in consultation with the un-empowered SA, with those files of the DSO/DRDO which pertained to proposals for incurring expenditure by the laboratories of the DSO/DRDO during those early years.

In short, at a time when capital expenditure sanctions were urgently required to be accorded to enable the DSO/DRDO to build, at least, the minimum of infrastructure and facilities that were required by our laboratories for undertaking the development of facilities or technologies or to execute hardware development projects for the Services, the second SA and, to a lesser extent, the first, too, could not do as much as they had intended to do. Both the non availability of a separate and adequate budget allocation for the fledgling DSO/DRDO and its laboratories and the complexity of the process that was involved in obtaining any kind of sanction for expenditure to be incurred by the DSO/DRDO had come in the way during the tenure of the first two SAs. That had meant that for the first two or, even, three decades of the existence of the DSO/DRDO there had been had been little progress in the development of military technology in our country. And, that had happened despite the fact that Professor Kothari, the first SA, had done a magnificent job while planning for and setting up the DSO/DRDO as our national R & D organization for laying the foundations of military technology in India and had spared no effort to make our respective PM and Defence Minister aware of the importance of military technology in the safeguarding of the security and the sovereignty of our country. However, as mentioned, Professor Kothari, the first SA, had, finally, insisted on returning to his academic work in the University and handing over the job of the SA to the next incumbent, Professor Bhagavantham.

It was during the closing years of that SA that I had joined the DRDL. I had, in fact, briefly met him in our laboratory, on two occasions during the first few months of my joining the DRDL. Interestingly, soon after I had met him for the second time I had learnt that on that occasion he was, in fact, bidding us farewell prior to his imminent retirement due to superannuation. As known, Professor Bhagavantam had served as our second SA-cum-DG DRDO for about a decade, probably. However, as we had realized in later years, although he had managed to serve as a SA till he had been superannuated he had not been able to do enough justice to his job as the DG DRDO as regards the build-up of the DRDO and the development of military technology in India. As mentioned, not having been accorded the financial and associated powers of a Secretary to the government, he had been handicapped. It is possible that he had felt that any attempt on his part to persuade the Defence Minister and the Prime Minister to initiate the restructuring of the MOD – by setting up a separate department of defence R & D within the MOD and thus empowering the SA-cum-DG DRDO to function, within the MOD, as an empowered Secretary (Def R & D) – may not have succeeded and yet caused an upheaval in the entrenched bureaucracy. However, it is, also, true that, by not having made that effort at bringing about the much-needed change in the higher defence management structure, the second SA had paid a heavy price in terms of the damage that the continuation of the status quo of an un-empowered DG holding the charge of the DSO/DRDO had inflicted to the cause of the build-up our military technology base on a fast track and had delayed the process of making amends by a decade and more.

Interestingly, thanks to the good work that had been done by his predecessor, ie the first SA (Professor Kothari), the second SA, Professor Bhagavantam, had seen some of the beneficial changes that Professor Kothari, with his remarkable foresight and rare dynamism, had initiated, materialize. For instance, it was during Dr Bhagavantham's time that the decision of our government, taken earlier, ie during Professor Kothari's time, to bifurcate most of the British-era Technical Development Establishments (TDEs) of our Army was implemented. Each TDE was, thus, bifurcated into two organisations, ie an Inspectorate and a Laboratory, and thus created

(a) a number of Inspectorates, which, thereafter, dealt only with the inspection and quality assurance work at Ordnance Factories and was, eventually, detached from the Indian Army and placed under a Director General of Inspection (DGI) under the Secretary, Department of Defence Production & Supply, and
(b) a number of R & D Establishments or a Laboratories, under the control of the SA, each such Laboratory having been given a portion of the technical manpower of the erstwhile TDE but very little or nothing by way of R & D infrastructure for the reason that the TDEs had not been equipped with the infrastructure, required for technology development.

This implementation process had eventually brought into being all of the 'older' laboratories of the DRDO, eg the ARDE, the ERDL, the DMRL etc, and, also, a few financial sanctions for building appropriate R & D facilities for those 'older' laboratories. But, as mentioned, there was very little that had been done, during that time, for equipping the 'new' laboratories, ie those R & D laboratories and establishments which had been conceived but could not have been actually built by the visionary first SA, Professor Kothari, eg the DRDO's guided missile laboratory in

Hyderabad, thc DRDL, which had earlier been known as the Special Weapons Development Team (SWDT) and located at the DSO/DRDO's complex in old Delhi.

Therefore, Professor Nag Chaudhuri, the third SA-cum-DG DRDO, had a major job waiting to be done, namely

(a) the build-up of those newly-formed laboratories, which were largely the products of Professor Kothari's foresight but, in reality, no better than mere start-ups till then, as suitably equipped as R & D laboratories, and

(b) getting all of the laboratories, both the older and the newly-formed ones, adequate funds for both the acquisition of the required test facilities etc and the recruitment of hundreds of young scientists of various technological disciplines to cater to the need for scientists with required technological skills,

(c) getting adequate funds for technology development projects, keeping in view the need for undertaking, as soon as possible, the required staff projects for the development of state-of-the-art weapons and equipment,

(d) getting all of the laboratories to prepare detailed plans for all of the above activities on a war-footing and getting them to implement those on a tight schedule as soon as the required funds are sanctioned by our government, and, finally

(e) selecting, in consultation with the Services, a limited number of hardware development projects to be undertaken by those new laboratories in a phased manner, a task which had, also, called for developing effective rapport with our military with a view to instilling their confidence in the DRDO's ability to deliver goods.

Unfortunately, as mentioned, Professor Bhagavantam had not possessed the wherewithal to effectively undertake that job. For instance, the SWDT, the fore-runner of the DRDL, had been conceived by Professor Kothari in the early nineteen fifties as a nucleus for initiating work for the development of our own guided missiles, ie the fore-runner of the guided missiles development laboratory which would, in Professor Kothari's vision, later grow into one of the largest of DRDO establishments, with its charter for the indigenous development of complete guided missile systems and related technologies, albeit, with the support of other laboratories of the DRDO and, also, non-DRDO institutions of our country. But, in reality the DRDL, the successor of the SWDT, located in the outskirts of Hyderabad, had seen no growth for nearly a decade, thanks to the fact that the second SA, by having remained un-empowered, had been much handicapped. More to the point, the same lapse had, also, caused a major setback in the development of our military technology enterprise in other areas of weapon development, too. And, viewed from the present, the tragedy seems all the more if one considers the fact that of the two newly 'liberated' nations, both of which were equally capable intellectually, despite having been exploited by the rulers for decades, of building self-reliant military technology, namely India and China, only one, ie new China, had taken the required measures without loss of time and thereby made rapid strides in developing self-reliant military technology and succeeded in making its own weapons and equipment. In short, during the tenure of second SA the continuation of status quo had contributed very largely to the rendering of the DRDO totally ineffective. And, in the process, our laboratory, the DRDL, with neither 'inherited' infrastructure nor funds available for building, even, a semblance of technology development facilities, had suffered, even, more grievously.

And, I had been a witness to that sorry state of affairs when I had joined the DRDL in December 1969. Neither the users, ie the Army/Navy/Air Force, nor the defence production units comprising the ordnance factories (OF) and the defence PSUs (eg the HAL ie the Hindustan Aircraft Limited, and the BEL or the Bharat Electronics Ltd) had any regard or respect for the defence laboratories and their scientists in those years. In fact, both the mandarins of the defence ministry comprising the departments of defence and of defence production and supply, and our Services, ie the seniors of our Army/Navy/Air Force, had by then developed an apathy and worse for the DSO/DRDO. It was evident, therefore, that both the scientists of our own laboratory, the DRDL, and the other DRDO establishments had, for no fault of theirs, become objects of ridicule for many years. Everyone who mattered had been aware that practically none of the so-called staff projects, meant for meeting the user's requirements, had been successful, and their deadlines had continually to be extended by the users, ie the concerned Service. Those first two decades, ie all of the fifties and sixties, had, therefore, remained a period of ineffectual existence. One sign of that shocking state of affairs was that even after two decades and more there was no budget head for allocation of funds for the DSO/DRDO. The measly funds that were budgeted for the DRDO had been clubbed with the allocation for our Army (and, later, with the Dept of Defence Production & Supplies) and were utilized, almost entirely and year after year, for meeting the salaries bill and such like.

That our government had been a party to an important organ of its national security infrastructure remaining in such a sorry state of ineffectual existence was a sad commentary on our system of governance and the manner and style functioning of our political parties in power then. In short, our government had, in this respect, failed to fulfill its obligations to our Constitution, although national security and sovereignty were of the utmost concern for our nation all of that time, thanks to the continuing hostility of two of our immediate neighbours. And, strangely enough, the parties in opposition seemed not to have, even, been aware of this sorry state of affairs, either, and that, despite the continuing threats, posed by those two our neighbouring countries. A fact which had, also, reflected, inevitably, on the quality of our newly-independent country's functioning as a parliamentary democracy. In fact, but for a few members of our parliament then, our elected representatives on both sides of the political divide, especially their leading members, had been negligent and had not cared to point out that our government had a constitutional obligation to protect the nation's sovereignty and to enhance national security and, therefore, to promote the build-up of self-reliance in weapons and equipment for our Military. In short, neither our leaders under the Prime Minister nor the leaders of the opposition had spoken out in favour of maintaining a balance between the two priorities of nation building, ie Defence and Development. However, as mentioned, although the first Prime Minister had failed to provide the required priority of resources, his choice of the first SA had been an excellent one, and Professor Kothari had done as well as any one could have as the un-empowered first incumbent to the position of the SA cum Director General of the newly-constituted DSO, as the DRDO was called in those early days and the following years, albeit for a decade thereafter.

It ought, also, to be mentioned in this connection that there had been something noteworthy in the conduct of our first Prime Minister, the legendary Jawaharlal Nehru, insofar as his perceptions on the nation's defence and security infrastructure were concerned. The same visionary Prime Minister who had given less priority to the strengthening of our military and, especially, to the development of military technology in India in the early years of his stewardship had been a votary of science and technology and self-reliance in all other spheres of nation-building from day one. As history has borne out, he had, despite his pre-occupation with the disastrous aftermath of the Partition, initiated remarkably vigorous actions to establish the process of self-reliance in the economic sphere through the both the development of Science and Technology and the growth of our civil-sector (ie non-defence) manufacturing Industry and our Agriculture. He had, also, planted the seeds of the much-needed social revolution in the entire country by bringing in reforms in our education, our social justice system and, especially, the measures directed towards the empowerment of the weak. He had, thereby, set in motion the process of our national reconstruction on a high gear.

That the same leader, however, would make an exception in the case of our country's Military and Military Technology build-up by relegating the need for making investments in national security concerns to a lower priority had, therefore, surprised many of our countrymen in the later years. The surprise had been all the more, especially, in the case of Military Technology, because, unlike in the case of the Indian Military, ie our Army/Navy/Air Force, which had been securely established pre-Independence, the infrastructure for the development of Military Technology in India had been non-existent during the colonial rule and needed to be built from the scratch, literally, by creating a well-resourced DSO/DRDO and installing an empowered SA-cum-DG DSO/DRDO as its chief. However, the fact that, having selected a very capable and a great visionary person like Professor Kothari as our first SA, our Prime Minister had failed to follow it up with making adequate investments in the development of military technology in our country, had soon become evident from the manner in which he had played down the importance of the DSO/ DRDO in comparison with the three other national-level R & D organizations of our country then, ie the Council of Scientific & Industrial Research (CSIR), the Atomic Energy Organisation (AEO) and the Indian Space Research Organization (ISRO).

In retrospect, it seems that an explanation for that apparent inconsistency could be found if one recalled that right from the beginning – and despite the glaringly aggressive act of Pakistan whose trained militia had intruded into the Indian territory of Kashmir soon after Independence – our government, under Prime Minister Nehru, had continued to give less priority to the demands of national defence, eg the expansion of our military to the required size and the development of military technology from the scratch, than to the build-up of the other national level R & D organizations of our country, eg the Atomic Energy, the Space Research and the Scientific & Industrial Research enterprises. In fact, Prime Minister Nehru had given the latter activities of nation-building so much importance that, having selected and empowered three eminent scientists of our country then as the heads of those enterprises, he had kept those three departments directly under his charge and given each of those enterprises a larger amount of resources and incentives. However, although those actions, taken by our Prime Minister then, were and are justifiably regarded as right for many reasons including the reason that those actions had signaled the importance of the growth of science and technology for a newly-independent nation he had gone tragically wrong in giving a second place, in many a respect including the allocation of resources, to an issue of prime importance to a nation's independent existence, namely our military and its efficient functioning. There were a few other important items of nation-building, too, which had figured in his priority list, too, but he had missed out on the importance of maintenance of a healthy military to preserving national security.

The only reason – for according lower priority to the build-up of our military and our military technology enterprise – seems, therefore, to be that when it came to the allocation of precious resources for the military and, especially, the build-up of military technology our first Prime Minister and his colleagues, veterans all of India's freedom movement, had had serious misgivings about the likely wastefulness of military related expenditure, the most important one being the perception that for a poor and non-aligned country like ours investing into the build-up of infrastructure for indigenous-weapons development ought not be regarded as important an issue as the other priorities of nation-building. Nehru and the other leaders of our freedom movement, led by Mahatma Gandhi, the apostle of non-violence, had an understandable abhorrence for war-fighting and, therefore, an innate dislike for the Military as an organ of the State. Add to that the fact that our independent India's Army had its roots in the British India's colonial Army, with its intimate association, in the past, with a repressive British regime which had often used that colonial Army to suppress our freedom movement. And, it would seem right to conclude that the first government of our newly-independent country, led by our first Prime Minister Jawaharlal Nehru, and a cabinet comprising other leaders of our freedom movement, had not been able to assimilate instantly the implications of the altered situation when, overnight, the British Indian Army, minus its British masters, had transformed itself into an Indian military comprising Army/Navy/Air Force, a military force poised to play the role of a newly-independent nation's own armed forces, ready to preserve and enhance our security and sovereignty. Consequently, our leaders had found it difficult to reconcile themselves with the position that the departure of the British rulers had instantly turned the British Indian Army into a patriotic national Army of our own and to eschew their long-held distaste for the Indian commissioned officers and Indian other ranks of the pre-independence era, whose loyalty to the British during the two centuries of the colonial rule had often brought them in direct conflict with our freedom fighters. Consequently, in the early days of Indian independence our first Prime Minister had sadly missed the opportunity to instantly accept the essentiality of the role of our newly-independent country's Military in nation-building. And he had failed to grasp the urgent need for making our Military largely self-reliant in weapons and equipment by building a viable Indian DTIB at the earliest opportunity.

That failure had been further aggravated by another co-incidence. Our Prime Minister had consulted – and placed his faith in – a senior British scientist on the question of building independent India's own defence research organization. That was, probably, unfortunate, considering the fact that our erstwhile rulers had a vested interest in perpetuating the dependence of our country on Great Britain in all spheres of economic activities for as long as possible and, especially, in the continuation of our dependence on Great Britain in the sphere of the most lucrative business of all, namely the supply of arms. In fact, that decision to consult a senior British scientist on this matter, taken by our first Prime Minister, had, in retrospect, turned out to be an unfortunate one for a newly independent nation and the future of its national security infrastructure including its defence science organization. And, not so unexpectedly, that senior British physicist, Professor PMS Blackett, who was a former Scientific Adviser to the British government, had rendered an incorrect advice, one that had, inevitably, reflected his inclination to support his own country's economic and political interests, as against a newly independent nation's. In any event, Prof Blackett had advised Prime Minister Nehru to make only a notional investment in building our own defence technology base and had recommended, instead, the setting up of only a tentative defence science organization for the reason that a newly independent India did not, in his opinion, possess the requisite scientist manpower and the scientific wherewithal to commence developing its own weapon related technologies in the foreseeable future. He had, thereby, implied that independent India would find it impossible to, even, master adequate knowledge in advanced science and technology in the near future, let alone make a start in the actual development of sophisticated weapons and equipment. He had, thereby, ruled out our achieving a semblance of self-reliance in weapons and equipment in the immediate future. Unfortunately, that advice, which ought to have been rejected, had, probably, influenced our Prime Minister's perception on our own scientists' ability to build a viable defence technology base on a fast track and on the necessity to develop our own weapons and equipment at the earliest. And, that had happened despite the otherwise-savvy Prime Minister's deeply-held conviction that the genius of India would assert itself immediately after independence and that Indian scientists and technology managers would soon prove that they were no less capable of developing science and technology than their western counterparts.

In other words, although as a visionary our first Prime Minister had been second to none and although he had taken many other notable initiatives to launch our newly independent country on the road to socio-economic transformation, he had opted for putting the investment of resources in military technology on a back burner. Consequently, although he had selected a very capable scientist and a competent manager to lead the newly-formed Defence Science Organisation (DSO), which was later renamed the DRDO, things had turned out to be dismal as far as self-reliance was concerned. And, despite Professor Kothari's most remarkable efforts at laying a sound foundation for the future growth of military technology in India he, our first SA-cum-DSO-chief, had neither received adequate support at the level of our political leadership nor been given, even, a fraction of the resources which were required for building a proper defence R & D infrastructure from scratch. That was regrettable, to say the least: Our country had thereby lost very valuable time, namely all of two decades and more, in making a proper start in military technology development. As known, for a non-aligned nation like ours, with countries like Pakistan and China on its borders, the achievement of a reasonable degree of self-reliance in weapons and equipment without loss of time ought to have been accepted as an important factor in the preservation of our sovereignty. In fact, throughout history none of the developed nations – and, even, intellectually-capable but economically less-developed nations like the former Soviet Union (FSU) and new China – had ever neglected this basic principle of national security. In the case of new China – which, like independent India, had been a newly-liberated nation of the world then and had possessed a good amount of intellectually-capable human resources but lacked adequate resources for simultaneously building its civil-industrial might and its military technology base on a fast track, the political leadership had given the same high priority to both building its national economy through energizing its civil-industrial complex and to the task of building its DTIB. As revealed in selected documents some twenty years later, new China's management structure for the build-up of its DTIB had, at its highest level, all of the top political leaders including Chairman Mao, and each of those top political leaders had actively participated in the deliberations of those high-level committees pertaining to its DTIB. In contrast, none of our top political leaders, on either side of the political divide, had ever brought up the subject of self-reliance in weapons and equipment as an important subject for discussions in our Parliament, let alone take part in deliberations on the build-up of our DTIB or the development of weapons and equipment.

In any event, as stated, Professor Kothari had not agreed to serve for too long as the SA and had gone back to his job as the Professor of Physics of Delhi University after a short spell in the MOD as our SA. It is not clear if his decision to take leave of the job of the SA had, in some measure, been due to his, finally, waking up to the fact that it would be futile to try to build a meaningful military technology base in our country in the absence of adequate support from our government or to his frustration at having remained, as an SA, all but a minor player amongst the mandarins of the South Block. As mentioned, however, he had done a magnificent job as our first SA, even, though he had, by choice, continued to serve as a SA on a salary of one rupee per month, reportedly, while retaining his position as a Professor of Physics of Delhi University. It is clear, however, that he had desisted from making his views known to the posterity on whether he, as the first SA and the first chief of the DSO/DRDO, had been frustrated by the continuation of our government's policy of denial of a higher priority to the build-up military technology in our country and the consequent denial of adequate funds to the DSO/DRDO and the empowering the SA. In any event, no attention had been paid by our government till the early seventies to the issues pertaining to the need for the build-up of military technology on a fast track and the role of the SA in the management structure of our MOD. Therefore, the issues pertaining to the empowerment of the SA and to the allocation of adequate funds for the build-up of military technology had remained unattended to for all of two decades and more. And that, despite the fact that the two other national-level R & D organizations, namely the Atomic Energy and the Space Research organisations, had, from their very inception, been structured and funded properly and their chiefs, duly empowered, had functioned, as Secretaries to the government, directly under the Prime Minister.

The choice of the nuclear physicist, Dr BD Nag Chaudhuri, as the third SA, had, fortunately for our country, been an excellent choice, too. As he had left the position of a Member of the Planning Commission to take over as our SA-cum-DG DRDO, he had, as mentioned, been given the powers of a Secretary to our government while functioning in his new appointment. He had, also, possessed, in good measure, the makings of a visionary leader, somewhat like his illustrious predecessor, Professor Kothari, the first SA. Probably, also, emulating two eminent scientists who were the chiefs of two other national-level R & D organizations, namely the great physicists Professor Homi Bhaba and Dr Vikram Sarabhai, Professor Nag Chaudhuri had, also, gone about his job most enthusiastically from day one. Having already had adequate experience of dealing with the red-tape of our administration during his tenure as a Member of our Planning Commission and having, fortunately, also, possessed the kind of management capabilities that was sorely needed for overcoming some of the other hurdles one faced in those early years while leading the development of military technology in our country without loss of time, he had proved most effective in bringing about the required administrative changes as quickly as the rules of our government had allowed. For instance, he had quickly identified the DRDO's development priorities, selecting, specifically, for his attention, a few items of high-technology weapon systems, whose development, in his judgement, necessitated the allocation of a higher priority and had earmarked greater resources, in all forms, for those laboratories which were primarily concerned with the technologies involved in the development of those high-priority weapon systems. And, as known, the development of guided missiles, in particular, had figured as one of those few high-priority DRDO programmes. During the very first year of his stewardship, therefore, he had made available, for the very first time, considerably more resources to the DRDL and its supporting laboratories than to some of the older laboratories. And, as our country's record of achievements in guided missiles, in particular, has shown, his vision and his stewardship, during his brief tenure as the SA-cum-DG DRDO, had largely succeeded.

However, that startling change in the DRDO's style of functioning, with the arrival of Professor Nag Chaudhuri as our SA, had not had an easy passage. In fact, there were many reasons why he had faced difficulties, but the primary reason was that there was skepticism all round, about the DRDO's and the DRDL's ability to swing it. And that skepticism had its origin, primarily, in one unfortunate fact, namely that our defence procurement system had, by then, been so fully attuned to the culture of imports that the case for acquisition of high-tech weapon systems through indigenous development had seemed to have had no takers. Not unexpectedly, the DRDO scientists' morale had been at the lowest ebb when Professor Nag Chaudhuri had arrived at the scene. It needs to be stated in this connection, however, that our military, by itself, had very little say in this particular matter then, since, by tradition, our Armed Forces had refrained from commenting publicly on our government's policies on higher defence management and, therefore, had never voiced any opinion on the importance of building our country's own weapon development capabilities. However, our military could have cautioned our government against the prevailing culture which discouraged indigenous development of weapons by reinforcing the practice of acquiring weapons and equipment through import and licensed-manufacture only. One reason why our military had not done so was that it had perceived, from the early days of our independence, that as far as self-reliance in weapons and equipment is concerned our political leadership had no real conviction in practising what it preached. In fact, the nexus of the corrupt among our politicians and the corrupt within our government servants had increasingly developed a vested interest in keeping the practice of procurement of weapons largely through imports alive and well.

In short, even, as late as in the late sixties our government and our parliamentarians alike had remained totally wedded to the belief that investing in the build-up of our own defence R & D capability on a fast track and, consequently, in the making of our DRDO accountable for delivering goods at the earliest opportunity was not a national priority. Inevitably, therefore, our political leadership had remained reconciled to letting our MOD's defence procurement organization meet both the short and the long term requirements of our military through only the import of arms from industrially developed foreign countries. Post independence, therefore, the nexus of the corrupt among our politicians and the corrupt inside our bureaucracy had managed to continue unabated the import of arms and, thus, to prevent our country for nearly three decades from, even, making a start in the building of self reliance in weapons and equipment.

Not surprisingly, it had suited our military, too, to import ready-to-use and, often, well-proven weapons and equipment of western origin. That was so, as known, because the development of high technology systems is not an easy task, especially for as ill-equipped a development organization as our DSO/DRDO then were. In fact, our military, too, had had no love lost for an ill-equipped and ineffective DSO/DRDO and, therefore, no sympathy, whatsoever, then for our defence scientists' plight, ie their inability to obtain funds and equip their laboratories to deliver goods. In short, our military, too, were totally attuned to the MOD's culture, then, of acquisition of weapons by either wholesale import or a mix of the import of an initial lot of ready-to-use weapons and ammunition and the licensed manufacture of the balance number by our Ordnance Factories and/or the concerned defence public sector units (DPSU), a method of procurement that helped our military to always keep its preparedness in as high a state of readiness as possible. In fact, in an environment of this kind both our political leadership and its minions, the civil servants, had given in to the practice of acquisition-by-import-only, and our military, the users, had, by and large, felt satisfied by giving only lip-service to the concept of self-reliance.

However, in the beginning, this mind-set – favouring acquisition-by-import – had developed slowly. That was because, in those early years, most of the decision-makers, the civilian bureaucrats, who had the last say on the import of arms including the selection of the suppliers, had been honest but had felt helpless: Because of the non-availability of indigenously developed weapons they could not have openly opposed the import of arms. In short, in the beginning most of the decision-makers, both the political masters and their minions, had no axe to grind while approving the import of arms, but with the passage of time that had changed, and the acquisition of arms by import-only had become the accepted practice. And, that had happened only because of our government's inability, in the first two decades of our Independence, to prioritize the growth of military technology on a fast track by empowering and investing in the nascent DSO/DRDO and thus making our DTIB accountable for developing and establishing the manufacture of indigenously developed weapons in a planned manner. Consequently, by the early nineteen sixties the arms-import lobby had taken deep roots. As known, things had rapidly changed thereafter, and by the mid-sixties two other factors had come into play and become the real determinants for India's arms procurement methods. One, the cold war had brought in its wake the erstwhile Soviet Union's abiding friendship with non-aligned India, and that friendship, driven unmistakably by mutual convenience, had made us dependent, in a very large measure, on the abundant supply of all kinds of high-tech weapons and equipment of Soviet origin. Second, the phenomenon of corruption had steadily crept in and commenced vitiating our system of governance and corrupting a section of both our elected leaders and their salaried minions, a process which, in turn, had led to the formation of the much-derided nexus of corrupt politicians and corrupt bureaucrats, a nexus which had, finally, loomed large over all sections of our governance system.

In any event, as mentioned, right up to the early nineteen seventies, the DSO/DRDO did not, even, figure in the loop for decision-making on the import of arms, and the DSO/DRDO had, to all intents and purposes, been kept out of the loop for decision-making, with the result that the DRDO were out of sync with both the Dept of Defence and the Dept of Defence Production & Supplies, each of which had played a major role in perpetuating the practice of meeting most of the requirements of our Army/ Navy/Air Force by resorting to import only. Thus, almost unbelievably, right up to 1971-72 neither the Department of Defence, which is entrusted with looking after the Army/Navy/Air Force, nor the Department of Defence Production & Supplies, which has, under its administrative control, both the Directorate General Ordnance Factories

(DGOF) and the Defence Public Sector units (DPSUs), were, in reality, obliged to make sure that the DRDO's charter as regards weapon development would not be compromised by the perpetuation of the practice of arms-procurement by import-only. In other words, for all of the first two decades and more of our Independence the resource-denied DSO/DRDO had kept been kept engaged in the pursuit of activities which were either unproductive or insignificant. There were a few exceptions, however, eg providing expertise to the Ordnance Factories in the matter of investigations of failures of licence-manufactured arms and ammunition of foreign origin, diagnosing manufacturing snags during the production of such items etc. Incidentally, the bulk of the weapon development related activities of the DRDO during those early years of our military technology related ventures were undertaken in the name of competence-building and suffered from the lack of adequate funding. But, inevitably, because of the circumstances prevailing then, those activities would yield very little benefit, even, if a few among those were later re-designated as 'staff projects', largely, because our Army/Navy/Air Force would oblige the concerned laboratories of the DRDO by agreeing to have those projects viewed by our government as staff projects with a view to assisting the DRDO in the matter of obtaining the required financial sanction without delay.

In any case, most of the competence-building activities of those early years which were undertaken prior to 1971, including a few which were later re-designated as staff projects, had, eventually, proved unproductive and unsustainable. And, that was so, primarily, because those development projects had been undertaken on the basis of an assumption which had – inevitably under the prevailing circumstances – proved unsustainable, namely that the two wings of the MOD, namely the DRDO and the Defence Production organization, each with its own independent management and its own charter of responsibilities, would somehow be able to ensure that the concerned ordnance factories and defence public sector units would fully and unfailingly support the defence R & D laboratories in the expeditious production of prototypes at all stages of the development programme and, eventually, in establishing the bulk production of the indigenously developed system. In fact, any arrangement which envisaged that the two wings of our DTIB, the Development and the Manufacture wings, would work in sync would prove impossible to implement unless the two wings are made to function under an integrated management. And, in the absence of a reliable and full-proof arrangement for prototype production any kind of weapon development activity would, inevitably, either meet with failures or yield too little too late. That, indeed, had been the altogether sad outcome of almost all of the DSO/DRDO's development project activities of the first two decades of our Independence. And, although this much-needed organizational restructuring of our country's defence production organization is still awaited and had been so then, too, the new SA, Professor BD Nag Chaudhuri, the first SA-cum-DG DRDO who had been vested with a semblance of financial powers, had, right from the beginning of his tenure, tried to make up for the lost time by building on a fast track, at some of our laboratories, eg the DRDL, a bare minimum of the much-needed infrastructure and technology development facilities with a view to expediting capacity-building in the development of prototypes for high-technology components and subsystems. However, while doing so he had, also, been obliged to address urgently another important problem, namely the problem of keeping all of his laboratories and their scientists engaged, in the interim, ie till financial sanctions for major development projects materialize, in meaningful development-related activities.

That had meant the figuring out of both a bare minimum number of the much-needed technology development activities and the early sanctioning of a few of such staff projects as would provide the DRDO an effective learning process. He had perceived that it was a combination of those two types of activities, which together would yield the promotion of much-needed confidence among the users, ie our military, in the competence of the DRDO to undertake the development of a few state-of-the-art weapon systems. The objective, in short, was to reverse the earlier trend at the earliest and to win the confidence of our military in our country's own capability in the field of military technology and to get them to support the sanctioning by our government, at the level of the Cabinet, of a few real-value staff projects without further loss of time. And, since there was an urgency in accomplishing that objective there was an urgency, also, in closing the few insignificant, if low-cost, project activities pertaining to guided missiles, which were not meaningful. In short, the task of selecting worthwhile technology development projects for our laboratory and its supporting laboratories could not have brooked any delay.

And, since that process had, also, implied that the DRDL's and the DRDO's scientist-manpower and technology build-up facilities would, inevitably, witness an unprecedented rate of growth during the intervening period, the magnitude of the problem – ie creating and sustaining more and more infrastructure and technology-competence building activities, keeping in pace with the required rate of build-up of scientist manpower etc – could have overwhelmed many others in his shoes. However, the new SA had quite soon – and rather satisfactorily, as it had turned out – solved that problem.

He had done so, presumably, after agonizing over the problem for long. But, from what we, as the concerned scientists of the DRDL then, had seen, as 'outsiders' (ie from outside the circle of the new SA's confidantes), it had had seemed clear that the new SA had studied the issue at great length by undertaking a series of visits to all of those relevant laboratories and by holding debates and discussions with a number of senior and not-so-senior scientists of those laboratories before making his decisions on each aspects of his plan of action. For instance, one of the earliest learning-experience that I had gathered in those early days of my work in the DRDL had occurred during my participation in two such group discussions with the new SA during his first two visits to the DRDL. Those had happened in quick succession and, also, soon after his taking over charge as our SA. In the case of our laboratory the group that had participated in that discussion had comprised our Director then and the few heads of the then DRDL's technology divisions. And, since those few heads of technology groups of the DRDL then had given our views freely to the new SA, Professor Nag Chaudhuri, there were lots of exchanges with both the SA and amongst ourselves as to the options available as regards both infrastructure build-up and future projects in the field of guided missiles. And, as I recall, the new SA had demonstrated a remarkable ability to listen to our views individually and collectively and to bear with us for long hours on both of those two occasions, and since the technologies related to guided missile cover a lot of specializations he had, also, impressed us on those two occasions with an amazing knowledge of nearly all branches of science and technology.

I may mention that prior to the arrival of the new SA our laboratory had been engaged in one, so-called, staff project which had dragged on, mostly hopelessly, for nearly a decade, for a number of reasons but, primarily, because of the lack of infrastructure for developing the technology for propellant-surface inhibition. Particularly, for developing the inhibition technique for making a long-duration, solid rocket sustainer engine's cigarette-burning propellant grain. It was one of those cases where the main project, for the development of an indigenous Anti-Tank Missile (ATM) system of an obsolescent kind, had been taken up as a competence building activity in the beginning but had later been designated as a user-sponsored staff project. There were, in addition, a few other projects and activities of lesser import, each handled by either one or two or a combination of a number of technology groups of the DRDL, each of those technology groups ill-equipped and understaffed then, to say the least. And, each of those competence building projects had been aimed at building competence in specific areas of missile technology, eg (a) the development of a 'work-horse' for liquid propellant rocket engine development activities, (b) design studies on a few types of solid propellant rocket engines, (c) design studies, focused on missile aerodynamics and structures, (d) guidance and control engineering study projects, and (e) the development of instrumentation as a support facility for both static testing of rocket engine parameters and other applications. However, in the near total absence of the wherewithal, there had been no meaningful progress for many years and no hope, even, of overcoming that impasse. As I recall, under those circumstances, especially the absence of sorely-needed resources, which had prevailed in the DRDO for nearly a decade by then, the handful of scientists of the then DRDL, thirteen or fourteen in all, spread thin over six or seven areas of the guided missile technology, had largely lacked the required degree of confidence and motivation for making any kind of real progress. In short, it had struck me then that for most of those early years of the guided missile development activity most of our efforts had, probably been unproductive. But, equally clearly, the primary responsibility for perpetuating that sorry state of affairs lay with our government's refusal to provide resources for guided missile R & D activities for nearly two decades by then and not with the handful of scientists who had started the SWDT and later formed the DRDL, including its Director.

The new SA had, no doubt, taken all of that into account and yet assessed that, given the required resources and an appropriately supportive leadership at the DRDO headquarters and at the level of our then-tiny and ill-equipped laboratory, the missile scientists would rise to the occasion and fulfill his expectations. In other words, he had concluded that the laboratory, DRDL, had great a potential for growing into an effective nodal laboratory for the development of guided missiles in our country. He had, also, assessed, not unsurprisingly, that all the unproductive activities of the past, including the so-called staff project for an indigenous ATM, had largely been a fruitless exercise for many years and had, by then, become largely unproductive activities, devised to keep the few scientists of our guided missile laboratory then notionally engaged. An example which pertains to that ATM development project would, probably, better illustrate the point. As a new entrant to the missile propulsion group I had, during my early days, gone into the reasons for the failure of the prototype ATM's propulsion engine, a solid propellant rocket motor which had a sustained-burning, cigarette-shaped, double-base propellant grain, inhibited on its outer surface. That propellant grain had been outsourced from a sister laboratory within the DRDO, namely the Explosives Research & Development Laboratory (ERDL), whose charter included the development of solid propellant grains. As one of the earliest military technology establishments of our country, which was tasked with the development of explosives of all varieties, that laboratory, the ERDL, like other establishments eg the Armament R & D Establishment

(ARDE) and a few other laboratories of ther DRDO, had been born at the very inception of the DSO/DRDO post-Independence, when a military explosives inspection unit of the British Indian Army, manned by scientists, had been bifurcated into two, namely (a) an inspection agency, under the Director General Inspection (DGI), for ensuring quality during the manufacture of military explosives for our Army/Navy/Air Force by the ordnance factories of our country, and (b) a research and development laboratory of the DSO/DRDO, charged with the development of all classes of military explosives, ie the ERDL. However, our laboratory, the ERDL, had not been in a position then, in the early nineteen sixties, to undertake such a task, thanks to the decades-long denial of resources for the much-needed build-up and up-gradation of the infrastructure of the laboratory.

As regards a state-of-the-art, cigarette-burning, solid propellant grain with its high-tech inhibition technology, which would prove adequate as a long-burning sustainer propellant grain, that old-established laboratory had been an ill-equipped, totally inappropriate source of supply of propellant grain for the booster motor of the DRDL's ATM project. A source which had no expertise nor infrastructure for developing the recently developed variant of the existing double-base solid propellant which was extruded, namely a double base propellant which was cast and, therefore, called cast double base propellant since it lent itself to being cast in cylindrical shape and inhibited on its sides for allowing long-duration end burning, and had, therefore, tried to make do with conventional extruded double base propellant since it did not process the infrastructure for developing either that type of propellant grain or its inhibition technology. And, yet the DSO/DRDO top management and, possibly, also, the scientists of the then newly-established SWDT/DRDL in its early years, had, in their anxiety to keep the activities of the missile laboratory going, overstepped their capability and embarked on such a project, namely the development of a state-of-the-art guided missile, ie the wire-guided ATM. And they had done so on the premise that our ill-equipped and poorly-funded explosives R & D laboratory, the ERDL, would somehow be in a position to develop successfully the required cigarette-burning propellant grain of the ATM by overcoming the associated problem of developing the required inhibition technique on their own. The result: Even after nearly a decade of development work, put in by the DRDL, the ERDL and other laboratories, and, also, years of flight trials, each of which had been designed with a view to testing a host of components and subsystems (eg guidance, control, propulsion etc), the ATM prototype had failed, largely for the reason that the prototype's propulsion system had met with failure due to the failure of the indigenously developed inhibition technique.

Some of the other indigenously developed subsystems of that prototype ATM had, also, not fared well, either. One example would illustrate the position. One of the most critical components of that indigenous ATM was the guidance wire, which transmitted the signals of the wire-guided ATM, ie a piece of very thin, insulated copper wire, which continuously unreeled during the flight of the missile after its launch. The efforts at developing an indigenous prototype of that component had taken half a decade, probably, and yet no satisfactory indigenous prototype had been in sight when, in early 1970, I had joined the laboratory. And that indigenous guidance wire-prototype's failure, as indeed the failure of a few other prototype-components, eg the end-burning propellant of the solid rocket engine, had been caused for the same kind of reason: It had been outsourced from one of the few small-scale, indigenous electric cable manufacturers, then in business in our country, which had been, somewhat unfairly, persuaded by the DRDL to undertake the job of developing and producing such a prototype guidance wire but had, in the end, failed in its efforts to develop the sophisticated guidance wire for the simple reason that it had neither the required expertise nor the wherewithal for acquiring the kind of sophisticated equipment which are required to be used to produce such guidance-wires. In fact, even the tentative specification for the indigenous prototype guidance wire, which the DRDL had drafted and supplied to the prospective manufacturers and which formed the basis of that attempted prototype development, had been far from helpful, because the concerned scientists of the DRDL themselves lacked adequate knowledge of the wire and the process know-how. That attempt at outsourcing that component had obviously been done by the development team by ignoring this reality as well as the fact that the cable manufacturers then in operation in India were incompetent to develop such a sophisticated item in the absence of know-how and appropriate facilities. The position had, in fact, been hopeless on all counts, because it was known by the DRDL that no Indian manufacturer would be able to obtain any kind of technology assistance on the production of that item from any western country at that point of time, even, if it had tried very hard to get such assistance.

The reason for that was simple, too. It was none other than that the only manufacturer and supplier of such ATM guidance wires in the West was a manufacturer in Belgium, a member country of the NATO led by the USA, and it had, therefore, been in no position to supply to our country that guidance wire or any such material for advanced weapons or components or their manufacturing process. As known, India had then been a leader of non-aligned countries, with as friendly a relation with the Soviets as with the USA and, therefore, an US-adversary in the eyes of the USA during those cold-war years. That ban against the supply of military technology as well as advanced-technology weapons to a non-aligned country like ours, which had been imposed by the USA on all of its allies during the cold war, had, in fact, lasted well after the end of the cold war, too, thanks to a number of post-cold-war technology-control measures that were taken by the US-led western countries against India, too. It was no surprise, therefore, that none of the indigenous prototype guidance wires had proved equal to the task.

As expected, the missile scientists of our laboratory had entirely been in agreement with the new SA's perception as regards the priorities and options for initiating the growth process without further loss of time by putting a stop to the hapless ATM project and other, open-ended activities, which, in the name of competence-building, had kept our laboratory 'engaged' for a decade but had contributed little by way of providing a learning process. A very timely and wise decision by the new SA that had thus saved other laboratories, too, eg the ERDL, which were working in support of the ATM project, from frittering away precious resources. As a result, at that time, two major activities had simultaneously been sanctioned by the new SA. In the process, the DRDL, for the very first time after nearly a decade, had been given a set of two very worthwhile and challenging tasks and relieved from the burden of continuing with its decade-old, unproductive activities. And it was those two inter-related development activities, as explained in the following text, that had kept the Laboratory fully engaged for the next five to seven years.

Of those two programmes, the first one had been aimed at preparing the laboratory and equipping it with the essential technology facilities in each field of expertise related to missile technology. It had enabled each division to take up immediately the task of designing and putting in place the test and prototype fabrication facilities relevant to its area of expertise, eg aerodynamics, structures, propulsion, guidance, control, instrumentation, system design, computer science etc. It ought to be noted that an air of urgency had, for the first time, been felt by the DRDL. And, keeping the priorities of our facilities build-up and the availability of budget allocations on an year-to-year basis, the facilities which were to be built and the order in which those were to be built had quickly been decided upon and approved in principle by the SA, in consultation with the scientists of the DRDL, as mentioned. It was thus that the DRDL scientists of that era had managed to design and to build the minimum required facilities for the Laboratory within the next one year or so. Those included most of the essential test facilities, eg the static test facilities for large-thrust solid rocket booster enigines and long-duration liquid propellant sustainer engine. The propulsion group (which was, incidentally, divided then into two divisions, ie one dealing with Solid rocket engine technology and the other liquid propellant rocket engines), the missile structures group, the aerodynamics group, the missile Control and Guidance groups etc were thus equipped with most of the less-expensive but specialized test facilities in a relatively short period and for the first time. A large Workshop, with a few of the sophisticated prototype component fabrication facilities such as a few numerically-controlled machines for mechanical component making etc, had, also, materialised. The build-up of those technology development facilities, either for prototype testing or for fabrication of prototype components for both mechanical assemblies and optoelectronic and microelectronic components, had been essential, because (a) in their absence the development of some of the essential components of missile subsystems, whose fabrication or testing could not have been outsourced but had needed to be dealt with in-house would have suffered, and (b) the development of the complete missile assembly as an integrated system, which, among other things called for the use of sophisticated large-body dimensions measuring instruments, large environmental conditioning facility etc etc, was the preserve of the nodal laboratory only, ie the DRDL.

It ought to have been evident by now that the build-up of our own testing and/or fabrication facilities, briefly outlined in the previous paragraph, had left out those facilities which were available outside the DRDO but within our country, eg some of the Indian Institues of Technology (IITs), other university departments, eg the Indian Institute of Science (IISc), the national-level research laboratories, eg the National Aeronautical Laboratory (NAL) and all public-sector manufacturing companies which were equipped with specialized fabrication facilities, eg the Bharat Heavy Plates and Vessels (BHPV), as well as a few of the well-managed and adequately-equipped private sector companies, eg the Larsen & Toubro (L & T), which were willing to respond to the requests of DRDO laboratories and to undertake the fabrication of prototype components and sub-assemblies and, in the event of the success of the guided missiles development programme, to undertake bulk production. Similarly, the DRDO laboratories which were closely connected with the nodal laboratory, the DRDL, and were, in fact, associates of the DRDL in the programme for the development of guided missile systems, had, also, built additional facilities to supplement their own fabrication and/or test facilities.[*] For instance, the entire task of developing the prototypes of the missile-warheads had to be undertaken jointly by the armament group of laboratories of the DRDO, namely the ARDE, the ERDL and the TBRL (Terminal Ballistics Research Laboratory), which together were required to undertake the detailed design and the development of the various types of missile-warheads, following the acquisition of the relevant design-inputs through the static and dynamic-testing of missile-warheads, using simulated targets etc.

The development of most of the electronics components and subsystems was largely outsourced by making use of either the appropriate DRDO laboratories, eg Electronics Research & Development Establishment (LRDE) and Defence Electronics Research Laboratory (DLRL) etc or, as in a few cases, the Public Sector Units (PSU) of the relevant specializations, eg the Bharat Electronics Ltd (BEL), the Hyderabad unit of the Hindustan Aircraft Limited (HAL) etc. Incidentally, those very DRDO and non-DRDO laboratories and PSUs were, also, used extensively, later, for the outsourcing of the development of electronics components and subsystems in the case of the four guided missile projects of the IGMDP. As far as ground equipment of Project Devil were concerned our Laboratory had, rightly, utilized both a DRDO laboratory dealing with engineering equipment and the public and private sector manufacturing companies of our country. One defence PSU, in particular, the Bharat Earth Movers Limited (BEML), had come in handy in this venture and, later, was made use of very largely for the IGMDP. And, through all this, ie the very first missile-technology-facilities-build-up cum the guided missile system development project, the project Devil, the third SA had, without the least loss of time, built up the much-needed guided missile development capability of the DRDO and, therefore, of our country in a remarkably short period of three years or less.

I ought to mention that the facilities build-up activities that were undertaken by us under the first programme had been done under a cluster of five or six project sanctions, given by the SA. Each of those projects had, in fact, fitted the description of a competence building activity, thus justifying the incurring of expenditure on competence building. By, sometimes, clubbing two or three of such competence-building activities into one project we had managed to ensure that no more than five or six government letters, giving the required expenditure sanctions, had needed to be signed by an undersecretary, once the SA had given his approval of the work. That procedure of clubbing a few activities under each project and thus reducing both the paperwork and the number of files that had to be processed in each case had enabled us to expedite the process of obtaining of sanctions and commencing and completing the build-up of a large number of essential but less-expensive test facilities in the shortest possible time. That had, of course, proved possible, for the first time in the history of the DSO/DRDO, only because the third SA, Professor BD Nag Chaudhuri, had both possessed, at least, a minimum of the requisite financial powers, ie the powers of a Secretary to the government in any department or ministry, and the gift of a remarkable talent as a research administrator. On our part, ie on the part of the missile scientists of the DRDL of that era, the record of accomplishments was, also, impressive in that the amount of design studies that each technology group had undertaken then, without loss of time, and the speed with which most of those technology groups had then built the relevant testing and fabrication facilities and, in most cases, completed them on time, too, could be considered remarkable.

The second programme, which was sanctioned by the SA a few months after the sanctioning of the first programme, had been devised as an essential learning process, aimed at making our Laboratory and, in a limited sense, the associated DRDO laboratories which were to undertake the development of components or subsystems or materials, specific to their expertise, gain an experience in the execution and the management of a multi-prong missile system development project. The most important objective of that programme had been to provide, through the execution of that programme, a kind of on-the-job training to the DRDL scientists in the management of a multi-prong, multi-institution, high-tech system development enterprise, involving large scale outsourcing of development activities to a host of DRDO and non-DRDO agencies which had the relevant facilities and expertise. The programme had, also, put in place an effective monitoring system which had kept track of the progress of each activity with a view to taking corrective actions without loss of time. However, that missile system development programme had, of necessity, been sanctioned in two stages. In the first stage, a choice had to be made of a suitable guided missile system, and a study of the feasibility of developing and manufacturing the indigenous version of that missile system had to be undertaken by the DRDL, as the nodal laboratory, in association with the supporting laboratories and prototype manufacturers of our country. That had involved seeking out sources of expertise in various fields, both within the government-owned institutions, ie the DRDO laboratories, other national-level scientific organizations, our universities, ordnance factories, public sector manufacturing companies etc, and outside, ie, research institutions and manufacturing centres in our private sector. In the second stage, ie after the studies on the choice of the missile system, to be developed under that training programme, had been completed, culminating in the selection of the preferred system, and, also, the feasibility study pertaining to that missile development task had been completed, the concerned laboratories had to undertake the actual development task including the establishment of its manufacturing protocol.

In our case, fortunately, the studies pertaining to the choice of the missile system had, as expected, readily indicated that because of many reasons there was, then, only one older-vintage missile which best suited the objective of that on-the-job training programme. During the first stage of the Project Devil, therefore, the feasibility of indigenisation of that 'model' missile, including its host of ground equipment, had been studied, and, as expected, the feasibility study had been completed, successfully, within a record time of two to three months only. It may be mentioned in this connection that our feasibility study had confirmed that although the actual development of such a missile system would not be an easy task in view of the fact that most of the advanced technologies, then relevant to such a complex guided missile system, were present in that guided missile system our scientists, including those of the project management team, would likely gain very valuable experience and design-insight while in handling such a development task, namely the Project Devil.

To sum up, we had finished the task of the feasibility study for Project Devil on a war footing. At this point a few words about our choice of that particular surface-to-air missile (SAM) system for our learning process, ie for Project Devil, would, probably, be appropriate. By selecting that SAM, a surface-to-air missile of the second generation, which was obsolescent by then, as our model missile for Project Devil and, thereby, making the relevant user-service our associate in the execution of Project Devil, both the DRDO and the other agencies of our country, which had participated in Project Devil then, had benefited immensely. Also, although that older-vintage SAM had, as mentioned, reached obsolescence by then that 'model' missile had, in fact, proved very effective in terms of fulfilling the principal obective of that exercise, ie Project Devil, namely honing the missile related technology development capabilities of the DRDL and its associated laboratories while, also, imparting the relevant project management skill to the senior scientists of the Project Devil. In any event, the execution of Project Devil during 1971- 75, following the successful completion of the relevant feasibility study, as well as its follow-up activities, namely a feasibility study for the indigenization of a later-generation SAM, had resulted in the development of a number of new technologies by our laboratory including the solid rocket ramjet technology. And it was those two programmes, put together, namely the Project Devil and its follow-up technology-development activities, that had kept both the DRDL and its associated laboratories fully engaged in developing missile related technologies, in a focused manner, during the years 1972-1980 and had, in this process, prepared the DRDO well for successfully launching the now-famous IGMDP soon thereafter.

In short, the Project Devil and the manner in which it had been executed by the DRDO had not only laid the foundation for our country's future success in developing a variety of guided missile systems, including the ballistic missile, under the IGMDP but had, in the long run, also contributed immensely to the enhancement of our national security and the safeguarding of our sovereignty by providing our country with the capability to develop a ballistic missile, eg the Agni, for our own strategic weapon.

Incidentally, there had been a few other reasons, too, why the selection of that older-vintage SAM as the 'model' missile for Project Devil had proved so very beneficial. For instance, since one wing of our armed forces, alone among the three wings, had, at that point of time, such a missile system in actual deployment for many years, the operational staff and the engineering crew, which had looked after that system had been in an excellent position to offer valuable inputs to the scientists of Project Devil on the finer points of the operation and maintenance of a complex system. Second, that model missile had, in many ways more than any other guided missile system of the world then, made use of a host of sophisticated, if less-refined, contemporary technologies and thus had provided an unique opportunity to our scientists to study the finer points of the design of guidance, control, propulsion etc of a complex guided missile system of that era. Third, having been tactically deployed for a decade or so by then, that 'model' missile system had undergone many cycles of repair and maintenance by our military's engineers and technicians, and that experience, gained by the highly-qualified engineers of the user service, had been shared with our missile scientists and proved invaluable for Project Devil. In fact, the inputs, provided to our scientists by those engineers, had resulted in the incorporation of quite a few hardware modifications and design changes, all of which, in turn, had yielded an indigenous missile which was an improved version of the original Devil missile.

As known, historically, all second-generation industrially-developed countries, eg Japan and, later, Soviet Russia and China had acquired their skill in undertaking ab-initio design and development of complex engineering products by first undertaking a series of in-depth design and development studies on newly-developed industrial products, marketed by an older first-generation developed country. This phenomenon, sometimes derisively termed 'copying', is better known in the circle of erudite engineers and inventors as reverse-engineering. In a sense, the decision of our missile scientists of that era to simulate a 'learning process' by undertaking a project like the Project Devil had been inspired by the same kind of thinking, namely acquiring the development skill on a fast track by undertaking a piece of reverse engineering of a complex system. However, right from the beginning of that process, ie the feasibility study leading through the entire gamut of developing the system-, sub-systems- and component-designs to the fabrication and testing of the prototypes of components and subsystems and, finally, the assembly and testing of the complete missile system including its ground equipment, most of it undertaken by the scientists and engineers of our own laboratory, other laboratories in and outside the DRDO and the prototype manufacturers, we had, also, received extra-ordinary help from the specialist engineers, technicians and the operational crew of the concerned user service. What that had meant in terms of the methodology that we had followed was that some of the principles of a procedure, popularly known as 'reverse engineering', had been adopted. That was largely because the same methodology had been successfully made use of, often, by many engineering development agencies of the industrially developed countries of the world whenever a 'new'-design equipment had first been launched in the market by a competitor. In short, it had been the practice wherever possible legal challenges, associated with suspected violation of the patent rights of an original manufacturer, could be circumvented. In fact, most of the industrially developed countries had been known to have achieved quicker success in developing a later-design equipment by first 'learning the ropes' through taking recourse to reverse engineering. In a competitive world of technology and innovations most of the manufacturers of industrially developed countries had, while developing a new-design or an improved version of an earlier-design equipment, made full use of the tools of reverse engineering to gain valuable insights into the technology of an earlier-vintage equipment, developed by a competitor.

It has, also, been common knowledge that in Japan's case, particularly, its rapid rise as an industrially developed country had its roots, in good measure, in its uncanny ability to make use of reverse engineering with a view to tapping into the latest advances in technology that had already been made by its competitors, namely the designers and manufacturers of the developed countries of Europe and America. In fact, it was that special ability that had marked one of Japan's most enviable intellectual traits and had helped Japan transform its economy and industry in the shortest possible time both before and after the second world war, even, though its exploitation of the same ability in another field, namely military technology, had led that country, also, to developing weapons on a fast track and to military misadventures, particularly, during the second world war and had brought about the temporary economic ruination of Japan immediately after that war.

In our case, however, there was another advantage: The knowledge of the system that we had gained from the user service had proved very valuable in the execution of the Project Devil. That is primarily because the technological inputs which had been received from the user service had, also, included valuable information on the designs of some of the missile components and subsystems that the user service's specialists had acquired over the years, often, during investigations into occasional failure of a component or a subsystem or while undertaking a modification for improving the functioning of a component.

There were other reasons, too, why that particular SAM had been selected as our 'model' missile for the Project Devil. It was apparent by the early nineteen seventies that there was a possibility that under the prevailing circumstances of a raging cold war, when our non-aligned country had maintained equidistance from both the sides, our user service might find it difficult to procure a later-design SAM from either the USSR or the USA-led western countries in order to replace on time its stock of the obsolescent and aging SAM and be obliged to make do, for a few more years, with an interim solution. And, that interim solution could mean either extending the life of the obsolescent and aging missiles through the refurbishment of certain components of the missile or replacing the entire stock of the aging SAM by newly-manufactured missiles of the same kind. There was, therefore, a possibility that the successful development of an indigenous version of that obsolescent SAM – under Project Devil – could lead to an actual production, by our own ordnance factories, of that indigenous missile or, at the least, the immediate production of some of the components of that obsolescent SAM. In short, during those difficult days of the cold-war era and an enhanced threat to our national security, that had just then been posed by Pakistan, there was yet one more reason for selecting that particular SAM for the Project Devil.

For all of the above-mentioned reasons the execution of Project Devil had proved to be an inspiring task. And, our laboratory, the DRDL, had been infused with a new spirit of adventure, and our scientists had, for the very first time, felt fully energized and ready to plunge into that inspiring work with an unprecedented enthusiasm. Consequently, two major activities, namely the designing and building of the infrastructure pertaining to the development of guided missiles, in general, comprising both test facilities and fabrication workshops, and the expeditious development of an indigenous version that SAM under Project Devil, had been speedily sanctioned, one after the other, although, in each case, the giving of a financial sanction had, as expected, been preceded by a process of intense scrutiny and deliberations by the our government. However, even before those project proposals had been formulated by the respective technology divisions of the laboratory the new SA, Dr Nag Chaudhuri, had held two historic meetings at our laboratory with each of our senior scientists, covering all areas of missile technology. In retrospect, one can only guess that while the SA had, during those discussions, exchanged detailed notes with his scientists on both the essentiality and the nature of the facilities that were required to be built by us, the SA had, also, sounded out the Services, ie the Indian military, on the future requirements of tactical missiles of all kinds. In other words, during those early days of his taking charge of his new office, the SA had, in all likelihood, assessed both the future potential of his own organization, the DRDO, and its laboratory, the then-miniscule DRDL, and the views of our military on our country's future requirements of tactical guided missiles. And, apparently, at some point of time within the very first few weeks of his arrival the new SA had decided to take a plunge by strengthening both the DRDL and the supporting laboratories within the DRDO through the build-up of infrastructure and facilities and the taking up of Project Devil both for its own sake, ie as a learning process, and for assisting the user service in obtaining an interim solution for the problem of its aging missiles. And, he had lost no time in making both of these project activities a reality.

Incidentally, in the midst of those deliberations, the SA had, also, initiated an allied activity, namely the induction of young scientist manpower in the DRDL and a few other DRDO laboratories on high priority. As it had turned out, that action had been the first one in a series of actions taken by the new SA, soon thereafter, in furtherance of his plans for building technology capabilities of the DRDO as a whole, ie not only in guided missiles but, also, in a few other areas of advanced weapon systems, eg combat aircraft, the main battle tank and selected naval systems. And, fortunately for our laboratory, he had commenced acting on his plan for the induction of scientist manpower by asking the DRDL first to do it, ie to recruit bright young graduates of the relevant engineering disciplines from the campuses of the reputed institutions of our country including our IITs. And, that action had, in fact, been very well timed, too: As far as guided missile development was concerned it had been slotted in just a few weeks prior to his sanctioning the two major development activities for our laboratory in quick succession, namely facilities build-up and the Project Devil.

And it was that lead time, ie the gap between the induction of manpower and the sanctioning of the two development activities in succession, that had given us the opportunity to reach a threshold of a minimum of scientist manpower in various disciplines before commencing our work on the first activity, namely the build-up of facilities. Although that had involved a great amount of work, namely sending out urgent notices for interviews, visiting in quick time some five or six venues for interviews in cities in the east, west, north and south of our country, most venues based at the IITs, and giving offer letters on the spot to the selected candidates for temporary appointments and, finally, putting those young engineers on their arrival at our laboratory through an induction process before getting to deploy them on actual jobs, our laboratory had been able to accomplish the task on a tight schedule and deploy the young scientists on project work without loss of time. And, since, as mentioned, the SA had decided to start the young-scientist induction process with first augmenting manpower for guided missiles it had been our laboratory which had sent out the first campus-selection board comprising three members, namely one each representing airframes and structures (Shri Rama Rao, then head of missile-structures), electronics and computer science (Shri JC Bhattacharya, then head of control engineering) and self (then head of missile propulsion). In fact, a team of only three or four of us from among the heads of technology divisions who, by virtue of our education, had broadly represented expertise in five or six of the relevant engineering disciplines had immediately been constituted by our Director and given the job.

The idea was to select young graduates by visiting the campuses of our universities and engineering colleges and offer them provisional appointment letters on the spot. That action enabled our laboratory's technology divisions to have those young engineers report for work without loss of time and to put those young engineers through their paces by immediately inducting them into the activities pertaining to design and development. We had taken up this job of recruitment of young engineers on high priority because our laboratory had felt confident that (a) sanctions for funds for the facilities build-up would be given immediately, (b) those sanctions for facilities build-up would be quickly followed by the according of sanction for the project itself, ie the Project Devil, and (c) the appointments of the young engineers whom we had selected on the campuses and recruited provisionally would be regularized by the time we had given them adequate training on the design and development work and inducted them into actual development activities pertaining to the our Project.

As I recall, we, the three members of our laboratory's first selection committee for recruiting young scientists at the campuses, had, in fact, quickly gone to work and, after obtaining the concurrence of those institutions, commenced visiting those campuses in a planned manner. That was, probably, in early 1972. And, although quite a large number of the graduating students of the concerned IITs and university colleges of engineering of our country then (eg Madras, Kharagpur, Jadavpur, Shibpur, Calcutta, Delhi, Banaras, Roorkee etc) had appeared at our interviews at each centre we had realized that not many of those who had graduated in the more 'attractive' (ie more paying) disciplines, eg Mechanical, Electrical and Electronics engineering, would, finally, join up. Therefore, while we had to put in extra efforts, as I recollect, to attract enough graduating students of those 'higher-paying' disciplines to jobs in our Service, ie the Defence R & D Service (DRDS), we had no difficulty in recruiting enough of the fresh graduates as far as the other disciplines were concerned.

And, as I recall, our experience in recruiting young scientists during that first campus-selection drive for young scientist positions in our laboratory had become a subject of interesting discussion with our SA later, probably, because our selection committee's experience had offered a few lessons for other laboratories, too.

As it had turned out, we did manage to get our quota of the required number of fresh graduates in the so-called more-lucrative disciplines, too. That was because we had anticipated the likelihood of some of the selected candidates of those disciplines not, finally, accepting our job offers and had selected a few more candidates than required and issued an 'extra' number of appointment letters. It was generally known, however, it was difficult to attract good graduates in those more-'attractive' disciplines to our kind of government service. And, by the mid-seventies it became loud and clear that there would be more choice of good candidates in such disciplines as Civil Engineering, Production Engineering, Instrumentation, Aeronautical and Chemical engineering than in the more-attractive disciplines like the mechanical, electrical or electronics engineering (and, later, the computer sciences and engineering, as known).

Since the SA had decided against the frittering away of the DRDO's limited resources by deploying the DRDO laboratories, primarily, on programmes for the development of three or four major weapon systems and platforms, all of the concerned nodal laboratories (eg the DRDL, the Aeronautical Development Establishment or the ADE, the Combat Vehicle Research & Development Establishment or the CVRDE, the Naval Science & Technology Laboratory or the NSTL etc) and their supporting laboratories for the development of weapon systems or of special materials (eg the Defence Electronics Research Laboratory or the DLRL, the Electronics and Radar Development Laboratory or the

LRDE, the Defence Metallurgical Research Laboratory or the DMRL, the ARDE, the ERDL, the TBRL, the R & D Engineers etc) had undertaken the selection and recruitment of young scientists during those three years of Dr Nag Chaudhuri's stewardship. In fact, all important laboratories of the DRDO, functioning in those priority areas, had managed to induct, in those few years, a sizeable number of young scientists, in one go and for the very first time, thanks to the vision and dynamism of Dr Nag Chaudhuri. It was gratifying, particularly, for those three of us, the heads of three different technology divisions of the DRDL in those early years – who, as members of our laboratory's first campus-recruitment committee, had started that young-scientist recruitment drive by visiting the campuses of our country and interviewing a very large number of fresh graduates – to see that many of those young engineers who had been inducted during those early years have performed very well and that a large number of them have reached senior positions. To give an example, one recently-retired scientist whom we had recruited in 1971/72 from an IIT campus as a young mechanical engineer, had, in due course, become the Director of the DRDL and, eventually, had later taken over as the Scientific Advisor cum DG DRDO.

In mid-1974 Dr Nag Chaudhuri had moved on to take up another challenge, offered by the same Prime Minister, Indira Gandhi, namely the job of establishing an altogether new type of institution for teaching and research in our country, namely the Jawaharlal Nehru University (JNU) with its sprawling campus in New Delhi, an adequately-funded Central University, primarily, for post-graduate studies and research. It was that Prime Minister, as known, who had, in the first place, induced the professor to leave the academia to join the service of our government, first as a Member of our Planning Commission and then as the first 'empowered' SA cum DG DRDO to fill a newly-created vacancy of a Secretary to the government in our MOD. That job of Professor Nag Chaudhuri, namely the Vice Chancellor of a richly-funded graduate school of our country, which was the only one of its kind in our country and needed someone capable of building it up from scratch into an internationally reputed centre of excellence for advanced studies and research in most of the social sciences and in a few branches of science, too. It goes without saying, however, that by the time Dr Nag Chaudhuri had moved out of the MOD our organization, the DRDO, had acquired a new stature. Most of its laboratories, including the DRDL, had already been equipped with a large number of technology development faacilities and had, also, put those into use, while the other laboratories, having built some of their technology development facilities earlier, were well on the way to completing the rest of the build-up. As for the scientist-manpower component of that build-up, the DRDO as a whole had successfully inducted into its laboratories quite a few hundreds of young scientists, probably, some ten times the number the DRDO had had before its expansion which had been brought about by our third SA, Professor Nag Chaudhuri.

Our organization, the DRDO, had by then commenced functioning every inch like it ought to have done some two decades back. As for the DRDL, it had continued on the growth-path for a few more years – by building newer technology facilities (eg a prototype manufacturing unit for fabricating special micro-electronic chips) and putting them to use, while remaining engaged on Project Devil and its follow-up activities, the development of selected, additional technologies. For instance, the successor missile, the SA 3, had a proven propulsion system, namely the integrated solid rocket ramjet engine, which was one of the first of its kind then and needed to be developed urgently as a missile propulsion device for future applications in the field of surface-to-air defence. Similarly, a solid rocket propellant which is universally used for long burning solid rocket sustainer engine of the ATM, namely the long-burning grain of cast double base propellant, with its sophisticated inhibition technique, had to be developed. The laboratory had, also, developed the technology of the guidance system for long-range SSMs. However, in January, 1976, as mentioned, I had been transferred to the DRDO=s headquarters and had joined its newly-formed Directorate of Rockets and Missiles. By then our laboratory, the DRDL, had successfully completed a major part of Project Devil, while, also, working on technology development activities pertaining to other classes of missiles. Just before I had handed over charge and moved away from the Laboratory in Hyderabad the indigenous prototype of the solid rocket engine of Project Devil had, also, been tested jointly by us, the DRDL, and our Air Force in flight at a missile-test range, not too far from our laboratory.

Of the futuristic technology development activities in many areas of missile technology, eg propulsion, guidance, control etc, which had commenced during the last two years of my work in the DRDL and had already made good progress before Professor Nag Chaudhuri had left, most had been successfully completed and had found application in our next generation of projects, eg the longer-duration liquid rocket sustainer engine, the inertial navigation system (INS), the solid-propellant rocket-ramjet engine, the structural test facility, computer simulation facility, environmental tests facility. Some of those were the work of joint efforts by the DRDL and some of its supporting laboratories, eg the ERDL. For instance, the facility for developing cast double base solid propellant and its inhibition technology for long-duration burning had been co-located with the Solid Rocket Propulsion Division inside the DRDL campus and received the required administrative support of our laboratory but functioned under the ERDL management in Pune. In other words, that wing of the ERDL had been conceived as an adjunct facility of the Solid Propulsion division of the DRDL. As for manpower, there were by then nearly two hundred young scientists of all disciplines in the DRDL, contributing enthusiastically to those development activities which had ushered in a new era in the DRDL. All in all, it had been a quantum jump in DRDL's scientist manpower, which had made combined strength of the DRDL, comprising young and senior scientists of various disciplines, nearly twenty times in about 5 years. That plus a phenomenal success in facilities build-up had made the DRDL largely equipped by then to function as a nodal laboratory for developing guided missile systems.

Chapter 7

Sadhan Dutt and Engineering Consultancy In India

There was an intervening period between my retirement from the Air Force in Jan 1989 and my taking to a scholarly pursuit in the early 1993. And, during that period, for nearly three years, I had worked for a reputed engineering consultancy company in our private sector as an executive director, and that experience, too, had proved unique in many ways.

As I recall, the opportunity to join the engineering-consultancy practice had come about somewhat unexpectedly. Just before I had reached my superannuation from our government's service at an early age of fifty seven I had been persuaded by my wife not to give up professional work at such an early age and to offer my service as an engineering professional to the Chairman of an engineering consultancy company in our private sector, whose success, both as an engineer and as an enterpreuner, had been a legend by then. And, more importantly, I had, also, been persuaded by my wife to believe that that legendary chief of that reputed engineering consultancy company of our country would likely respond favourably if someone, with my credentials, were to offer his professional services to that company. So, after some hesitation, I had sent a letter to that gentleman only a week before my retirement from government service. However, since our government's rules for post-retirement employment then had allowed one to look for a job a full six months ahead of one's retirement and, also, since most people would initiate such actions months in advance of their retirement I had known that I had been very late in initiating my action.

However, that legendary Indian chief of engineering consultancy then, Mr Sadhan Dutt, whom I had neither met before nor known much of, had, to my surprise, responded promptly. And, soon after my retirement and moving into our own house in New Delhi I was visited by an emissary from the New Delhi office of that engineering consultancy company and informed that I had been invited by the chief of his organization to meet up with him in his office in Calcutta for a discussion as soon as it was convenient for me to do so. However, although it had been quite a few weeks thereafter, probably, a month or more later, that I could undertake my travel to Calcutta to meet up with that gentleman he had been very prompt in making up his mind and letting me know – after only an hour's meeting with him, in fact, in his Calcutta office – that he would like me to join his organization as soon as possible. And he had followed that offer with a prompt letter, offering an appropriate position in his organisation, namely that of an Executive Director. However, although I had returned to New Delhi the following day itself and initiated the required action for obtaining the permission of our government for accepting that job offer it had taken me all of the next six months to obtain that permission for accepting that job offer. And, interestingly, that delay in my getting the approval of our government had occurred, way back in 1989, despite the fact that I have had no previous contact, whatsoever, with that company in my entire career, let alone an occasion when I had dealt with it in any manner as a senior officer of our government in either the recent or the distant past. That delay, I may add here, could have, however, been avoided if I had not been a stickler for rules, ie if I had circumvented the relevant rule in the manner in which, as I had found later, most retired seniors of our civil service then did and, probably, still do.

Thus it is that I had first applied for a job in a reputed engineering consultancy company of our country then, namely the Development Consultants Limited (DCL), and had, soon thereafter, met the chief of that organization, the legendary Sadhan Dutta, at the organisation's corporate headquarters in Calcutta in June or July, 1989.

I had remained with that organization for about three years. It was one of the two large and multi-discipline engineering consultancy companies in our private sector then, and, probably, nearly as large as the other government-owned consultancy company then was, namely the government-owned Engineers India Ltd, with its presence, then, in many other countries in Asia, Africa and North and South America. It was, also, the largest ever Indian-owned, private-sector, corporation which successfully conducted engineering-consultancy business in both India and outside.

Somewhat to my amusement, however, I had found soon after taking up that appointment that it was less known by its current name than by the names of two of its earlier avatars, namely the Kuljian Corporation (India) and the Development Consultants Pvt Ltd (DCPL). And, that was so despite the fact that its name had changed, successively, many years back from the Kuljian Corporation to the DCPL and, later, to the DCL. The reason why there had been three changes had to do, primarily, with the fact that the company had, unavoidably, gone through a transformation in its ownership structure in a step-by-step manner, from having been a branch office in India of the Kuljian Corporation of the USA through becoming an Indian subsidiary of a US-owned company, with headquarters in Philadelphia, USA, and bearing the same name to becoming a fully Indian-owned engineering consultancy company, bearing the name, the DCPL, or, later, the DCL, with a fully-owned subsidiary in the USA, named the Kuljian Corporation, the last change (ie dropping the word 'Private' from the registered name of the company) having been made in compliance with a change in company law, that had just then been brought about by our government and required a privately-owned Indian company, whose turn-over exceeded a certain upper limit to comply with the regulations which govern the functioning of public limited companies in our country.

The DCL's corporate headquarters, where I had joined work, was in Calcutta, housed in its own prestigious building on the Park Street, where it was in occupation of only one half of the floors, probably, leaving the other half with pre-existing tenants which were, also, reputed business houses. Since, however, the total work-force of engineers and management staff was very large then the DCL has, also, been in part occupation of another seventeen buildings in and around the Park Street. Bsides that corporate headquarters, the DCL, then, had, also, had zonal offices in the three other metropolitan cities of India, ie Mumbai (then Bombay), Delhi and Chennai (then Madras), each of which had its own design engineers and other staff. As stated, the DCL, with Mr Sadhan Dutta as its majority-share-holder, had, also, owned, from its beginning, the US-based Kuljian Corporation, with its headquarters in Philadelphia, USA, ie the company which had once fully owned the the DCL's previous avatar, the Kuljian Corporation (India). In short, the DCL, then, had, by virtue of its full ownership of its US-based subsidiary, the Kuljian Corpn, had a large business office in the USA and, also, in the UK and a few other cities in the middle east and South America, ie countries where the DCL had been engaged in engineering consultancy business for many decades by then.

I had served in that organization for a little over three years, ie for nearly two years at its headquarters in Calcutta and, later, for an year, at its New Delhi office. I ought to mention here that among all of the public limited companies of our country then, either in the public sector or in the private, the DCPL/DCL was rather 'special' in those early years of our industrialization, eg in the early nineteen sixties onwards. And, that was because of three reasons: (a) During the nineteen sixties to early nineteen nineties it was the only wholly-Indian-owned private-sector trans-national company (ie a multi national corporation, MNC, minus the mindset of a MNC, I believe), which provided major engineering consultancy service in many fields of engineering to industrial organizations, both our country and in the middle east and South America, (b) It was, for many decades, also, the only large company in India's private sector, which had operated successfully in a 'niche' area of technology-based business, namely engineering consultancy, and, finally, (c) Since the work of an engineering consultant, in its true sense, consisted only of rendering engineering design including detailed engineering and, also, if the client so desired, of providing assistance in the selection of – and the supervision of construction by – a suitable construction agency and, finally, the commissioning of the plant, it had tried to scrupulously follow that principle by not bidding for any construction contract in any case where the DCL had been selected as the project's engineering consultant.

Way back in the nineteen sixties and right up to the nineteen nineties the DCL was one of the few Indian companies which had operated globally in a line of business which had been regarded as a difficult area of business-operation by Indian-owned enterprises. However, although, as mentioned, Mr Sadhan Dutt, had been a pioneer in India in the field of engineering consultancy since the nineteen sixties and, also, probably, the first Indian engineer who had made business-inroads in foreign countries as early as the nineteen seventies in competition with some of the world-renowned engineering consultancy companies, it was only after I had joined his company in 1989 that I had grasped the full import of his achievements. In short, it was only then that the realization had dawned on me that his genius had brought forth a win-win situation for our country: Whereas the work of an Indian-owned engineering consultancy company, comprising design studies, detailed engineering, erection supervision, commissioning and certification, was undertaken wholly by a work force, made up of Indian engineers only and based largely in India, its competitors, eg the US-owned engineering consultancy companies and their equivalents in Western Europe, had to depend for the execution of the same kind of work on engineers and experts, based in the USA or Europe, and had, thereby, to incur expenditures, much higher than those borne by an Indian enterprise, ie the DCL or its earlier avatar, The Kuljian Corporation (India).

In other words, probably, the most important secret of Sadhan Dutta's success had been that, as a business leader, he was, in one important way, well ahead of his competitors in the industrially developed world. In those early years of Indian independence he, alone, had perceived and, also, implemented the concept of outsourcing well before any company in the developed countries had grasped the significance of out-sourcing as a major cost-cutting measure, even though those competitors, all companies of Europe and the USA, were much larger enterprises than the DCL was in India. He had an additional advantage, too: He had foreseen that in his particular line of business a combination of two well-managed engineering consultancy companies, both owned and managed by an Indian national, namely a small-sized consultancy company, based in the USA and employing a fewer number of engineers and managers, and a large engineering consultancy company, based in India and manned by a large pool of Indian engineers and designers possessing the required skill, would make it possible to deliver engineering consultancy services to projects anywhere in the world at an appreciably less cost and would, consequently, prove more competitive than the much larger multinational companies, based in the USA or Europe. Additionally, since under such an arrangement for delivering service most of the consultancy work would be produced by the Indian consultancy company, a much larger number of Indian engineers and managers would have to be employed by the Indian company, ie the DCL, than anyone had ever foreseen. It was thus evident that it was entirely due to the vision of Sadhan Dutta, both his Indian company, ie the DCL, and his country, ie India, had received huge benefits: There would be more revenue and greater profit for the DCL, while our country would earn higher corporate-tax revenue and generate more employment.

It had, also, been then that the realization had dawned on me that neither many in our country had, even, heard of Sadhan Dutta nor, as in the case of most his contemporaries at the helm of Indian industries, been aware of the full extent of his achievements. A man who had started his professional career as an engineering graduate of the Beneras University in 1945 but had soon, thereafter, proceeded to the USA under a government of India training scheme and, in the process, had developed such an insight in entrepreneur-ship that, on his return to India, he could achieve unprecedented success in the profession of engineering consultancy by setting up the first-ever Indian-owned transnational engineering consultancy company and making it grow into a world-wide organsation of repute.

As an aside I might, also, add that in the process he had, also, set another record of a sort: Since most of the professionally qualified Indians – and, especially, those of Bengali descent – are proverbially known to have shied away from setting up any kind of business of their own, the fact that Mr Sadhan Dutt, an Indian engineer of Bengali descent, had opted for starting up an engineering business enterprise in India and had then attained an unqualified success in growing that business into an world-wide enterprise has constituted a great achievement and ought to be recognized as such.

Mr Sadhan Dutt is no more, but his legacy remains. And, although my three years of work with the DCL had ended in February, 1993, it had, as I recall, provided me with an opportunity, once, to work in close proximity to that legendary man on one of the first-of-its-kind engineering consultancy projects then for the DCL, namely providing consultancy to an Indian public limited company, a public sector unit (PSU), at that, for the setting up a high-technology clean-room facility for the manufacture of special-quality silicon wafers, a high-end consultancy project, which was very close to his heart and the like of which the DCL had not handled before. When successfully executed during the years 1991 to 1994, that project had added a feather to the DCL's cap and had led to an yet another consultancy project on the same lines but for a more sophisticated wafer manufacturing project.

It was because of that work by the company on engineering a clean room facility for the manufacture of silicon wafers that I had the opportunity to observe – from close quarters and, during the early stages of that work, often on a daily basis – Sadhan Dutta's unique style of functioning as the chief of a worldwide organization. His ability to effectively delegate responsibility to a trusted deputy – and yet to keep himself abreast of each critical step of decision-making by that deputy without appearing to be overbearing – had been an interesting experience for me. He had given me a free hand to access a wide variety of the DCL's considerable infrastructure and expertise in the field of designing and engineering and, also, the service of an experienced manager in its associated company's, ie Kuljian Corpn's, US office to help me explore the availability of reputed clean room technology consultants and select an appropriate collaborator towards the making of preparation for the bidding, in an international competition, for a high-technology consultancy project in which the company had had no prior experience. That process had meant our setting up a consortium of two consultants, with the DCL as the lead company, and thus managing to have that DCL-led consortium 'qualify' as an acceptable bidder – for that altogether-new field of engineering consultancy – in competition with world-renowned clean-room technology engineering consultants of France, the USA etc., a feat that had meant the crossing of the first hurdle of the bidding process in that two-step race for winning the contract for that exciting work. He had, also, taken keen interest on that occasion in every step that we had taken during the entire process of bid-making,

(a) starting from the preparation of a joint response by the DCL-led consortium to the prospective client's original notice inviting tender through delineating the methodology for sharing the design-cum-detailing work etc, involved in the execution of the consultancy project, the consequent method of making of payments of consultancy-fees, separately, to the lead contractor and its US-based associate, ie the making of the major part of the fees, in only Rupees, to the DCL, and the 'minor' part of the consultancy fees, in US dollars, to the US-based member of the DCL-led consortium,

(b) through the making of a series of presentations to the expert committees of the client as well as addressing specific issues, raised by the prospective client's experts, and the making of the presentation to the top management, thereafter,

(c) to, finally, winning that high-technology consultancy contract in a matter of less than a year and in the face of stiff competition with the other two short-listed bidders, both of those large multi-national engineering consultants, specialized in clean-room and wafers-manufacturing technology.

The clinching of that altogether-new piece of consultancy work by a DCL-led consortium of engineering consultants from its conceptualization to its completion during 1989-1990 – and the actual delivery of that work by a large team of Indian engineers and only a handful of US-based consultants during the following 2 years – had resulted in the breaking of new grounds by the DCL in engineering consultancy in our country, as stated. And, it had been made possible as much due to the legendary Sadhan Dutta's ability to seize an opportunity as soon as it arose as to his ability to keep an open mind to accepting any forward-looking high-technology consultancy opportunity after doing the required due diligence. As exemplified in this case, his ready acceptance of the proposal that I had put forward in this case, namely (a) that the DCL, which had a large and highly-competent engineering work-force but had had no opportunity, so far, to gather consultancy experience in clean-room technology, join hands with a highly competent but much-smaller US-based consultancy company, that has an excellent record of prior work in engineering clean room facilities for silicon wafer manufacture, to form of a two-member consortium of engineering consultants, and (b) that the above-mentioned DCL-led consortium responds, by due date, to the Indian silicon-wafer manufacturing company's recent notice inviting tenders, a notice which had so far been overlooked, in fact, by the concerned senior of the DCL, had done the trick in this case, as stated already.

Soon, thereafter, there had been a change in circumstances in my case, however. With the eldest of our three daughters having married and moved away a little before that, our other two daughters, both highly educated and single then, had, also, at that point, left their home, ie India, in pursuit of their respective career plans, one for England and the other for the USA. We, as parents, had, therefore, decided to be supportive of them by making ourselves free to travel abroad on short notice. And, since I had already been toying for sometime with the idea of giving up my job and taking to scholarly activities as a free-lance academic I had, at that point of time, left my position with that reputed engineering consultants, the DCL, and joined the life of a free-lance researcher and occasional lecturer at graduate schools in India and abroad. And, since taking up engineering research – in continuation of my decades-long career in military technology – was no longer an option I had, in early 1993, taken up researching and writing on the technology related issues of international politics as a free-lance scholar and occasional lecturer.

Chapter 8

Terminal Ballistics and Warheads Research

The payload of a rocket-based weapon system, whether an unguided rocket or a guided missile, is the warhead. Whereas a space-launch vehicle (SLV), which is a guided rocket for a space-related application, carries either a satellite or a manned or unmanned experimental station, eg a specially-equipped scientific laboratory as its payload, both the unguided rocket-weapon and the guided missile carry one or more warheads, specifically made for destroying or defeating a designated target. And, since all warheads, whether those are fitted on unguided rockets or guided missiles, or are delivered by a manned aircraft, a drone, an artillery piece or a mortar, use high explosives or explosive-like materials for exploding the warhead and inflicting damage on its target the science and technology of warheads have a lot in common and constitute, therefore, a distinct area of research for military technologists. And, most of the developed nations which have made large investments in military technology, eg the France, the UK,

Germany, the USA, Russia and China, have some of their own R & D laboratories, equipped for undertaking research into terminal ballistics, ie the study of the terminal effects on objects, regarded as hostile targets that need to be dfeated, and its associated phenomena, as well the developmental testing of various kinds of warheads of both the rocket-based weapons and the other weapons. In the USA, for instance, the R & D organization of the Department of Defence (DOD) at Pentagon has a Ballistics Research Laboratory (BRL) in Maryland State, not far from its capital, the Washington DC, which laboratory historically dealt with warheads research and allied technologies.

Our country had established its own warhead research establishment, the Terminal Ballistics Research Laboratory (TBRL), soon after our independence, thanks, again, to the foresight and the leadership of Professor DS Kothari, the first Scientific Adviser of our country, as mentioned earlier. An early Director of that Laboratory was a pioneer in India's warhead research, namely Dr Sampuran Singh, a physicist by training, who had been an early entrant, as a scientist, to the fledgling Defence Science Organisation of India, ie the DRDO of today. Incidentally, quite a few of those early scientist-recruits of the defence science organization were selected by the Union Public Service Commission (UPSC) under the direct advice and encouragement of the first Scientific Adviser who, as already stated, had laid the foundations of the DRDO in all respects. Hence, the TBRL, too, had been planned well by the first SA in the early days of the DSO (ie the DRDO) and had, in fact, earned a name as a well-designed and appropriately equipped R & D institution of our country for decades – for undertaking the R & D of warheads – when I had taken over as its fourth Director, in July, 1985, ie some three decades after its formation. However, I did not have the good fortune of meeting the Director who had laid most of the foundation of the Laboratory and who was still living in the city, Chandigarh, I had been told, probably, because he was by then getting on in years.

Before proceeding further, however, let me state at the outset that in this chapter, writing very briefly on our country's work in warhead research, I will, of necessity, briefly touch upon only a few items of the interesting work that the TBRL had undertaken, in the past and during my time, in relation to almost all of the weapon system development projects of our country and, more importantly, in our guided missile development programme.

Critical Feature of Warhead Research

By virtue of the fact that research into explosives-physics and the development and testing of warheads entail the handling of very sensitive high explosives and the routine of experimentation with explosives-filled electro-mechanical and electronics devices it constitutes work that is fraught with danger to life and the limbs of the concerned scientists. Hence, the facilities of all warhead research institutions are, of necessity, built in two or more separate locations, away from each other. And, in the case of our Laboratory, too, the facilities for experimentation with warhead-related non-explosive devices as well as electronics measuring equipment of sophisticated nature, had been located and built within the city and, thus, had been co-located with such facilities as the centre for theoretical studies, the administrative departments of the Laboratory, the city-office of the Director.

But, the explosives laboratories and the prototype making facilities for warheads and their components and, also, other explosives-filled devices of all kinds were located in a very large and secure area, well outside the city limits and away from all habitations. All in all, the Laboratory bore the hallmark of a very large, modern and an appropriately-designed research and development establishment for warhead research, even, after nearly three decades of its existence, I had noted with admiration when I had joined that Laboratory.

And, all of it had been done in full compliance with the stipulated safety regulations pertaining to the storage of and, more importantly, the undertaking of experiments with high explosives, explosives-filled components, warhead prototypes and all types of complete warheads. I may mention in this connection that the building of that prime experimental centre of the Laboratory, as the core R & D centre of our country's warhead research, in that appropriately-vast open area, away from the city and all human habitations, had been made possible only due to the foresight and the generosity of one the few outstanding, if strong-willed, Indian political leaders of that era, namely an all-time famous Sikh political leader of the then East Punjab, who had placed large tracts of land in his state at the disposal of the government of India to enable our country to build that extensive experimental centre of the TBRL, popularly known as the Range.

Warheads, Guided Missiles and Weapon Platforms

The effectiveness of a weapon system, eg an unguided rocket-weapon or a guided missile or an ammunition which is discharged by a mortar or a piece of artillery, or an aircraft bomb, and, therefore, the effectiveness of any weapon-platform, eg a self-propelled Artillery, an armoured tracked vehicle or a tank, a fighter or a bomber aircraft, a naval craft of any kind, each of which is fitted with one or more of those weapons, eg guided missiles, long-range guns, torpedoes etc, depends, in the final analysis, on the effectiveness of warheads, ie their terminal effects. Therefore, as in other industrialized countries, the warhead research and development work of the TBRL had been an integral part of each of our weapon-system development programmes of our country, eg the multi-barrel rocket launcher, the Arjun MBT and the IGMDP. And, since during nearly two decades of work on our missile programme, in the nineteen eighties and the nineties, say, the IGMDP, with its mandate for four types of tactical-application guided missiles and of the Agni technology-demonstrator ballistic missile, had, probably, featured as the most pervasive of the weapon system development programmes of our country, the TBRL had been involved during those two decades, most intensely, in the work of the IGMDP, in particular.

And, inevitably, that development activity for the IGMDP had largely comprised collaborative R & D work with the ARDE on the design of the warheads and the static and the simulated dynamic testing of some fifteen types of conventional (ie high explosives) missile-warheads for a total of four tactical missies of the IGMDP, some of those warheads incorporating sophisticated sub-munitions. And, therefore, as a major participant laboratory of the IGMDP, jointly working with the DRDL, the lead laboratory, the TBRL had necessarily to work closely with the DRDL for the entire duration of the IGMDP. And, as the Director of the TBRL then, I recall, I had, on some occasions, witnessed some of the dynamic testing of prototypes of missile-warheads at the TBRL's experimental centre, ie the so-called Range, in the company of the Director of the DRDL, the esteemed Dr Abdul Kalam. That was well before Dr Kalam had handed over the charge of the DRDL and of the IGMDP's programme management board and taken over as the SA cum Secretary (Def R & D) and the Chairman of the apex Guided Missile Board.

Simulated Environmental Tests

It is not often that a large experimental centre of a warhead Laboratory that handles research and development activities pertaining to both the physics of explosives and the ballistics of warheads, also, undertakes within its precincts some of the advanced environmental tests, eg simulated environmental tests for missile-borne equipment and selected components of guided missiles . One experimental facility for conducting such an environmental test, namely the facility for checking the integrity and the unimpaired functioning of a component or an equipment, when subjected to high accelerations, comprises a rocket-propelled sled that, when triggered, travels from rest and quickly gains a very high speed within seconds by traveling a few kilometers or less on a specially-constructed and sophisticated rail track. This test facility thus enables any material or equipment, strapped on its sled, to be subjected to the stresses of high accelerations. The design and construction of such a sophisticated test facility had constituted one of the more interesting engineering programmes. Historically, the first Rail Track Rocket Sled (RTRS) of the world had, probably, been constructed and put into use many decades back by Germany, but, at least, three other nations, namely the USA, the former Soviet Union and France, had, probably, caught up with Germany in no time, since each of those industrially developed nations had, even before the second world war, also, commenced serious work on rocketry and in control and guidance engineering and had invested heavily, soon after that war, into the R & D of both Space launch vehicles (SLVs) and Guided Missiles, including long-range ballistic missiles.

Conventional Warheads and Ballistic Missiles

Only thirty to forty years back a surface-to-surface guided missile (SSM), if intended to destroy or defeat targets at distances in excess of 100 kilometers, say, was not regarded as cost-effective if its warhead could not cause the kind of destruction that only a smaller-size nuclear warhead can inflict. It is for that reason that the 'original' Prithvi missile, which had been developed under the IGMDP a decade back and has since been deployed by our Artillery regiments, has a shorter range. However, the continued progress being made in research into the technology of conventional warheads and, especially, into the development of a class of missile-warheads, which incorporates sub-munitions and thereby makes the warhead much more effective against certain classes of surface-targets, has increased the cost-effectiveness of such shorter-range SSMs as a tactical-application weapon. Increasingly, therefore, better classes of missile-warhead, eg warheads which contain more sophisticated sub-munitions that are designed to be more effective against such targets as enemy-troop concentrations, storage parks of armoured-vehicles etc, are being developed for such 100 to 200 kilometer-range ballistic missiles as are meant to be deployed only in tactical mode. It is likely, therefore, that in the case of our Prithvi missile, too, such a longer-range SSM of up to 150 kilometer-range, say, has been developed or is being developed for purely tactical-application – as are a variety of more-effective missile-warheads for it, ie missile-warheads of the kind which will make the deployment of such a tactical-application-but-longer-range Prithvi missile entirely cost-effective.

Chapter 9

Guided Missiles Vis-À-Vis MBT and LCA

Introduction

India's spectacular success in the development of both guided missiles and missile warheads including the nuclear-warhead has been universally acknowledged. Three of the four types of tactical-application guided missiles of the IGMDP, each with its own variety of sophisticated high explosives warheads, are now in production and deployed by our military. And, the twin successes of our ballistic missiles and the nuclear warhead development programmes have provided India with a deterrent weapon, capable of keeping at bay both of our nuclear-armed neighbours which constantly threaten our security and sovereignty. There have, also, been two other, important fall-outs of that success, namely the withdrawl by the USA of a host of technology control regimes, that were imposed on our country by the USA and its allies, even, before the inception of the Cold War, and the subsequent improvement in our relationship with all of the industrially developed countries of the world, led by the USA. In short, our twin success in guided missiles and both types missile-warheads have proved to be the two most important achievements of our country's military technology enterprise.

Unfortunately for our country, however, the disconnect between the success in guided missiles and their warheads development, on the one hand, and the failure in the case of most other indigenous-weapon making programmes, on the other, has not been adequately addressed, even, now. And that, despite the fact that our government had, since the days of our dynamic Prime Minister, Mrs Indira Gandhi, reversed its earlier policy of denial of resources to and commenced the making investments in military technology, a policy reversal that has enabled us to build, since long, a sizeable infrastructure for both the Development and the Manufacture wings of our DTIB. In fact, our country now owns a fairly large military-industrial complex (MIC), comprising both a sizeable amount of defence R & D facilities, overseen by the Dept of Defence R & D, on the one hand, and a very large network of OFs (Ordnace Factories) and DPSUs (Defence Public Sector Units), controlled by the Dept of Defence Production & Supplies, on the other, even if most of the defence production facilities had been built, primarily, for the licensed-manufacture of imported weapons of both Western and Russian origin.

There are two big differences, however, between our country and those other democracies which, too, have large MICs of their own, namely (a) in the manner in which our country exercises control over our DTIB, as opposed to how other democracies do so and (b) in respect of the management structure that our government has instituted for overseeing the functioning of our DTIB vis-à-vis the position in those countries.

Parliamentary Control

As regards (a), while in other industrialized countries, with elected governments, eg France, the USA and the UK, both the achievements and the shortcomings in making state-of-the-art weapon systems of their own are constantly kept in public view, thanks to the functioning of the built-in systems for the exercising of checks and balances by respective Parliaments and Legislatures, in our case the absence of any kind of informed debate by our elected representatives makes for an all-pervasive apathy towards the issue of self-reliance in weapons and equipment. The result: A total lack of accountability and an unabated flow of all types of imported weapons of the conventional kind since the day of our independence and the failure, even, to take note of the disconnect between the two utterly-dissimilar experiences of our country, namely our DTIB's success in developing deterrent weapons and its failure in making conventional ones, let alone instituting measures for correcting the position.

Management Structure

As regards (b) above, ie the management structure of our DTIB, while all countries have an integrated management for development-cum-manufacture of weapon systems our government has to this day failed to institute an integrated management system for our DTIB. While several superficial actions have been taken by our government from time to time in the form of instituting studies by individuals and committees, featuring, invariably, retired bureaucrats without the required expertise, for finding out what needed to be done to overcome the problem of our DTIB's singular failure to undertake successfully the development-cum-manufacture of our own tactical (ie not strategic) weapon systems nothing of substance has emerged. The net result:

We have a dismal record in the making of our own weapons of the conventional kind, eg the LCA and the MBT. Having researched and written on this subject for many years now, including a book ('Military Technology & Defence Industrialisation: The Indian Experience'), I will try, in this chapter, to briefly explain why none of the half-hearted measures, taken by successive governments of our country, to make amends has worked. And I will argue that nothing short of an overhaul of the management structure of the Indian DTIB will address adequately the problem of our country's inability to achieve a reasonable degree of self-reliance in conventional weapons.

While the most outstanding success of our government's policy-making post-independence was in prioritizing the build-up of our industrial base through the promotion of scientific education and research, a success that owes its origin largely to Prime Minister Nehru's breath-taking vision, the most debilitating feature of that policy-implementation was its failure to accord due recognition to the need for building our country's national security infrastructure in a manner that befitted a newly-independent country in order that our newly-independent country achieved a reasonable level of self-reliance in weapons and equipment without loss of time. That was, probably, the most unfortunate failure, also, of the same Prime Minister, the esteemed Jawaharlal Nehru, the leader of a newly-liberated nation which, although non-aligned, had endured unrelenting threat to its security and sovereignty from its immediate neighbourhood from the day of its inception and had needed a strong and self-reliant military from the very beginning of our Independence. And, that failure on our Prime Minister's part had manifested itself in several forms but, primarily, in his failure (a) to replace the former colonial system of governance in relation to defence by a system of higher defence management that befits a sovereign nation and that, in fact, exists in every independent nation of the world, (b) to make adequate investments in the development of military technology on a fast track with a view to attaining the required degree of self-reliance in weapons and equipment on priority, as opposed to perpetuating the practice of meeting our military's requirements exclusively by the import of arms and (c) by instituting that system of management for weapon development-cum-manufacture, which, alone, ensures an unified control over the processes of developing and manufacturing weapons, a system which, also, exists in every nation which makes arms for its own military and for export. The result: Both our military's war-fighting capability post-Independence and the build-up of self-reliance in weapons and equipment that buttresses war-fighting had been most adversely affected and remains so, even, today.

Keeping the development of military technology as our the subject of discussion, however, it needs to be emphasized that the failure to institute of an appropriately-unified management structure for our country's defence technology and industrial base has been the one all-encompassing reason why, even, after 1971-72 – when our third Prime Minister, IndiraGandhi, had both signaled a change in policy, as evident from the commencement of allocation of funds for the development of our military technology, on the one hand, and the institution of an empowered head of our DRDO through elevation of the position of the SA-cum-DG DRDO to the level of a Secretary to government, on the other – our country could not achieve a reasonable degree of self-reliance in weapons and equipment, far less generate revenue for our country by export of arms. The fact that, even, after a lapse of another four decades from that period our country has been far from being self-reliant, except for the guided missiles and the deterrent or strategic weapon, is a testimony to the existence of that all-encompassing reason.

A DTIB, by definition, consists of three components, namely the infrastructure for Development, for Manufacture and for Maintenance. While the infrastructure for Maintenance belongs to the realm of the military and is, therefore, outside the scope of our present discussion it is the other two components of our DTIB, which we need to examine in relation to our continuing failure to develop successfully our own weapons and equipment of the conventional kind, eg the MBT and the LCA.

Pre-independence the management of both the Ordnance Factories (OFs), of which there were only a few, and the Technical Development Establishments (TDEs) that were attached to those Ordnance Factories for the primary purpose of overseeing inspection but, also, to undertake, if notionally, the so-called incremental development activities in relation to the military's armaments in production, had vested in the British Indian Army's Commander-in-Chief (C in C), ie the Army Headquarters India. As known, the C-in-C India reported directly to the Chief of the Imperial General Staff (CIGS) in London, the supreme commander of all Armies of the British Empire, who had his office in the British MOD in Whitehall, London. Therefore, in colonial India the C-in-C, India, alone, was responsible for all things military in the Indian colony, including the defence of India's borders, and not to the Viceroy of India. Till 1947, the Army Headquarters, India, had functioned, therefore, as an extension of the headquarters of the CIGS in London, and, therefore, had formed an integral part the MOD of the government in Great Britain. Till 15 August, 1947, therefore, the Viceroy and his Executive Council had no jurisdiction over matters pertaining to either the British Indian Army or the defence of the borders of colonial India. And, since the

C-in-C India had, understandably, not been empowered to undertake in India any activities, even, remotely resembling the ab-initio development of new weapons for the military in India, the few TDEs and Ordnance Factories, which had existed in colonial India, had been engaged only in what, in effect, is the 'licensed' production of weapons and equipment on the basis of drawings and specifications that were supplied by the British MOD. In short, each of those few items of armament, which were under production in the Ordnance Factories in India till 1947, had already been developed successfully in the UK earlier and was in free-flow production in the Royal Ordnance Factories in Great Britain.

It is not surprising to learn, therefore, that at the dawn of our independence there was not, even, a semblance, in our newly independent country, of the kind of DTIB that had existed for a century or more in industrially developed countries, including Great Britain itself, let alone any knowledge of their DTIB's management structure, namely a system of integrated management for development-cum-manufacture which had made it possible for the DTIBs of industrially developed nations to successfully develop military technology and manufacture weapon systems of their own. And, therefore, on attaining independence our government had neither inherited nor had seen any evidence on the ground of the kind of DTIB management organization that had existed in ALL industrially-developed and arms-producing countries for many decades, including Great Britain itself. Tragically, also, none of our leaders of that era, highly-educated freedom-fighters all, who had, in August 1947, assumed the responsibility to govern our country, had cared, even, to learn from the experience of the industrialized countries of the world how to manage successfully our own DTIB with a view to ensuring success in making indigenous weapons and, thereby, in the attainment of a reasonable degree of self-reliance in weapons and equipment. Therefore, our Prime Minister, Jawaharlal Nehru, and his government had failed to set up of an integrated management system for weapons development-cum-manufacture.

And, that failure had resulted, as known, in our DTIB functioning in a divided manner under the supervision of two independent authorities, one for Development and another for Manufacture but both reporting to the country's Defence Minister. While the DRDO, headed by its own DG cum Secretary (Def R & D), presides over the Development function, a Secretary (Def Prod & Supply), a senior administrator, also sitting in the MOD and reporting to our Defence Minister, controls the Manufacture function, in isolation of the Development function, by 'supervising' the work of the Chairman, Ordnance Factories Board, on the one hand, and the CMDs of a number of DPSUs, on the other.

Apparently, our first Prime Minister and the other founding fathers had overlooked one fundamental truth: The reason why those industrially developed countries which, also, have viable military industrial complexes had achieved success in both the civil-sector industry and their arms production enterprises is that those countries have in place the same type of management structure in both their civil-use industries and their military industrial complexes, namely an integrated management for overseeing both the development of new products and the manufacture of such products. As stated, our successive governments have utterly failed to do so and adopted a non-integrated management structure for the development-cum-manufacture of armaments. And, that despite the fact that successive governments had been aware of the fact that an integrated management system exists in each of our private-sector industries which develop their own products and undertake the manufacture of those products.

It is for this reason that the Indian experience in the case of the development of our own weapons has uniformly been dismal. In our case, the design and development work for developing a prototype MINUS the manufacture of the prototypes – at all stages of the development phase – are conducted by DRDO laboratories under the control of the SA-cum-DG DRDO-cum-Secretary (Def R & D), who is a professional Scientist-Engineer with adequate knowledge of and experience in technology development and management. But, the making of the prototypes themselves, during the development phase, as well as the establishment of bulk production remain the responsibility, at the highest level of 'management', of a senior official of our government's administrative service, who bears no accountability as regards the success or failure of the development-cum-manufacture of indigenous weapons, namely the Secretary (Def Prod & Supplies) or, at one level below that, of the Chairman, Ordnance Factories Board, or the CMD of the concerned DPSU, as applicable, none of which two senior officials remains, once again, accountable for the success or failure of the development-cum-manufacture of our own (ie indigenous) weapon systems.

And, because of that absence of an integrated management, in our MOD, for controlling the functioning of our DTIB, a management system which is geared for overseeing – and accountable for the success or otherwise of – both the Development and the Manufacture wings of our DTIB, the running of every major-weapon development programme of our country, eg the MBT, the LCA etc, called frequently for co-ordination, as regards time-bound activities, between the concerned DRDO laboratories (which, as already mentioned, cannot undertake prototype manufacture on their own but depend entirely on the concerned Ordnance Factories or DPSUs for that task) and the corresponding Ordnance Factories or DPSUs, which, alone, as mentioned, are equipped with the machines and the manpower, ie the process-expertise, that are required for manufacturing the prototypes. It is this situation, therefore, namely the making of compromises on the time-frames for completion of design-tasks at every stage of the evolution of the design and development of the prototypes, that results often in the whole project being delayed, even though that progress of the project had been overseen by a duly-constituted steering committee, with the DRDO and the concerned Ordnance Factory/DPSU(s) represented on that committee.

Not so strangely, therefore, such indigenous weapon development programmes would often call for interventions by the Scientific Advisor, at one end, and the Secretary, Defence Production and Supplies, on the other. That is so, because there is an inherent conflict of priorities between the uninterrupted production of an existing item or component by the concerned OF or the DPSU, whose primary task, even, today remains the production of imported weapons under a foreign manufacturer's license, and the making of prototypes of indigenously designed components and subsystems for a DRDO laboratory on a fast-track. And it occurs, inevitably, in each and every case of the development-cum-manufacture of indigenous weapon systems. It goes without saying, therefore, that such an arrangement – meaning, the present system of non-integrated DTIB management for the development-cum-manufacture process – proves eminently unsuitable for running any weapon development programme of our country on a pre-designed time-schedule.

With the recent change in the ruling-party-composition of our central government, post-General Election 2014, there are indications that a change in our government's thinking on the opening of doors of our military-industrial complex to the private sector of India or, even, to public-private collaboration to allow for the welcoming of technological expertise of reputed manufacturers of advanced weapon systems in some of the industrially developed countries. However, although such a change in policy, if it is actually implemented by our new government, will not be out of place and will, in fact, prove beneficial, as evident from the fact that most of the industrially developed countries of the world including, lately, even, France had adopted the US practice of entrusting arms manufacture to reputed corporations in the private sector, it would be advisable in our case, for a number of important reasons, to be selective and proceed with caution. That will ensure that the entire business of developing and manufacturing new weapons is not transferred to the private sector, in its entirety, in the foreseeable future. One of the important reasons why it would neither be feasible nor advisable for us to transfer the whole responsibility pertaining to weapon systems development and manufacture to our private sector is that in our case the entire infrastructure and expertise for the development of weapon systems, both in terms of the engineering hardware and in terms of the high explosives contents, have been built and acquired by and belong to our government only and ought to be fully made use of in the foreseeable future, a fact that must be taken into account while admitting our private sector into arms manufacture.

One consequence of our country changing its policy in future and admitting the private sector into arms manufacture will be that a spirit of competition will ensue, and our government-owned production units' inability to match the efficiency of the private sector will highlight the fact that the private sector, unlike our government, undertakes both development and manufacture of weapon systems under an integrated management. And, that will make it evident that the management structure of our country's DTIB needed to be changed by our government without loss of time to allow the integration of arms development management with arms manufacture management. Incidentally, both Russia and China which, unlike the industrially developed countries of the west, eg the USA and France, have not allowed privately owned corporations to undertake arms manufacture, also, develop and manufacture their weapon systems under an integrated management structure, because each of their State-owned weapon development-cum-manufacturing enterprises has an integrated management board. In short, India alone now lives with its problem of un-integrated management for development-cum-manufacture of weapon systems, except for two cases, namely the development-cum-manufacture of our guided missile and its warheads including the deterrent warhead.

The Contrast Between Success In Strategic Weapons and Our Experience With The Conventional Systems: The Role of Integrated Management

Though it may not be widely known, even, now that, unlike in the case of our conventional weapon systems development programmes, eg the MBT and the LCA, we had, while developing our guided missiles and our deterrent warheads, managed to scrupulously adhere to the principle of an integrated management for Development-cum-Manufacture. But, even in those two cases, ie the nuclear warhead and the guided missile, where our country had ensured that the same management and personnel had undertaken the supervision of work during both the development and the bulk manufacture phases, we had achieved success by taking two different routes in order to ensure that an integrated management for development-cum-manufacture oversees both the development and the manufacture functions. Whereas in the case of our strategic warhead we had, from all indications, achieved that condition by ensuring that we follow the same practice which had been followed by all five of the 'original' nuclear-weapon nations of the world, namely that the same management and personnel undertake both the development of the prototype and, later, the manufacture of that product in bulk, that has not been the case in our guided missiles development, because of the lack, even, now, of an integrated management structure that would ensure that both the development and, later, the manufacture functions would be undertaken under the same management, an inadequacy that had, however, been overcome, thanks to late by Dr Abdul Kalam, the leader of the guided missiles programme, through the making of an innovation, namely the creation of an environment of virtual integration of management for both the development and manufacture functions.

As in the case of the guided missiles, the success in the case of our nuclear warheads had, also, come about after years of painstaking work by our scientists, which had followed the spectacular success, as known, of their earlier research work that, as known, had culminated in the demonstration of a peaceful nuclear explosion (PNE) by our country in 1974 under the leadership of our then Prime Minister, Mrs Indira Gandhi. And, it goes without saying that the contributory factor for that success had, also, been the same as the one which had earlier made the nuclear weapon projects of the USA and the other four nuclear-nations a success. In short, as far as one can tell, the same combination of the scientific-leadership and the development work process that had resulted, finally, in the success of the development of our first prototype nuclear-warhead had, thereafter, been made use of by our government for the so-called manufacture of that warhead.

Military Technology and Governance: The Case of India

As mentioned, the failure of our founding fathers and, especially, of our first Prime Minister in taking cognizance of the fact that the defence and national security infrastructure management system that we had inherited from our British rulers had been built by the British only to suit colonial India, ie to perpetuate the colonial rule and was, therefore, most inappropriate for an independent nation had resulted in our government's failure to instantly reject that set-up and to replace it by one that befitted an independent nation. And, that failure had done an incalculable damage to a non-aligned country like ours, surrounded, as we were and are, by two of the most hostile nations of the world.

While much had since then been justifiably said by some of our international security studies (ISS) analysts about two aspects of that failure on the part of first Prime Minister, namely the one that impacted directly on our military's war-fighting capability, ie the non-integration of our Army/Navy/Air Force's command structure into one entity for the purpose of conducting war-fighting under a joint command and the deliberate distancing of our Army/Navy/Air Force Headquarters from the core of our MOD's decision-making apparatus, most of those analysts had failed to draw our attention to yet another, equally-important, aspect of our country's shortcoming in governance. And, that was the inability of independent India's successive governments to achieve, even, a semblance of self-reliance in conventional weapons and equipment for war-fighting. That failure which ought to have caused the greatest of concerns to each one of our succeeding Prime Ministers and ought to have resulted in an immediate overhaul of our DTIB's management structure had, curiously, not done so.

As known, like the DTIBs of all industrially developed countries, ours, too, consists of three components, namely

(a) the defence production units comprising our ordnance factories (OFs) and defence public sector units (DPSUs), which together constitute the Manufacture wing of our DTIB,
(b) the laboratories and R & D establishments of the DRDO which are engaged in the development of both military technology and the hardware and the software of weapon systems to meet our military's operational requirements, ie the Development wing of the DTIB, and
(c) the weapon repair and maintenance organizations of our Army/Navy/Air force, which represent our DTIB's Maintenance wing. It is, therefore, the combined effort of the (a) and (b) wings of our DTIB that is tasked with the responsibility for bringing about national self-reliance in weapons and equipment.

Therefore, the occurrence and the persistence of our country's failure to achieve, even, a modicum of self-reliance in conventional weapon systems, eg the combat aircraft and the armoured fighting vehicles, despite the large-sized investments, made by our country in the build-up of our military-industrial complex, can only be explained by the fact that our higher defence management structure and, especially, the management system of our DTIB, which is so unlike those of the industrially developed and the not-so-developed countries, needs to be put right without delay.

As known, every equipment manufacturer in the industrially-developed world – be it a company which develops and manufactures power-generation equipment, like the General Electric of the USA, or a company that develops and produces advanced-weapon systems for its own country's military, eg the Aerospatialle of France and the General Dynamics of the USA, regards the development any kind of new equipment (or chemicals or materials or metals, for that matter) and its bulk production as one integral function which can only be successfully discharged by one integrated management, ie the CEO or the Board of Directors of that company or corporation. Also, as evident from the working of companies or corporations manufacturing weapon systems, this is true irrespective of whether the manufacturer is a government-owned company, as in Russia, China and, partly, France, or an unalloyed privately-owned corporation, as in the USA, Sweden, and, increasingly, France.

In our case, however, ie in the case of our indigenously developed, 'conventional' weapon-systems, eg the MBT and the LCA, there are two separate organizations for Development and Manufacture, each with its own equivalent of a CEO (and a Board of Directors, as applicable). And, those two organizations share responsibility for undertaking the development-cum-manufacture of our indigenously developed weapon systems. Whereas our MOD's SA, ie the Secretary (Defence R & D)-cum-DG-DRDO, who has full control over only the DRDO laboratories and their functioning, bears full responsibility for 'developing' a new weapon system he has no control over our country's weapon systems manufacturing organisations and, therefore, on the appropriately equipped production centres and, therefore, the facilities for making the prototypes, or for solving the problems connected with the transfer of technology, that often come in the way of the establishment of bulk production of a newly developed system. That is because the control over the Manufacture of weapons and equipment is exercised by a senior official of our administrative service, namely the Secretary (Defence Production & Supplies) of the MOD, who exercises this control by 'overseeing' the work of both the Chairman of our Ordnance Factories Board (OFB) and the CMDs/Boards of Directors of our DPSUs, one of which two types of manufacturing organizations in our country bears the responsibility for the bulk production of our indigenously-developed weapon systems. As already mentioned, this kind of divided management structure of our country's DTIB, which is utterly at variance with the kind of integrated DTIB management system that prevails in every industrially developed country including Great Britain itself, prevails, even, to this day only in our country's DTIB, ie only in the arms industry of our country. In the other sector of our country's industrial world, however, namely the non-defence industry, ie in the companies which both develop and manufacture non-defence items and market those goods, whether those items are meant for public consumption, eg consumer electronics, or utilized for making other machines, eg heavy engineering equipment, sets up the same kind of integrated management for both Development and Manufacture as prevails in both the defence and non-defence sectors of the industrially developed countries of the world.

And, the reason why the management structure of our country's DTIB is so inappropriate – and so unlike that of the DTIBs of all of the other industrially developed countries which, also, undertake the development of weapon systems and their manufacture and market those – is not far to seek, either. Our political leaders, while taking over the responsibility for governance of our newly independent nation in 1947, had neither possessed the required foresight as regards national security nor been willing to comprehend the higher defence management system of an independent nation which is, also, industrially developed. Nor had they felt the necessity, in 1947 or, even, , also,industry, including a weapon manufacturer, of an independent and industrially developed nation followed. It is that unfortunate circumstance which had made the leaders of our newly independent country and its government blind to the fact that in all industrially developed countries which, also, undertake the manufacture of arms and equipment follow the same management practice for both the defence and non-defence industry, namely an integrated management system, with one individual or one board of directors remaining accountable, undertakes both the development of a new weapon and its manufacture. In other words, although it should have been noted by our first Prime Minister that the British themselves had, in their own country, instituted the same type of integrated DTIB management structure that had prevailed in other industrially developed countries of the world, the newly formed government of our country had not opted to do so. They had, instead, decided to only tinker with the higher defence management structure that our newly-independent country, ie its newly-formed government, had inherited from the British rulers during the transfer of power. In short, it was, probably, more by default than by design that our political leadership had put into place an altogether inappropriate management structure for our DTIB.

It goes without saying that in colonial India no organization for indigenous development of weapons or equipment for the British Indian Army/Navy/Air Force had existed. And, only a handful of items of ordnance and ammunition of British design and origin, most of those close to being obsolescent, had been in production in the few Indian ordnance factories that had been built by the British in India for that purpose. It will, also, be of interest to note that during the British rule it was the British Commander-in-Chief (C-in-C) of the British Indian Army who had wielded the administrative and functional control on those OFs from his (ie the British Indian Army's) Headquarters in New Delhi. Also, as known, the C-in-C, India, had, during the British rule, reported directly to the Chief of the Imperial General Staff (CIGS), one of the highest-level functionaries, then, of the British government, and the headquarters of the CIGS were an integral part of the British MOD in the White Hall in London. Therefore, our political leadership post-Independence had, in fact, had an ideal opportunity to study the integrated DTIB management system that had prevailed in each of the industrially developed countries, including Great Britain itself, and to put into place in our newly-independent country's newly-formed MOD the same type of integrated management system for both developing our own weapons and, later, manufacturing those indigenously developed weapons and equipment for both supplying those to our own Army/Navy/Air Force and exporting those to other, friendly nations. However, as mentioned, our leaders had defaulted on this and opted for an altogether inappropriate DTIB management structure which prevails to this day and has prevented our country from attaining self-reliance in conventional weapons and equipment.

A Virtual Integration of DTIB Management and Success In Guided Missiles Programme

As stated earlier, despite our government's failure to integrate our DTIB management structure two of our weapon development programmes, namely the IGMDP and the nuclear warhead, have met with success. As, also, stated earlier, the reason for that apparently-contra phenomenon is the fact that only in those two cases of indigenous weapon development it has been possible for our country to overcome the management-related hurdles that have so far prevented the development-cum-manufacture programmes of the other weapon systems development programmes, eg the MBT and the LCA, to attain the same kind of success. However, the circumstances associated with those two cases, ie our guided missiles and our deterrent warheads, have been different. Whereas the success of our deterrent warhead programme has been achieved in a straightforward manner, ie by ensuring that both the development of the prototype nuclear warhead and, later, the production of that item, albeit in small quantities, had been undertaken under a truly integrated management, that has not been the case in the guided missiles programme.

That is because, unlike the deterrent warhead development programme, the development of guided missiles had involved, in a more substantive manner, overcoming the same type of problem that had hobbled the other development programmes, eg the MBT and the LCA, namely the necessity for depending on an organization outside the DRDO for making prototypes, at ordnance factories and DPSUs which, as known, are controlled by the Dept of Defence Production. In short, in the case of the IGMDP the problem of an un-integrated management system could not be done away with in the manner it was done in the case of our nuclear warhead. However, the problem was solved by taking recourse to creating a virtual integration of development management with manufacture management for only a specific purpose, the guided missiles related work, thanks to the genius of Dr Abdul Kalam, the leader of the IGMDP. In short, the integration of managements for Development and Manufacture had been brought about in those two cases, either in actuality, as in the case of our strategic warhead, or in a virtual mode, as in the case of our guided missiles.

In short, while the success of our strategic warhead programme owes its origin to the actual presence of an integrated management during both the Development and Manufacture phases, in the case of our guided missiles programme it had been ensured that the development related work which had been undertaken at the site of the bulk production units, eg the fabrication of prototypes of components, subsystems and assembled units, at various stages of the development work as well as the work related to transfer-of-technology-cum-establishment of bulk manufacture, which, necessarily took place at the end of the development phase, had been undertaken jointly by development scientists and production engineers under the umbrella of a virtually integrated management. And, as stated, that virtual integration of management could only be achieved in this case because of the role that Dr Kalam had played at every stage of the execution of the guided missiles programme. And, as stated, it was only his genius that could achieve what had amounted to a virtual integration of the management of development-cum-manufacture of each of the five types of guided missiles of the IGMDP, and he had done that by ensuring that, in essence, the services of the same kind of assembly of scientists, supervisory personnel and the process/machines, which were employed during the development phase, were, also, utilized, effectively, during both the prototype-manufacture stage and the establishment of bulk production, thus making doubly sure that our country's 'classical' non-integration of management, that has adversly affected the successful development of our other indigenous weapons, eg the MBT and the LCA, do not occur in this case. In short, the difficulties that are, continually faced by our scientists in the making of the prototypes as expeditiously as the project schedule demanded and the difficulties and the delays that our country experiences in establishing bulk production of an indigenously developed weapon, thanks to the absence in our country's DTIB of an integrated management for development-cum-manufacture, were made irrelevant in the case of our guided missiles programme. It would, therefore, be interesting to inquire why it has been possible to do so ONLY in those two cases, ie the strategic warhead and the guided missiles programme and not in the other cases, eg the MBT and the LCA.

First, as regards the development of our strategic warheads, which had preceded the development of our guided missiles, our country had, of necessity, adopted the same kind of integrated development-cum-manufacture process as had been followed the world over, ie in all five nuclear-weapon nations which had done this work long before we had done it. In other words, in this case we had done away with the role that the Dept of Defence Production and Supplies play in the cases of conventional weapons, eg the MBT and the LCA, by making sure that both the Developer and the bulk Manufacturer reported to the same authority, ie the integrated Management.

Second, in the case of our IGMDP, ie our guided missiles programme, our country has been exceptionally fortunate in getting to appoint an exceptional technology manager as the leader of the programme, namely Dr Abdul Kalam. It was the unique mixture of his unusual personality traits, his foresight, his organizational skills and his ability to both work unceasingly and 'manage' people, all of which are his assets and his alone – that had made it possible for the DRDO to get our government to specially sanction, for the very first time, a number of innovative organizational and financial measures for the IGMDP, largely devised by Dr Kalam, and it is that factor that had facilitated the overcoming by the IGMDP of almost all of the proverbial problems that the non-integration of our DTIB management structure has spawned. It was precisely the institution of those innovative measures, coupled with the style of leadership that was the hallmark of Dr Kalam's personality, that had resulted in the creation of a virtual integration of our DTIB management structure in the case of the IGMDP. In short, only in the case of the IGMDP including the Agni long-range ballistic missiles the DRDO had been able to bring about a set of organizational innovations that had ensured both the unhindered development of all of our guided missiles including the expeditious making of the prototypes of components and subsystems of all kinds by all of the designated component-developers-cum-manufacturers in both the public and the private sector and the consequent smooth transition of the Development phase into the Manufacture phase.

Unlike conventional weapon development programmes, eg the MBT and the LCA, the IGMDP had, for its smooth functioning, obtained the sanction of our government for instituting an unique three-tier programme management structure that had ensured the most-expeditious removal of all obstacles that had traditionally prevented a complex indigenous weapon development programme from making progress in the expected manner. That is because the apex body of the IGMDP's management structure, which had the Director DRDL (ie the Leader of the IGMDP, Dr Kalam) as its Secretary and his 'superior', the SA cum Secretary (Defence R & D), as its Chairman, had been given full freedom by our government at its highest level then (ie the Cabinet Committee for Political Affairs or the CCPA of those times) to directly contact the Secretary of any Department or Ministry, concerned with the progress of the IGMDP, eg the Department of Defence and the Dept of Defence Production & Supplies of our MOD, the Ministry of Finance, the Chiefs of the three Services etc, in the event a lower-level functionary of any one of those Departments or Ministries had proved ineffective in removing any bottleneck in an expeditious manner. It was primarily for this reason, coupled with the reason that the leader of the IGMDP, Dr Kalam, had been most informed and energetic in pursuing his task throughout the duration of his term as the Director of the DRDL the IGMDP had succeeded in developing and then establishing the manufacture of four types of guided missiles of our own design in the most reasonable time-frame.

In short, in the case of the IGMDP Dr Kalam had been able to overcome all of the problems that no other conventional-weapon development prgrommes of our country could surmount. And, since the IGMDP has had necessarily to use the services of a very large number of our OFs and DPSUs, both of which enterprises belong to a separate entity, namely the Dept of Defence Production, and, therefore, are controlled, at the highest level of management, by the Secretary (Def Production & Supplies) of the MOD, that outcome had surprised everyone connected with any one of the five projects of the IGMDP then. More so, because the scientists working for each of those five projects, including the Agni project, had had necessarily to deal with both the design and the making of a host of prototypes of all kinds, eg components, subsystems and, even complete systems (eg the solid rocket-ramjet engine), and the making of each of those prototypes of a component or a subsystem had involved the taking of service of an OF or a DPSU. Incidentally, a guided missile, typically, has a wide variety of electrical, mechanical, electronic, electro-mechanical and electro-chemical (eg a battery) items, each of which had, in the case of the IGMDP, to be designed and developed – through the process of prototype-making and testing – by either a DRDO laboratory or the scientists of another institution in the public sector (eg an IIT, the BEL, the HAL, etc) or by the private (eg the L & T). But, as known, despite the enormity or that task, especially, the contingency of having to deal with likely slippages, that had imperiled the success of other weapon development projects of our country for decades, those imponderables had not stalled the progress of the IGMDP. That is to say that, even, in the face of the existence of our country's non-integrated DTIB-management system, the projects of the IGMDP had made spectacular progress. And, all of that success had come about only because of the genius of Dr Abdul Kalam, whose capacity for organizational innovation and whose style of functioning had succeeded in creating a virtual integration of our country's DTIB's management system in the case of the projects of the IGMDP.

In this connection I ought mention one organizational innovation that Dr Kalam, as the leader of the IGMDP, had brought forth in support of the objective of creating a virtual integration of the management system of our DTIB: He had engineered the triggering of a major expansion of one of our country's hitherto-less-known DPSUs, namely a late-entry, small-size DPSU which was set up by our government, in the mid-nineteen sixties, probably, for the licensed manufacture of only one type of guided missile, at that juncture, namely an ATM of French origin but which had, nearly three decades later, been given a much bigger task, namely that of manufacturing five types of indigenous guided missiles that were developed under the IGMDP.

That IGMDP-induced organizational innovation, namely the re-equipping and the expansion of that erstwhile-small-size DPSU, had, as known, resulted, at that point of time, into that DPSU growing into a much bigger and better-equipped DPSU such that it could, thereafter, take on the production, simultaneously, of both a number of types and a much larger quantity of indigenous guided missiles that were being developed then under the IGMDP. Incidentally, that DPSU, the Bharat Dynamics Ltd (BDL), although administratively 'controlled' by the Dept of Defence Production & Supplies of our MOD, in all probability, was, however, effectively 'functionally-controlled' and 'supervised' by the Scientific Adviser-cum-Secretary (Defence R & D), because he had, right fron its inception, been the Chairman of the Board of Directors of that DPSU. That practice, so unlike what prevailed in other DPSUs, eg the HAL, the BEL etc, where either the Secretary (Defence Production & Supplies) himself or, as in most cases, a nominee, deputed by him, chairs the Board of Directors, was very unique, indeed, in its functional nature. And, Dr Kalam, with his foresight, had fully made use of that uniquely advantageous situation to achieve his objective, namely to get our government, ie the Dept of Def Production & Supplies of our MOD, to expand manifold and further empower that DPSU, ie the BDL. That was one initiative that had been, very rightly, fully seized by Dr Kalam at both a critical juncture of the progress of work of the projects of the IGMDP and without any loss of time. And that action had, by itself and in a very large measure, helped him achieve what he had badly wanted to achieve then as the leader of the IGMDP, in order that an environment of virtual integration of development management with manufacture management is created with respect to the projects of the IGMDP, in particular.

There are a host of other organizational innovations, conceived and successfully engineered by Dr Kalam, which have made the IGMDP a success. For instance, his resolve to get our government to agree to establish, in and around the DRDL, a cluster of other laboratories and quasi-laboratories, each dedicated to the development of a specific technology and/or prototype-production of components that embodied that technology, eg the development and prototype-manufacture of a special kind of microelectronic chip for a specific missile-guidance system, a sophisticated subsystem of a guided missile, had made it possible to build and put into use those government-owned high-technology laboratories in and around the DRDL , an achievement that had ensured that the work of the IGMDP could be undertaken in the environment of a virtually-integrated development-cum-manufacture management. And, that particular achievement of Dr Kalam, namely the conceiving and bringing to fruition that cluster of high-technology, development-cum-manufacturing facilities, fully owned by our government and dedicated to the making of some of the most sophisticated components of a variety of guided missiles, had contributed very substantially to the success of the IGMDP. It had enabled the IGMDP projects to make progress in an environment of a virtually integrated management system for the development-cum-manufacture of the indigenous missiles by enabling it to avoid all of the pitfalls of our DTIB's inherently dysfunctional management structure, which promote failures.

Dr Kalam's contribution to the success of our guided missile programme, therefore, has been phenomenal, to say the least. And, since he had continued to work for the DRDO well after his leaving the DRDL, ie by moving from the DRDL to take over the job of the Scientific Advisor-cum-Secretary (Def R &D) and, later, by assuming the position of the Scientific Advisor to our Prime Minister, his over-a-decade-long presence in our government's military technology enterprise had largely contributed to the continuation of the success in our guided missiles programme, as evident from the successes of our shorter-range and longer-range 'Agni' missiles and the development of many a variant of our Akash and our Trishul missiles and, even, the success of the sea-launched cruise missile through an Indo-Russian collaborative process and the undertaking of a co-development project.

However, there are a few early but clear signs now that the gains of the previous era could be frittered away, slowly but inevitably, due to the inability of the recent

DRDO-leadership to win the confidence of the present government. Since, however, the need for making serious investments in the attainment of self-reliance in weapons and equipment as well as the need for attaining early success in our weapon-development programmes continue to be real and urgent, the integrity and the honesty of purpose, that distinguish the present Prime Minister and the Defence Minister our new government, will likely ensure that the new incumbents to the posts of the SA and the DG DRDO-cum-Secretary (Defence R & D) would duly receive our government's support and encouragement in the discharge of their tasks. However, despite the change in the alignment of political leadership and the emergence of an honest leader as our Prime Minister there is no indication whatsoever if our country's higher defence management structure will be reshaped by the new government and our DTIB's dysfunctional management structure will be replaced by an integrated management system in the foreseeable future.

A few words about our MOD's rehashed procurement executive, which was put in place about two years back, will be in order. The so-called new system for procuring weapons and equipment for our Army/Navy/Air Force had been devised, primarily, by our civilian bureaucracy, presumably, after a token consultation with the three chiefs of our Army/Navy/Air Force and promulgated with considerable fanfare and publicity, as known. On the face of it, the reorganized system for the acquisition and procurement of weapons and equipment for our military

(a) seems logical, if only an exact copy of the one which all developed countries have adopted since long,
(b) satisfies our MOD's real decision-makers which, as known, are none other than the seniors of our country's administrative service, who, alone, manage the procurement wing of our MOD's Dept of Defence in association with the MOD's Department of Defence

Production and Supplies, which is, also, manned by the same administrative service, and

(c) enjoins on the DRDO to cede some grounds to our military's long-standing demand that the DRDO would henceforth confine its activities to ontrolling only two areas, namely (1) the development of a selected number high technologies and (2) the development-cum-manufacture of only those weapon systems which incorporate high technology, leaving the task of the development of all other weapon systems, eg combat aircraft, guided missiles, armoured vehicles etc to other players, namely our OFs, our DPSUs and our private sector companies.

In short, the policy rehash, a few years back, for re-defining the functions of our procurement executive, has undertaken a revolutionary tinkering, on paper, with the charter and the management-structure of our DRDO but has singularly failed to grasp the real problem, namely the absence, in our DTIB, of an integrated management system for managing the process of development-cum-manufacture of indigenous weapons under an unified authority. Incidentally, the fact that the lapses, which had resulted in our late-delivered LCA and our much-delayed MBT, were inevitable under the prevailing circumstances have never figured in the reports of the so-called expert-committees, each of which had, almost inevitably, only recommended some tinkering with procedures and/or institution of some irrelevant changes in the functioning of the DRDO but remained entirely comfortable with the position that the responsibilities for the Development and the Manufacture functions of our DTIB are vested in two independent authorities, (a) namely a senior scientist who, as the DG DRDO-cum-Secretary Def R & D, remains accountable for the success of the Development function and a generalist administrator who, as the Secretary (Defence Production & Supplies), who 'manages' the Manufacture of weapons by exercising his prerogative of bossing over the Ordnance Factories Board and the Chairmen/CEOs of our DPSUs. And, that untenable system of managing the making of our own weapon systems still prevails in our country only because of one reason: The power of the vested interests, lurking within our system of governance, continues to ensure that a succession of our political masters do not see the truth that the process of development-cum-manufacture of indigenous weapon systems, like that of any other sophisticated product of a manufacturing industry, ought to be managed by one unified management, ie one technocrat CEO or one Board of Directors, who or which remained accountable to one Minister of the cabinet.

Chapter 10

Success Despite Dysfunctional Defence Production Management: Achieving The Unachievable a Legacy of Scientist Leader Abdul Kalam

Our success in guided missiles development had come about due as much to the work of our missile scientists since the early nineteen seventies, when our government had, for the very first time since Independence, abandoned its earlier policy of denial of resources and commenced investing in military technology, as to the quality of the leadership that had been provided by Dr Abdul Kalam, almost a decade later, in making our guided missiles programme a spectacular success.

However, although I had met Dr Kalam, for the first time, a decade prior to his joining the DRDO, ie during my first visit to the research centre of the ISRO (ie the SSTC, later renamed the VSSC, as a member of the first-ever four-member DRDO-delegation to the ISRO in 1971-72, it was only when Dr Kalam had joined the DRDL, a decade later, that I had had the opportunity to get to work with him as my senior colleague on the guided missiles programme and, thereby, to see him from close quarters both as a scientist and as an individual. By then I had moved from the DRDL to the Rockets & Missiles Directorate and been engaged in preparing the DRDO proposal for the sanctioning of the IGMDP in consultation with both our own laboratories and their associates including other stake-holders in and outside the DRDO.

Therefore, as soon as Dr Kalam had joined the DRDL as its Director I had the privilege for the next few months – and a rare privilege, indeed – of having to meet up with Dr Kalam, almost on a daily basis, while putting the finishing touches on the DRDO proposal for the launching the IGMDP. And, since that process had gone on for two or three months and had ended only on the day we had, finally, obtained our government's sanction for the IGMDP my work-relationship with Dr Kalam had been both intense and highly satisfying during that period. All the more, in fact, because we had to work really hard for ensuring that all of the requirements, both in terms of the financial allocations for each of the five projects and in respect of the method of the execution of those five projects through the institution of a 3-tier management structure, are unequivocally sanctioned by the relevant cabinet committee under the chairmanship of the then Prime Minister, the late Indira Gandhi, and spelt out un-ambiguously in the government letter.

It is not known by most analysts who have written on the subject but ought to be mentioned, once again, that (a) it was only Dr Kalam who had clearly envisioned the three-tier management structure, with both financial powers of each tier of management clearly defined and the major stake-holders unfailingly represented at each tier of that management structure, and (b) it was, again, Dr Kalam who had insisted on our ensuring that all of those details were mentioned unambiguously in the government's letter, sanctioning the programme. And, as known, Dr Kalam had scrupulously made use of each of those two authorisations, while leading the IGMDP, in order that all red tapes were cut effectively and all avoidable delays, at every stage of the progress of each project, are determinedly eliminated.

As a result, the fact that all of those details of the IGMDP management structure were incorporated in the government letter had contributed as much to success of the IGMDP, despite the inbuilt defect in our dysfunctional defence management structure, as the ability of Dr Kalam, the leader of the IGMDP, to negotiate skillfully through all of the hurdles that had to be circumvented at each stage of the progress of the IGMDP.

It was an altogether new experience for me – especially, during the first one year – to watch Dr Kalam at work from close quarters. Already a reputed scientist-manager of our country by then – by virtue of the fame that he had recently earned as a scientist of the ISRO for leading the development and the launch of the first successful satellite launch vehicle, the SLV-3 – Dr Kalam, whom I had met and known since his younger days as an epitome of honesty and simplicity, had further amazed me during that period, an amazement that had continued to enliven the rest of my IGMDP years, which had ended, as stated, with my retirement at an early age. His utter disregard for 'status', his unrelenting dedication to work and a total absence of any sense of 'entitlement' were to be seen to be believed. And, I have had the opportunity to have experienced that during all of my remaining seven or eight of the DRDO years.

As soon as he had joined the DRDL as its new Director, Dr Kalam would often visit the DRDO headquarters for getting things done for his laboratory and, more importantly, for ensuring that the IGMDP is sanctioned in the correct form and on a fast-track. And, on each of those occasions, especially, during the first few months, Dr Kalam would, invariably, drop in on my office, also, unannounced or otherwise. And, he did that in order to let me in on his views on all of the issues pertaining to the planning for and the sanctioning of the IGMDP, views that were considered by him most important for the successful execution of the IGMDP in an expeditious manner. His concerns had included, particularly, the way each of the supporting work-centres had estimated both the cost of their work and the expected date of the completion of that piece of work, be it technology development or the development of component or a subsystem. One of his important concerns, as I recall, was that the DRDO proposal for the IGMDP must not only reflect the need for instituting the kind of management system that he had considered essential for the successful execution of the IGMDP but, also, spell out the kind of management structure that he, the designated chief of the Programme, had recommended, namely a three-tier system, with clear enunciation of both the limits of financial power and the types of functional responsibility that each level of that system, ie the Project Management Committee (PMC) for each project, the Programme Management Board (PMB) and, finally, the Guided Missile Board (GMB), would be assigned in order that the government letter for the IGMDP clearly spelt out those details.

All of those informal discussions with Dr Kalam and the formal meetings which had followed those discussions, either in Dr Kalam's office in the DRDL or in the office of the SA in the Department of Defence R & D of the MOD, had clearly shown that Dr Kalam, as the designated leader of our guided missiles programme, had a clear vision of both the enormity of the task ahead of him and a detailed plan for ensuring the exercise of the required checks and balances by the relevant level of the 3-tier management system that would be put in place during the execution of the five, individual guided-missile projects of the IGMDP on a fast track. And, it needs be said here that most the points that were made by Dr Kalam during those informal discussions between Dr Kalam and us, the seniors among the ex-DRDL scientists, then working at the DRDO headquarters, had been included in the DRDO's proposal for the IGMDP, that I had drafted, and had, eventually, received the approval of the relevant cabinet committee of that era, namely the Cabinet Committee for Political Affairs (CCPA), chaired by the then Prime Minister, Mrs Indira Gandhi. And, the Integrated Guided Missile Development Programme (IGMDP) had been formally launched the day that our government had issued the letter sanctioning the IGMDP.

I may point out here that we had managed to fast-track the passage of the DRDO proposal for the sanctioning of the IGMDP through a host of government departments, ie the ministries and agencies which were either genuine stakeholders (eg the Finance, the Defence, our Army/ Navy/Air Force, the Ordnance Factories Board etc) or such agencies as had very little stake in the missile development programme but a 'right' to be consulted a priori, we had no problem in getting the then cabinet committee to approve our proposal. Once as we had obtained that sanction for the IGMDP Dr Kalam, as the designated chief of that Programme, had quickly set up a liaison office of the IGMDP in New Delhi to make sure that of all the follow-up actions that had needed to be taken by various agencies of the government are taken without the least delay. And, it was that action, namely the setting up of that 'expeditor'-unit that had played a major role in ensuring that each project under the IGMDP proceeded without any delay that was avoidable.

As we had expected, the focus of action had, thereafter, shifted from our headquarters to our laboratory, ie the DRDL, and that had resulted in my having to visit Hyderabad frequently, thereafter, because Dr Kalam had insisted that I participate in both the formal project committee meetings and the follow-up discussions that would invariably take place in his office. That was, probably, because he had wanted to make sure that, as a scientist who had both worked in the DRDL and, later, handled all of the work connected with the processing the sanction of the IGMDP, I would, on my return to the DRDO headquarters, make sure that the senior staff at the concerned directorates of the DRDO headquarters as well as the departments of defence and of defence production and supplies would pay immediate attention and resolve quickly any problem that had been highlighted in the project committee meetings.

I may, also, mention here that most of those informal meetings in Dr Kalam's office, which followed the meetings of the project management committees in the early years of the IGMDP, ie during my time, had, inevitably, dealt with some of the issues concerning occasional differences of opinion between two participating laboratories of the missile programme or between the headquarters and the DRDL as regards project priorities, personnel policy etc. And, I had the rare privilege, as a person from the DRDO headquarters, to watch from close quarters, on some of those occasions, how deftly but firmly Dr Kalam, as the leader of the IGMDP, had managed to deal with such sensitive issues without having to yield any ground, on any matter, which he, as the leader of the IGMDP, had considered sacrosanct. A few years later, when I had left Delhi and moved to Chandigarh to join the TBRL as its Director, as mentioned, I would, again, have the opportunity to deal with Dr Kalam at work on a regular basis, eg during his periodical visits to the TBRL in connection with IGMDP-related tests and trials of various types of missile-warheads' prototypes, periodical meetings of the Programme Management Board (PMB), of which Dr Kalam was the Chiarman and the Directors of participating Laboratories members etc. Incidentally, it was, probably, on one such occasion, just before I had retired from the IAF and ended my association with the DRDO, and a meeting of the PMB had been hosted by my laboratory, the TBRL, that I had my last opportunity to see Dr Kalam at work from close quarters.

As mentioned, my work-relationship with Dr Kalam had continued as before, even, after I had left the headquarters of the DRDO and taken over the TBRL as its Director. But it had, inevitably, undergone a change in character once I had moved to a laboratory as its Director. The TBRL, which is the warhead research laboratory of our country, had, inevitably, been a major participant of the IGMDP, but, while Dr Kalam, as the Director of the DRDL, had continued to be the chief of the IGMDP, dealing with all aspects of that programme, including the development of each and every subsystem of each type of guided missile, my primary responsibility pertaining to the IGMDP had become an altogether different one in content. I, as the Director of the TBRL, had, from now onwards to shoulder the responsibility, associated with the development of a wide variety of tactical warheads for all of the five types of tactical guided missiles, that were being developed under of the IGMDP. Consequently, apart from participating, formally, in the Programme Management Board meetings of the IGMDP, which were chaired by Dr Kalam and held, often, in the DRDL but, also, on a few occasions, in one or the other of the participating Laboratories of the DRDO, eg the TBRL. I had assumed the additional responsibility of managing the work of my laboratory in relation to the development of all the tactical missile warheads relevant to the IGMDP. However, I had continued to be amazed to see how hard Dr Kalam could work every day of the week and how inspirational that ability to work so hard and the total lack of ostentation, that was the hallmark of Dr Kalam, would prove to be for our young scientists at every work centre of the IGMDP. On one such occasion, when Dr Kalam had been witnessing, in my company, a prototype-warhead's performance-trial at the testing range of the TBRL I had, also, been amazed to watch from close quarters another trait of Dr Kalam, namely his extraordinary ability to engage young scientists – in that instance, two physicists of the TBRL in detailed discussions on what each individual had contributed by way of research in relation to a particular component of the prctotype warhead that had then been undergoing a functioning test.

As mentioned, my work relationship with Dr Kalam had changed in character after I had taken over my new appointment. Apart from participating in the formal meetings of the Programe Management Board, chaired by him, we had, often, also, got engaged in informal discussions, specifically, on some of the critical issues pertaining to the ongoing work on missile-warheads. One such issue, for instance, had been the design of a test procedure for subjecting a sensitive missile-warhead prototype to a dynamic environment of high acceleration, and, once again, both our concerned scientists, ie warhead specialists, who had designed that test procedure, and I were amazed to see how knowledgeable and well-informed Dr Kalam had made himself, beforehand. That had been, for me, yet another reminder of the fact that Dr Kalam had, indeed, possessed a scintillating mind.

Till my retirement in January 1989, Dr Abdul Kalam, the scientist, had remained, for me, a senior colleague who had filled the leadership role in the development of each of the five types guided missiles of the IGMDP in a manner that very few seniors in India's science and technology enterprise could have done. In short, although I had met him for the first time in 1970-71, when we both were young scientists, he a Scientist C in the SSTC/VSSC and I a mid-level guided missile scientist of the then-DRDL, a tiny guided missiles laboratory of our country, bearing the rank of a Squadron Leader, I had, thereafter, seen him grow enormously, both as a sub-system specialist and as a technology manager in his parent organization, the ISRO. Therefore, although Dr Kalam then had not taken a particular interest, as one of our country's senior scientists, in the work of the DRDO nor had he participated, in any manner, including as an observer, in the work of the DRDL in relation to the development of guided missiles, he had, nevertheless, achieved, almost, an instant success, as known, when he had joined the DRDO as the Director of the DRDL and the mandated Chairman of the Programme Management Board (PMB) as soon as the IGMDP had been formally sanctioned by our government. And, as the most dynamic Director of the DRDL during the next decade or so, Dr Kalam had retained that leadership position well past the time of my departure from the DRDO as the Director of the TBRL.

However, as known, a few years after my retirement Dr Kalam had moved from Hyderabad to New Delhi to take over the reins of the DRDO as the SA. And, he had served successfully for quite a few years in that position, too, before handing over charge as the SA-cum-DG DRDO. He had then worked for an year or two as the SA to our Prime Minister before leaving the defence R & D service, finally. As known, a few years later Dr Kalam had been elected the

President of our Republic and had served most effectively for five more years as, arguably, the best President that our country has had to date. His record, as a compassionate, hard-working and an utterly transparent Head of the State, with no axe to grind, is, probably, one which none of his predecessors had matched nor any one of his successor-Presidents may surpass. For his honesty and integrity he is still held in the highest esteem by all ordinary citizens of our country, especially the poor and the underprivileged, who constitute an overwhelming majority of our nation, even, today.

Afterword

I haven't dealt with nor speculated upon the organizational changes that may yet occur in our country's defence technology and industrial base. However, what has transpired so far suggests that, even, our new and industrious Prime Minister may not have the time or the inclination in the near future to deal with the problem of our country's dysfunctional DTIB management structure, which continues to make it impossible for us to achieve self-reliance in weapons and equipment. However, because of the induction of that new government, about an year back, which has resulted, for the very first time, not only into a smart and scrupulously-honest politician taking over as our Prime Minister but, also, in an energetic and scrupulously clean political leader being appointed the Defence Minister, there is yet hope that the problem our country's DTIB management system would receive this government's attention in due course.

Although I have no basis, whatsoever, for making any conjecture on the kind of changes, as regards our DTIB, that our new government may be contemplating, it is possible that a policy-driven effort will be made by the present

Prime Minister to bring about collaborative ventures between reputed engineering companies of our country and foreign weapons-manufacturers of repute with a view to getting our private sector to participate in the development and manufacture of indigenous weapon systems for our military and for export. And, in the event our government succeeds in making our private sector participate, in the not too distant future, in the development and manufacture of our own weapons that occurrence will, in turn, bring about the much-awaited integration of development management with manufacture management in relation, at least, to those of the indigenous weapon making programmes which would be pursued by our private sector.

The other point that I wish to make here is in support of what I have already stated in this book, namely that but for the role that late revered Dr Abdul Kalam had played in his DRDO years as the leader of our first-ever, integrated, guided missiles development programme that enterprise could not have become the unalloyed success that it has become despite our DTIB's dysfunctional management structure that still afflicts the functioning of our MOD.

Sadly, Dr Kalam is no more, much to the shock of millions of our countrymen who had known of his unparalleled honesty and his unbounded compassion for the poor and the underprivileged. Having made his acquaintance, as stated, as early as in the early nineteen seventies, when he had worked with the ISRO, I had had the unique privilege, a decade later, of having worked with him as a colleague on the guided missiles programme for several years. However, curious as it may seem, I had not met Dr Kalam, even, once after my retirement. That is, neither before nor after he had served as the President of our Republic wth the greatest of distinction. However, it had become evident to me well before my departure from the DRDO that Dr Kalam would most likely prove to be that scientist-leader who would not only prove capable, from day one, of mastering and managing the development of technologies as diverse as those of a guided missile but would most likely, also, succeed in overcoming the problem of our DTIB's un-integrated management structure and thus make our country's guided missiles development programme a total success.

And, to every one of our countrymen's utter delight, he had, indeed, proved to be that successful scientist-leader of our country well before he had become the much-beloved President of India.

Index